卞尺丹几乙し丹卞と
Translated Language Learning

Siddhartha
シッダールタ

An Indian Poem
インドの詩

Hermann Hesse
ヘルマン・ヘッセ

English / 日本語

Copyright © 2024 Tranzlaty
All rights reserved
Published by Tranzlaty
Siddhartha – Eine Indische Dichtung
ISBN: 978-1-83566-688-3
Original text by Hermann Hesse
First published in German in 1922
www.tranzlaty.com

The Son of the Brahman
ブラフマンの息子

In the shade of the house
家の陰で
in the sunshine of the riverbank
川岸の陽光の中で
near the boats
ボートの近く
in the shade of the Sal-wood forest
サルウッドの森の木陰で
in the shade of the fig tree
イチジクの木陰で
this is where Siddhartha grew up
ここはシッダールタが育った場所です
he was the handsome son of a Brahman, the young falcon
彼はブラフマンのハンサムな息子であり、若いハヤブサだった
he grew up with his friend Govinda
彼は友人のゴヴィンダと一緒に育った
Govinda was also the son of a Brahman
ゴーヴィンダもまたバラモンの息子であった
by the banks of the river the sun tanned his light shoulders
川岸で太陽が彼の明るい肩を日焼けさせた
bathing, performing the sacred ablutions, making sacred offerings
沐浴、神聖な清めの儀式、神聖な供物を捧げる
In the mango garden, shade poured into his black eyes
マンゴーガーデンで、彼の黒い目に影が差し込んだ
when playing as a boy, when his mother sang
少年時代に遊んでいたとき、母親が歌っていたとき
when the sacred offerings were made
神聖な供物が捧げられたとき
when his father, the scholar, taught him
学者である父親が彼に教えたとき

when the wise men talked
賢者たちが話していたとき
For a long time, Siddhartha had been partaking in the discussions of the wise men
シッダールタは長い間、賢者たちの議論に参加していた。
he practiced debating with Govinda
彼はゴヴィンダと討論の練習をした
he practiced the art of reflection with Govinda
彼はゴヴィンダとともに反省の術を実践した
and he practiced meditation
そして彼は瞑想を実践した
He already knew how to speak the Om silently
彼はすでに黙ってオームを唱える方法を知っていた
he knew the word of words
彼は言葉の意味を知っていた
he spoke it silently into himself while inhaling
彼は息を吸いながら心の中でそれを言った
he spoke it silently out of himself while exhaling
彼は息を吐きながら心の中でそれを言った
he did this with all the concentration of his soul
彼は全身全霊でこれをやった
his forehead was surrounded by the glow of the clear-thinking spirit
彼の額は明晰な思考の精神の輝きに包まれていた
He already knew how to feel Atman in the depths of his being
彼はすでに自分の存在の奥底にあるアートマンを感じる方法を知っていた
he could feel the indestructible
彼は不滅のものを感じた
he knew what it was to be at one with the universe
彼は宇宙と一体になることがどういうことかを知っていた
Joy leapt in his father's heart

父親の心は喜びにあふれた
because his son was quick to learn
息子は学習が早いので
he was thirsty for knowledge
彼は知識に飢えていた
his father could see him growing up to become a great wise man
父親は彼が成長して偉大な賢者になるのを予想していた
he could see him becoming a priest
彼は彼が司祭になるのを想像できた
he could see him becoming a prince among the Brahmans
彼はバラモンの王子になるだろうと予想した
Bliss leapt in his mother's breast when she saw him walking
彼が歩いているのを見たとき、ブリスは母親の胸の中で飛び跳ねた
Bliss leapt in her heart when she saw him sit down and get up
彼が座って立ち上がるのを見たとき、彼女の心は至福でいっぱいになった。
Siddhartha was strong and handsome
シッダールタは強くてハンサムだった
he, who was walking on slender legs
細い足で歩いていた彼は
he greeted her with perfect respect
彼は彼女に敬意を持って挨拶した
Love touched the hearts of the Brahmans' young daughters
愛はバラモンの若い娘たちの心に触れた
they were charmed when Siddhartha walked through the lanes of the town
シッダールタが町の路地を歩いていると彼らは魅了された
his luminous forehead, his eyes of a king, his slim hips
彼の輝く額、王様のような目、細い腰
But most of all he was loved by Govinda
しかし、何よりも彼はゴヴィンダに愛されていた

Govinda, his friend, the son of a Brahman
ゴーヴィンダは彼の友人であり、バラモンの息子である。
He loved Siddhartha's eye and sweet voice
彼はシッダールタの目と優しい声を愛していた
he loved the way he walked
彼は歩き方が好きだった
and he loved the perfect decency of his movements
そして彼は自分の動作の完璧な礼儀正しさを愛していた
he loved everything Siddhartha did and said
彼はシッダールタのしたことや言ったことをすべて愛していた
but what he loved most was his spirit
しかし彼が最も愛したのは彼の精神だった
he loved his transcendent, fiery thoughts
彼は超越的で燃えるような考えを愛していた
he loved his ardent will and high calling
彼は自分の熱烈な意志と高い使命を愛していた
Govinda knew he would not become a common Brahman
ゴーヴィンダは自分が普通のバラモンにはなれないことを知っていた
no, he would not become a lazy official
いいえ、彼は怠惰な役人にはなりません
no, he would not become a greedy merchant
いいえ、彼は貪欲な商人にはなりません
not a vain, vacuous speaker
虚栄心や空虚さを語る者ではない
nor a mean, deceitful priest
卑劣で欺瞞的な司祭でもない
and he also would not become a decent, stupid sheep
そして彼もまた、まともな愚かな羊にはならないだろう
a sheep in the herd of the many
多くの群れの中の一匹の羊
and he did not want to become one of those things
そして彼はそれらの一つになりたくなかった

he did not want to be one of those tens of thousands of Brahmans
彼は何万人ものバラモンの一人になりたくなかった
He wanted to follow Siddhartha; the beloved, the splendid
彼はシッダールタに従いたかった。愛され、輝かしい
in days to come, when Siddhartha would become a god, he would be there
将来、シッダールタが神になったとき、彼はそこにいるだろう
when he would join the glorious, he would be there
彼が栄光に加わるとき、彼はそこにいるだろう
Govinda wanted to follow him as his friend
ゴヴィンダは友人として彼に従いたかった
he was his companion and his servant
彼は彼の仲間であり、彼の召使いであった
he was his spear-carrier and his shadow
彼は彼の槍持ちであり、彼の影であった
Siddhartha was loved by everyone
シッダールタは皆に愛されていた
He was a source of joy for everybody
彼は皆にとって喜びの源でした
he was a delight for them all
彼は皆にとって喜びだった
But he, Siddhartha, was not a source of joy for himself
しかし、シッダールタは自分自身にとって喜びの源ではなかった
he found no delight in himself
彼は自分自身に喜びを見出せなかった
he walked the rosy paths of the fig tree garden
彼はイチジクの木の庭のバラ色の小道を歩いた
he sat in the bluish shade in the garden of contemplation
彼は瞑想の庭の青みがかった木陰に座っていた
he washed his limbs daily in the bath of repentance
彼は毎日悔い改めの風呂で手足を洗った
he made sacrifices in the dim shade of the mango forest

彼はマンゴーの森の薄暗い木陰で犠牲を払った
his gestures were of perfect decency
彼の身振りは完全に礼儀正しかった
he was everyone's love and joy
彼は皆の愛と喜びでした
but he still lacked all joy in his heart
しかし彼の心には喜びが全くなかった
Dreams and restless thoughts came into his mind
夢と落ち着かない考えが彼の心に浮かんだ
his dreams flowed from the water of the river
彼の夢は川の水から流れ出た
his dreams sparked from the stars of the night
彼の夢は夜の星から生まれた
his dreams melted from the beams of the sun
彼の夢は太陽の光で溶けてしまった
dreams came to him, and a restlessness of the soul came to him
夢が彼に現れ、魂の不安が彼に訪れた
his soul was fuming from the sacrifices
彼の魂は犠牲に憤慨していた
he breathed forth from the verses of the Rig-Veda
彼はリグ・ヴェーダの詩から息を吹き込んだ
the verses were infused into him, drop by drop
詩は一滴ずつ彼の中に染み込んでいった
the verses from the teachings of the old Brahmans
古代バラモンの教えの詩
Siddhartha had started to nurse discontent in himself
シッダールタは自分自身に不満を抱き始めていた
he had started to feel doubt about the love of his father
彼は父親の愛に疑問を感じ始めていた
he doubted the love of his mother
彼は母親の愛を疑った
and he doubted the love of his friend, Govinda
そして彼は友人のゴヴィンダの愛を疑った
he doubted if their love could bring him joy forever and ever

彼は彼らの愛が永遠に彼に喜びをもたらすかどうか疑っていた
their love could not nurse him
彼らの愛は彼を養うことはできなかった
their love could not feed him
彼らの愛は彼を養うことはできなかった
their love could not satisfy him
彼らの愛は彼を満足させることができなかった
he had started to suspect his father's teachings
彼は父親の教えに疑問を持ち始めていた
perhaps he had shown him everything he knew
おそらく彼は自分が知っているすべてを彼に見せたのだろう
there were his other teachers, the wise Brahmans
彼には他の教師、賢明なバラモンたちがいた
perhaps they had already revealed to him the best of their wisdom
おそらく彼らはすでに彼に彼らの知恵の最高のものを明らかにしていたのだろう
he feared that they had already filled his expecting vessel
彼は彼らがすでに彼の期待を満たしているのではないかと恐れていた
despite the richness of their teachings, the vessel was not full
彼らの教えは豊かであったが、その器は満ちていなかった
the spirit was not content
精神は満足していなかった
the soul was not calm
魂は穏やかではなかった
the heart was not satisfied
心は満たされなかった
the ablutions were good, but they were water
沐浴は良かったが、水だった
the ablutions did not wash off the sin

沐浴では罪は洗い流されなかった
they did not heal the spirit's thirst
彼らは魂の渇きを癒さなかった
they did not relieve the fear in his heart
彼らは彼の心の中の恐怖を和らげなかった
The sacrifices and the invocation of the gods were excellent
神々への捧げ物と祈りは素晴らしかった
but was that all there was?
しかし、それだけだったのでしょうか？
did the sacrifices give a happy fortune?
犠牲は幸運をもたらしたのでしょうか？
and what about the gods?
神々についてはどうですか？
Was it really Prajapati who had created the world?
世界を創造したのは本当にプラジャパティだったのでしょうか？
Was it not the Atman who had created the world?
世界を創造したのはアートマンではなかったのか？
Atman, the only one, the singular one
アートマン、唯一のもの、唯一無二のもの
Were the gods not creations?
神々は創造物ではなかったのか？
were they not created like me and you?
彼らは私やあなたと同じように創造されたのではないですか？
were the Gods not subject to time?
神々は時間の影響を受けなかったのでしょうか？
were the Gods mortal? Was it good?
神々は死すべき存在だったのか？それは善だったのか？
was it right? was it meaningful?
それは正しかったのか？それは意味があったのか？
was it the highest occupation to make offerings to the gods?
神々に供物を捧げることが最高の職業だったのでしょうか？
For whom else were offerings to be made?

他に誰のために供物を捧げるべきだったのでしょうか？
who else was to be worshipped?
他に誰を崇拝すべきでしょうか？
who else was there, but Him?
彼以外に誰がそこにいたでしょうか？
The only one, the Atman
唯一の存在、アートマン
And where was Atman to be found?
そしてアートマンはどこにあったのでしょうか？
where did He reside?
彼はどこに住んでいたのですか？
where did His eternal heart beat?
彼の永遠の心はどこで鼓動したのでしょうか？
where else but in one's own self?
自分自身以外にどこがあるでしょうか？
in its innermost indestructible part
最も内側の破壊不可能な部分
could he be that which everyone had in himself?
彼は誰もが自分の中に持っているものになれるだろうか？
But where was this self?
しかし、この自己はどこにあったのでしょうか？
where was this innermost part?
この一番奥の部分はどこにあったのでしょうか？
where was this ultimate part?
この究極の部分はどこにあったのでしょうか？
It was not flesh and bone
それは肉と骨ではなかった
it was neither thought nor consciousness
それは思考でも意識でもなかった
this is what the wisest ones taught
これは最も賢い人たちが教えたことだ
So where was it?
それで、それはどこにありましたか？
the self, myself, the Atman

自己、私自身、アートマン

To reach this place, there was another way
この場所に到達するには別の方法がありました

was this other way worth looking for?
この他の方法は探す価値があったでしょうか?

Alas, nobody showed him this way
残念ながら、誰も彼にこの道を教えなかった

nobody knew this other way
誰もこれを知らなかった

his father did not know it
彼の父親はそれを知らなかった

and the teachers and wise men did not know it
教師や賢者たちはそれを知らなかった

They knew everything, the Brahmans
バラモンたちはすべてを知っていた

and their holy books knew everything
そして彼らの聖書はすべてを知っていた

they had taken care of everything
彼らはすべてを処理した

they took care of the creation of the world
彼らは世界の創造を担当した

they described origin of speech, food, inhaling, exhaling
彼らは、言葉、食べ物、吸入、呼気の起源について説明した。

they described the arrangement of the senses
彼らは感覚の配置を説明した

they described the acts of the gods
彼らは神々の行為を描写した

their books knew infinitely much
彼らの本は無限に多くのことを知っていた

but was it valuable to know all of this?
しかし、これらすべてを知ることは価値があったのでしょうか?

was there not only one thing to be known?
知るべきことは一つだけではなかったのか?

was there still not the most important thing to know?
まだ知るべき最も重要なことはなかったのでしょうか?
many verses of the holy books spoke of this innermost, ultimate thing
聖書の多くの節は、この最も奥深い究極のものについて語っている。
it was spoken of particularly in the Upanishades of Samaveda
それはサマヴェーダのウパニシャッドで特に語られている。
they were wonderful verses
素晴らしい詩でした
"Your soul is the whole world", this was written there
「あなたの魂は全世界です」とそこに書かれていました
and it was written that man in deep sleep would meet with his innermost part
そして、深い眠りの中で人は自分の心の奥底と出会うであろうと書かれていた。
and he would reside in the Atman
そして彼はアートマンの中に住まうだろう
Marvellous wisdom was in these verses
これらの詩には素晴らしい知恵が込められている
all knowledge of the wisest ones had been collected here in magic words
最も賢い人々の知識はすべて魔法の言葉に集められていた
it was as pure as honey collected by bees
それは蜂が集めた蜂蜜のように純粋だった
No, the verses were not to be looked down upon
いいえ、その詩は軽視されるべきものではありません
they contained tremendous amounts of enlightenment
そこには膨大な啓蒙が含まれていた
they contained wisdom which lay collected and preserved
そこには収集され保存された知恵が含まれていた
wisdom collected by innumerable generations of wise Brahmans

無数の世代の賢明なバラモンによって集められた知恵
But where were the Brahmans?
しかし、バラモンはどこにいたのでしょうか?
where were the priests?
司祭たちはどこにいたのですか?
where the wise men or penitents?
賢者や悔い改めた人々はどこにいるのか?
where were those that had succeeded?
成功した人たちはどこにいたのでしょうか?
where were those who knew more than deepest of all knowledge?
あらゆる知識の中で最も深いものを知っている者はどこにいたのか?
where were those that also lived out the enlightened wisdom?
悟りを開いた知恵を生きた人たちはどこにいたのでしょうか?
Where was the knowledgeable one who brought Atman out of his sleep?
アートマンを眠りから目覚めさせた知識人はどこにいたのでしょうか?
who had brought this knowledge into the day?
この知識を現代にもたらしたのは誰でしょうか?
who had taken this knowledge into their life?
この知識を人生に取り入れたのは誰でしょうか?
who carried this knowledge with every step they took?
誰がこの知識を一歩一歩携えていったのでしょうか?
who had married their words with their deeds?
言葉と行動を一致させたのは誰でしょうか?
Siddhartha knew many venerable Brahmans
シッダールタは多くの尊敬すべきバラモンを知っていた
his father, the pure one
彼の父は純粋な人だった
the scholar, the most venerable one
学者、最も尊敬すべき者

His father was worthy of admiration
彼の父親は称賛に値する人物だった
quiet and noble were his manners
彼の態度は静かで高貴だった
pure was his life, wise were his words
彼の人生は清らかで、彼の言葉は賢明だった
delicate and noble thoughts lived behind his brow
彼の額の裏には繊細で高貴な考えが宿っていた
but even though he knew so much, did he live in blissfulness?
しかし、彼は多くのことを知っていたにもかかわらず、至福の中で生きていたのでしょうか？
despite all his knowledge, did he have peace?
あらゆる知識にもかかわらず、彼は平安を得ていたのでしょうか？
was he not also just a searching man?
彼もまたただの探求者ではなかったのか？
was he still not a thirsty man?
彼はまだ喉が渇いていなかったのだろうか？
Did he not have to drink from holy sources again and again?
彼は聖なる水源から何度も飲まなければならなかったのではないですか？
did he not drink from the offerings?
彼は供え物から飲まなかったのか？
did he not drink from the books?
彼は本から飲まなかったのですか？
did he not drink from the disputes of the Brahmans?
彼はバラモンの争いから利益を得なかったのか？
Why did he have to wash off sins every day?
なぜ彼は毎日罪を洗い流さなければならなかったのでしょうか？
must he strive for a cleansing every day?
彼は毎日浄化に努めなければならないのでしょうか？
over and over again, every day
毎日何度も

Was Atman not in him?
アートマンは彼の中にいなかったのでしょうか？
did not the pristine source spring from his heart?
その純粋な源泉は彼の心から湧き出たのではないだろうか？
the pristine source had to be found in one's own self
純粋な源泉は自分自身の中に見つけられなければならない
the pristine source had to be possessed!
純粋な源泉を手に入れなければなりませんでした！
doing anything else else was searching
他に何かをすることは検索することだった
taking any other pass is a detour
他のパスを取ることは遠回りになる
going any other way leads to getting lost
他の道を行くと道に迷うことになる
These were Siddhartha's thoughts
これらはシッダールタの考えでした
this was his thirst, and this was his suffering
これが彼の渇きであり、これが彼の苦しみだった
Often he spoke to himself from a Chandogya-Upanishad:
彼はしばしばチャンドグヤ・ウパニシャッドから自分自身に語りかけた。
"Truly, the name of the Brahman is Satyam"
「本当に、ブラフマンの名はサティヤムである」
"he who knows such a thing, will enter the heavenly world every day"
「そのようなことを知る者は、毎日天国に入るだろう」
Often the heavenly world seemed near
天国はしばしば近くに感じられた
but he had never reached the heavenly world completely
しかし彼は完全に天界に到達したことはなかった
he had never quenched the ultimate thirst
彼は究極の渇きを癒したことがなかった
And among all the wise and wisest men, none had reached it

そして、すべての賢者、最も賢い人々の中で、誰もそれに到達できなかった
he received instructions from them
彼は彼らから指示を受けた
but they hadn't completely reached the heavenly world
しかし彼らはまだ天界に完全には到達していなかった
they hadn't completely quenched their thirst
彼らは喉の渇きを完全に癒していなかった
because this thirst is an eternal thirst
この渇きは永遠の渇きだから

"Govinda" Siddhartha spoke to his friend
「ゴーヴィンダ」シッダールタは友人に語った
"Govinda, my dear, come with me under the Banyan tree"
「ゴヴィンダ、愛しい人よ、私と一緒にバンヤンの木の下へ来なさい」
"let's practise meditation"
「瞑想を実践しましょう」
They went to the Banyan tree
彼らはバンヤンツリーへ行きました
under the Banyan tree they sat down
彼らはガジュマルの木の下に座った
Siddhartha was right here
シッダールタはここにいた
Govinda was twenty paces away
ゴヴィンダは20歩離れたところにいた
Siddhartha seated himself and he repeated murmuring the verse
シッダールタは座り、詩をつぶやきながら繰り返した。
Om is the bow, the arrow is the soul
オムは弓、矢は魂
The Brahman is the arrow's target
ブラフマンは矢の標的である
the target that one should incessantly hit
絶えず狙うべき目標

the usual time of the exercise in meditation had passed
瞑想の通常の練習時間は過ぎていた

Govinda got up, the evening had come
ゴヴィンダは起きて、夜が来た

it was time to perform the evening's ablution
夜の清めの儀式を行う時間だった

He called Siddhartha's name, but Siddhartha did not answer
彼はシッダールタの名前を呼んだが、シッダールタは答えなかった

Siddhartha sat there, lost in thought
シッダールタはそこに座って考え込んでいた

his eyes were rigidly focused towards a very distant target
彼の目は非常に遠くの目標にしっかりと焦点を合わせていた

the tip of his tongue was protruding a little between the teeth
舌の先が歯の間から少し出ていた

he seemed not to breathe
彼は息をしていないようだった

Thus sat he, wrapped up in contemplation
彼はこうして、瞑想にふけりながら座っていた

he was deep in thought of the Om
彼はオームについて深く考えていた

his soul sent after the Brahman like an arrow
彼の魂は矢のようにブラフマンを追いかけた

Once, Samanas had travelled through Siddhartha's town
かつてサマナスはシッダールタの町を旅した

they were ascetics on a pilgrimage
彼らは巡礼中の苦行者だった

three skinny, withered men, neither old nor young
老いも若きもない、痩せて萎びた三人の男

dusty and bloody were their shoulders
彼らの肩は埃と血で汚れていた

almost naked, scorched by the sun, surrounded by loneliness

ほとんど裸で、太陽に焼かれ、孤独に囲まれて
strangers and enemies to the world
世界にとっての異邦人であり敵である
strangers and jackals in the realm of humans
人間の世界には見知らぬ人やジャッカルがいる
Behind them blew a hot scent of quiet passion
彼らの背後には静かな情熱の熱い香りが漂っていた
a scent of destructive service
破壊的なサービスの匂い
a scent of merciless self-denial
容赦ない自己否定の香り
the evening had come
夕方が来た
after the hour of contemplation, Siddhartha spoke to Govinda
瞑想の1時間後、シッダールタはゴーヴィンダに話しかけました
"Early tomorrow morning, my friend, Siddhartha will go to the Samanas"
「明日の朝早く、私の友人シッダールタはサマナスに行きます」
"He will become a Samana"
「彼はサマナになるだろう」
Govinda turned pale when he heard these words
ゴヴィンダはこの言葉を聞いて青ざめた。
and he read the decision in the motionless face of his friend
そして彼は友人の動かない顔からその決意を読み取った
the determination was unstoppable, like the arrow shot from the bow
その決意は弓から放たれた矢のように止められないものだった
Govinda realized at first glance; now it is beginning
ゴヴィンダは一目で理解した。今、それは始まった
now Siddhartha is taking his own way
今シッダールタは自分の道を歩んでいる

now his fate is beginning to sprout
今、彼の運命が芽生え始めている
and because of Siddhartha, Govinda's fate is sprouting too
そしてシッダールタのおかげでゴーヴィンダの運命も芽生えている
he turned pale like a dry banana-skin
彼は乾いたバナナの皮のように青ざめた
"Oh Siddhartha," he exclaimed
「ああ、シッダールタ」と彼は叫んだ
"will your father permit you to do that?"
「あなたのお父さんはそれを許可してくれるでしょうか？」
Siddhartha looked over as if he was just waking up
シッダールタはまるで目覚めたかのようにこちらを見た
like an Arrow he read Govinda's soul
彼は矢のようにゴヴィンダの魂を読み取った
he could read the fear and the submission in him
彼は彼の中に恐怖と服従を読み取ることができた
"Oh Govinda," he spoke quietly, "let's not waste words"
「ああ、ゴヴィンダ」彼は静かに言った、「言葉を無駄にしないようにしましょう」
"Tomorrow at daybreak I will begin the life of the Samanas"
「明日の夜明けに私はサマナの生活を始める」
"let us speak no more of it"
「これ以上は話さないでおこう」

Siddhartha entered the chamber where his father was sitting
シッダールタは父親が座っている部屋に入った
his father was was on a mat of bast
彼の父親は靭皮の敷物の上にいた
Siddhartha stepped behind his father
シッダールタは父親の後ろに立った
and he remained standing behind him
そして彼は彼の後ろに立ったまま

he stood until his father felt that someone was standing behind him
彼は父親が後ろに誰かが立っていると感じるまで立っていた

Spoke the Brahman: "Is that you, Siddhartha?"
ブラフマンは言いました。「それはあなたですか、シッダールタ？」

"Then say what you came to say"
「じゃあ、言いに来たことを言いなさい」

Spoke Siddhartha: "With your permission, my father"
シッダールタは言った。「お許しを、父上」

"I came to tell you that it is my longing to leave your house tomorrow"
「明日あなたの家を出たいと思っていることを伝えに来ました」

"I wish to go to the ascetics"
「修行僧のところへ行きたい」

"My desire is to become a Samana"
「私の願いはサマナになることです」

"May my father not oppose this"
「父がこれに反対しないように」

The Brahman fell silent, and he remained so for long
ブラフマンは沈黙し、長い間沈黙したままだった

the stars in the small window wandered
小さな窓の中の星はさまよっていた

and they changed their relative positions
そして彼らは相対的な位置を変えた

Silent and motionless stood the son with his arms folded
息子は腕を組んで静かに動かずに立っていた

silent and motionless sat the father on the mat
父親は黙って動かずにマットの上に座っていた

and the stars traced their paths in the sky
そして星々は空に軌跡を描いた

Then spoke the father
すると父親は言った

"it is not proper for a Brahman to speak harsh and angry words"
「バラモンが厳しい怒りの言葉を話すのは適切ではない」
"But indignation is in my heart"
「しかし、私の心には憤りがある」
"I wish not to hear this request for a second time"
「この要求を二度と聞きたくない」
Slowly, the Brahman rose
ゆっくりとブラフマンは立ち上がった
Siddhartha stood silently, his arms folded
シッダールタは腕を組んで静かに立っていた
"What are you waiting for?" asked the father
「何を待っているんだ?」父親は尋ねた。
Spoke Siddhartha, "You know what I'm waiting for"
シッダールタは言った。「私が何を待っているかはご存じでしょう」
Indignant, the father left the chamber
父親は憤慨して部屋を出て行った
indignant, he went to his bed and lay down
彼は憤慨してベッドに行き、横になった。
an hour passed, but no sleep had come over his eyes
1時間が経過したが、彼の目には眠りは訪れなかった
the Brahman stood up and he paced to and fro
ブラフマンは立ち上がり、あちこち歩き回った
and he left the house in the night
そして彼は夜中に家を出た
Through the small window of the chamber he looked back inside
彼は部屋の小さな窓から中を覗いた
and there he saw Siddhartha standing
そして彼はシッダールタが立っているのを見た
his arms were folded and he had not moved from his spot
彼は腕を組んでその場から動かなかった
Pale shimmered his bright robe

彼の明るいローブは青白く輝いていた
With anxiety in his heart, the father returned to his bed
父親は不安を抱えながらベッドに戻った
another sleepless hour passed
眠れない一時間が過ぎた
since no sleep had come over his eyes, the Brahman stood up again
眠気はなかったので、ブラフマンは再び立ち上がった。
he paced to and fro, and he walked out of the house
彼はあちこち歩き回って家を出て行った
and he saw that the moon had risen
そして月が昇っているのを見た
Through the window of the chamber he looked back inside
彼は部屋の窓から中を覗き込んだ
there stood Siddhartha, unmoved from his spot
シッダールタは動かずにその場に立っていた
his arms were folded, as they had been
彼は腕を組んでいた。
moonlight was reflecting from his bare shins
月の光が彼のむき出しのすねに反射していた
With worry in his heart, the father went back to bed
父親は心配しながらベッドに戻った
he came back after an hour
彼は1時間後に戻ってきた
and he came back again after two hours
そして彼は2時間後にまた戻ってきた
he looked through the small window
彼は小さな窓から外を見た
he saw Siddhartha standing in the moon light
彼はシッダールタが月明かりの中に立っているのを見た
he stood by the light of the stars in the darkness
彼は暗闇の中で星の光のそばに立っていた
And he came back hour after hour
そして彼は何時間もかけて戻ってきた
silently, he looked into the chamber

彼は黙って部屋の中を覗いた
he saw him standing in the same place
彼は彼が同じ場所に立っているのを見た
it filled his heart with anger
彼の心は怒りで満たされた
it filled his heart with unrest
それは彼の心を不安で満たした
it filled his heart with anguish
彼の心は苦悩で満たされた
it filled his heart with sadness
彼の心は悲しみで満たされた
the night's last hour had come
夜の最後の時間が来た
his father returned and stepped into the room
父親が戻って部屋に入ってきた
he saw the young man standing there
彼はそこに立っている若い男を見た
he seemed tall and like a stranger to him
彼は背が高くて、見知らぬ人のようだった
"Siddhartha," he spoke, "what are you waiting for?"
「シッダールタ」彼は言った。「何を待っているのですか？」
"You know what I'm waiting for"
「私が何を待っているかはご存じでしょう」
"Will you always stand that way and wait?
「あなたはいつもあのまま立って待つのですか？
"I will always stand and wait"
「私はいつも立って待つ」
"will you wait until it becomes morning, noon, and evening?"
「朝、昼、夕方になるまで待ちますか？」
"I will wait until it become morning, noon, and evening"
「朝、昼、夕方になるまで待つよ」
"You will become tired, Siddhartha"
「疲れるでしょう、シッダールタ」

"I will become tired"
「疲れちゃうよ」
"You will fall asleep, Siddhartha"
「あなたは眠りに落ちるでしょう、シッダールタ」
"I will not fall asleep"
「私は眠らない」
"You will die, Siddhartha"
「あなたは死ぬでしょう、シッダールタ」
"I will die," answered Siddhartha
「私は死ぬでしょう」とシッダールタは答えた。
"And would you rather die, than obey your father?"
「それで、あなたは父親に従うより死んだほうがましですか？」
"Siddhartha has always obeyed his father"
「シッダールタは常に父に従ってきた」
"So will you abandon your plan?"
「それで、計画を放棄しますか？」
"Siddhartha will do what his father will tell him to do"
「シッダールタは父の言うことに従うだろう」
The first light of day shone into the room
部屋に最初の光が差し込んだ
The Brahman saw that Siddhartha knees were softly trembling
ブラフマンはシッダールタの膝が静かに震えているのを見た
In Siddhartha's face he saw no trembling
シッダールタの顔には震えは見られなかった
his eyes were fixed on a distant spot
彼の目は遠くの一点に釘付けになっていた
This was when his father realized
その時、父親は
even now Siddhartha no longer dwelt with him in his home
シッダールタはもはや彼の家に住んでいなかった
he saw that he had already left him
彼はすでに彼を見捨てていたことに気づいた

The Father touched Siddhartha's shoulder
父はシッダールタの肩に触れた
"You will," he spoke, "go into the forest and be a Samana"
「あなたは」彼は言った、「森に入ってサマナになるのだ」
"When you find blissfulness in the forest, come back"
「森で至福を見つけたら、戻ってきてください」
"come back and teach me to be blissful"
「戻ってきて私に幸せになることを教えてください」
"If you find disappointment, then return"
「がっかりしたら戻ってきてください」
"return and let us make offerings to the gods together, again"
「戻って、また一緒に神々に供物を捧げましょう」
"Go now and kiss your mother"
「今すぐ行ってお母さんにキスして」
"tell her where you are going"
「どこに行くのか彼女に伝えなさい」
"But for me it is time to go to the river"
「でも私にとっては川に行く時間です」
"it is my time to perform the first ablution"
「初めての清めの儀式を行う時間です」
He took his hand from the shoulder of his son, and went outside
彼は息子の肩から手を取って外に出た
Siddhartha wavered to the side as he tried to walk
シッダールタは歩こうとしながら横にふらついた。
He put his limbs back under control and bowed to his father
彼は手足を元に戻し、父親に頭を下げた。
he went to his mother to do as his father had said
彼は父親の言う通りにするために母親のところへ行った
As he slowly left on stiff legs a shadow rose near the last hut
彼がゆっくりと足を固くして去っていくと、最後の小屋の近くに影が浮かび上がった。
who had crouched there, and joined the pilgrim?

そこにしゃがみ込んで巡礼者に加わったのは誰でしょうか?
"Govinda, you have come" said Siddhartha and smiled
「ゴーヴィンダ、来たな」シッダールタは微笑んで言った。
"I have come," said Govinda
「来ました」とゴヴィンダは言った

With the Samanas
サマナスとともに

In the evening of this day they caught up with the ascetics
この日の夕方、彼らは修行僧たちに追いついた
the ascetics; the skinny Samanas
修行僧、痩せたサマナ
they offered them their companionship and obedience
彼らは彼らに友情と服従を与えた
Their companionship and obedience were accepted
彼らの友情と従順は受け入れられた
Siddhartha gave his garments to a poor Brahman in the street
シッダールタは路上の貧しいバラモンに衣服を与えた
He wore nothing more than a loincloth and earth-coloured, unsown cloak
彼は腰布と、縫い目のない土色の外套だけを身に着けていた。
He ate only once a day, and never anything cooked
彼は一日に一度しか食べず、調理したものも食べなかった
He fasted for fifteen days, he fasted for twenty-eight days
彼は15日間断食し、28日間断食した
The flesh waned from his thighs and cheeks
太ももと頬の肉が衰えた
Feverish dreams flickered from his enlarged eyes
熱っぽい夢が彼の大きくなった目からちらついた
long nails grew slowly on his parched fingers
乾いた指にゆっくりと長い爪が生えてきた
and a dry, shaggy beard grew on his chin
彼のあごには乾燥したぼさぼさのひげが生えていた
His glance turned to ice when he encountered women
女性に出会うと彼の視線は凍りついた
he walked through a city of nicely dressed people
彼はきちんとした服装をした人々がいる街を歩いた

his mouth twitched with contempt for them
彼は彼らに対する軽蔑で口を歪めた
He saw merchants trading and princes hunting
彼は商人たちが商売をし、王子たちが狩りをするのを見た
he saw mourners wailing for their dead
彼は死者を悼む人々が嘆き悲しんでいるのを見た
and he saw whores offering themselves
そして彼は娼婦たちが自らを差し出すのを見た
physicians trying to help the sick
病人を助けようとする医師
priests determining the most suitable day for seeding
種まきに最適な日を決める司祭たち
lovers loving and mothers nursing their children
愛し合う恋人達と子供を育てる母親達
and all of this was not worthy of one look from his eyes
そして、これらすべては彼の目には映らないものだった
it all lied, it all stank, it all stank of lies
すべては嘘で、すべては悪臭を放ち、すべては嘘の悪臭を放っていた
it all pretended to be meaningful and joyful and beautiful
すべては意味があり、楽しく、美しいものであるかのように見せかけていた
and it all was just concealed putrefaction
そしてそれはすべて隠された腐敗だった
the world tasted bitter; life was torture
世界は苦く、人生は拷問のようだった

A single goal stood before Siddhartha
シッダールタの前にはただ一つの目標が残っていた
his goal was to become empty
彼の目標は空っぽになることだった
his goal was to be empty of thirst
彼の目標は渇きを癒すことだった
empty of wishing and empty of dreams

希望も夢もない
empty of joy and sorrow
喜びも悲しみもない
his goal was to be dead to himself
彼の目標は自分自身に死ぬことだった
his goal was not to be a self any more
彼の目標はもはや自分自身になることではなかった
his goal was to find tranquillity with an emptied heart
彼の目標は空っぽの心で平穏を見つけることだった
his goal was to be open to miracles in unselfish thoughts
彼の目標は、利他的な考えで奇跡を受け入れることだった
to achieve this was his goal
これを達成することが彼の目標だった
when all of his self was overcome and had died
彼の自我の全てが打ち負かされ、死んだとき
when every desire and every urge was silent in the heart
あらゆる欲望と衝動が心の中で沈黙していたとき
then the ultimate part of him had to awake
そして彼の究極の部分が目覚めなければならなかった
the innermost of his being, which is no longer his self
彼の存在の最も内側、それはもはや彼自身ではない
this was the great secret
これは大きな秘密でした

Silently, Siddhartha exposed himself to the burning rays of the sun
シッダールタは黙って太陽の灼熱の光線に身をさらした
he was glowing with pain and he was glowing with thirst
彼は痛みと渇きで赤く染まっていた
and he stood there until he neither felt pain nor thirst
そして彼は痛みも渇きも感じなくなるまでそこに立っていた
Silently, he stood there in the rainy season
彼は雨季に静かにそこに立っていた

from his hair the water was dripping over freezing shoulders
彼の髪から水が凍りつくような肩に滴り落ちていた
the water was dripping over his freezing hips and legs
水は彼の凍り付いた腰と足に滴り落ちていた
and the penitent stood there
そして悔い改めた者はそこに立っていた
he stood there until he could not feel the cold any more
彼は寒さを感じなくなるまでそこに立っていた
he stood there until his body was silent
彼は体が動かなくなるまでそこに立っていた
he stood there until his body was quiet
彼は体が静かになるまでそこに立っていた
Silently, he cowered in the thorny bushes
彼は黙って、とげのある茂みの中に身を潜めていた
blood dripped from the burning skin
焼けた皮膚から血が滴り落ちた
blood dripped from festering wounds
化膿した傷口から血が滴り落ちた
and Siddhartha stayed rigid and motionless
そしてシッダールタは固く動かずにいた
he stood until no blood flowed any more
彼は血が止まるまで立っていた
he stood until nothing stung any more
彼は何も刺さらなくなるまで立っていた
he stood until nothing burned any more
彼は何も燃えなくなるまで立っていた
Siddhartha sat upright and learned to breathe sparingly
シッダールタはまっすぐに座り、呼吸を控えめにすることを学んだ
he learned to get along with few breaths
彼は息を少なくして生きることを学んだ
he learned to stop breathing
彼は呼吸を止めることを学んだ
He learned, beginning with the breath, to calm the beating of his heart

彼は呼吸から始めて心臓の鼓動を静めることを学んだ
he learned to reduce the beats of his heart
彼は心臓の鼓動を抑えることを学んだ
he meditated until his heartbeats were only a few
彼は心拍数がわずかになるまで瞑想した
and then his heartbeats were almost none
そして彼の心拍はほとんど止まった
Instructed by the oldest of the Samanas, Siddhartha practised self-denial
最年長のサマナの教えを受けて、シッダールタは自己否定を実践した。

he practised meditation, according to the new Samana rules
彼は新しいサマナのルールに従って瞑想を実践した
A heron flew over the bamboo forest
竹林の上をサギが飛んでいた
Siddhartha accepted the heron into his soul
シッダールタはサギを魂の中に受け入れた
he flew over forest and mountains
彼は森と山々の上を飛んだ
he was a heron, he ate fish
彼はサギで、魚を食べました
he felt the pangs of a heron's hunger
彼はサギの飢えの苦しみを感じた
he spoke the heron's croak
彼はサギの鳴き声を話した
he died a heron's death
彼は死んだ
A dead jackal was lying on the sandy bank
死んだジャッカルが砂浜に横たわっていた
Siddhartha's soul slipped inside the body of the dead jackal
シッダールタの魂は死んだジャッカルの体の中に滑り込んだ
he was the dead jackal laying on the banks and bloated
彼は岸に横たわり、膨れ上がった死んだジャッカルだった

he stank and decayed and was dismembered by hyenas
彼は悪臭を放ち、腐敗し、ハイエナにバラバラにされた
he was skinned by vultures and turned into a skeleton
彼はハゲタカに皮を剥がされて骸骨になった
he was turned to dust and blown across the fields
彼は塵となって野原に吹き飛ばされた
And Siddhartha's soul returned
そしてシッダールタの魂は戻った
it had died, decayed, and was scattered as dust
それは死んで朽ちて塵となって散らばっていた
it had tasted the gloomy intoxication of the cycle
それは、そのサイクルの暗い陶酔を味わった
it awaited with a new thirst, like a hunter in the gap
それは隙間のハンターのように新たな渇きを待っていた
in the gap where he could escape from the cycle
彼がそのサイクルから抜け出すことができる隙間に
in the gap where an eternity without suffering began
苦しみのない永遠が始まった隙間に
he killed his senses and his memory
彼は感覚と記憶を殺した
he slipped out of his self into thousands of other forms
彼は自分自身から抜け出して何千もの他の姿に変わった
he was an animal, a carrion, a stone
彼は動物であり、死肉であり、石であった
he was wood and water
彼は木と水でした
and he awoke every time to find his old self again
そして彼は目覚めるたびに昔の自分を取り戻すことができた
whether sun or moon, he was his self again
太陽であろうと月であろうと、彼は再び自分自身に戻った
he turned round in the cycle
彼はサイクルの中で方向転換した
he felt thirst, overcame the thirst, felt new thirst

彼は渇きを感じ、渇きを克服し、新たな渇きを感じた

Siddhartha learned a lot when he was with the Samanas
シッダールタはサマナ族と一緒にいたときに多くのことを学んだ

he learned many ways leading away from the self
彼は自己から離れる多くの方法を学んだ

he learned how to let go
彼は手放すことを学んだ

He went the way of self-denial by means of pain
彼は苦痛を伴う自己否定の道を歩んだ

he learned self-denial through voluntarily suffering and overcoming pain
彼は自ら苦しみ、痛みを克服することで自己否定を学んだ。

he overcame hunger, thirst, and tiredness
彼は飢え、渇き、疲労を克服した

He went the way of self-denial by means of meditation
彼は瞑想によって自己否定の道を歩んだ

he went the way of self-denial through imagining the mind to be void of all conceptions
彼は、心があらゆる概念を捨て去ったと想像することで自己否定の道を歩んだ。

with these and other ways he learned to let go
彼はこれらの方法や他の方法で手放すことを学んだ

a thousand times he left his self
彼は千回も自分自身を捨てた

for hours and days he remained in the non-self
彼は何時間も何日も非自己の中に留まり

all these ways led away from the self
これらすべての道は自己から遠ざかる

but their path always led back to the self
しかし彼らの道は常に自分自身へと戻っていった

Siddhartha fled from the self a thousand times
シッダールタは千回も自己から逃げた

but the return to the self was inevitable
しかし、自分自身への回帰は避けられなかった
although he stayed in nothingness, coming back was inevitable
彼は虚無の中に留まっていたが、戻ってくることは避けられなかった
although he stayed in animals and stones, coming back was inevitable
彼は動物や石の中に留まっていたが、戻ってくることは避けられなかった
he found himself in the sunshine or in the moonlight again
彼は再び太陽の光や月の光の中にいた
he found himself in the shade or in the rain again
彼はまた日陰か雨の中にいた
and he was once again his self; Siddhartha
そして彼は再び自分自身に戻りました。シッダールタ
and again he felt the agony of the cycle which had been forced upon him
そして彼は再び、自分に課せられたサイクルの苦しみを感じた。

by his side lived Govinda, his shadow
彼の傍らにはゴヴィンダが影となって住んでいた
Govinda walked the same path and undertook the same efforts
ゴヴィンダも同じ道を歩み、同じ努力をしました
they spoke to one another no more than the exercises required
彼らは練習に必要なこと以外は互いに話さなかった
occasionally the two of them went through the villages
二人は時々村を通り抜けた
they went to beg for food for themselves and their teachers
彼らは自分たちと先生のために食べ物を乞いに行きました
"How do you think we have progressed, Govinda" he asked

「ゴヴィンダ、私たちはどれだけ進歩したと思いますか？」と彼は尋ねた。

"Did we reach any goals?" Govinda answered
「何か目標を達成できましたか？」とゴヴィンダは答えた。

"We have learned, and we'll continue learning"
「私たちは学びました、そしてこれからも学び続けます」

"You'll be a great Samana, Siddhartha"
「あなたは偉大なサマナになるでしょう、シッダールタ」

"Quickly, you've learned every exercise"
「あっという間に、すべての練習を習得しました」

"often, the old Samanas have admired you"
「昔のサマナ族はよくあなたを尊敬していました」

"One day, you'll be a holy man, oh Siddhartha"
「いつかあなたは聖人になるでしょう、おお、シッダールタ」

Spoke Siddhartha, "I can't help but feel that it is not like this, my friend"
シッダールタは言いました。「友よ、私はそれがそうではないと感じざるを得ません。」

"What I've learned being among the Samanas could have been learned more quickly"
「サマナ族の中で私が学んだことは、もっと早く学ぶことができたはずだ」

"it could have been learned by simpler means"
「もっと簡単な方法で学ぶことができたはずだ」

"it could have been learned in any tavern"
「それはどの居酒屋でも学べたはずだ」

"it could have been learned where the whorehouses are"
「売春宿がどこにあるかを知ることができたかもしれない」

"I could have learned it among carters and gamblers"

「私は馬車屋やギャンブラーの間でそれを学んだかもしれない」
Spoke Govinda, "Siddhartha is joking with me"
ゴヴィンダは言った、「シッダールタは私をからかっている」
"How could you have learned meditation among wretched people?"
「どうしてあなたは惨めな人々の中で瞑想を学べたのですか？」
"how could whores have taught you about holding your breath?"
「どうして売春婦が息を止めることを教えることができたんだ？」
"how could gamblers have taught you insensitivity against pain?"
「ギャンブラーがどうしてあなたに痛みに対する無感覚を教えたのですか？」
Siddhartha spoke quietly, as if he was talking to himself
シッダールタはまるで独り言を言っているかのように静かに話した。
"What is meditation?"
「瞑想とは何ですか？」
"What is leaving one's body?"
「身体を離れるとはどういうことか？」
"What is fasting?"
「断食とは何ですか？」
"What is holding one's breath?"
「息を止めるって何？」
"It is fleeing from the self"
「それは自分から逃げることだ」
"it is a short escape of the agony of being a self"
「それは自己であることの苦しみからの短い逃避である」
"it is a short numbing of the senses against the pain"
「それは痛みに対する感覚の一時的な麻痺です」

"it is avoiding the pointlessness of life"
「人生の無意味さを避けることだ」
"The same numbing is what the driver of an ox-cart finds in the inn"
「牛車の御者が宿屋で感じる麻痺と同じだ」
"drinking a few bowls of rice-wine or fermented coconut-milk"
「ライスワインや発酵ココナッツミルクを数杯飲む」
"Then he won't feel his self anymore"
「そうしたら彼はもう自分自身を感じられなくなるだろう」
"then he won't feel the pains of life anymore"
「そうすれば彼はもう人生の苦しみを感じなくなるだろう」
"then he finds a short numbing of the senses"
「すると、彼は感覚が一時的に麻痺してしまうのです」
"When he falls asleep over his bowl of rice-wine, he'll find the same what we find"
「彼が酒を飲みながら眠りに落ちたとき、私たちと同じものを見つけるだろう」
"he finds what we find when we escape our bodies through long exercises"
「彼は、私たちが長い訓練を通して肉体から逃れたときに見つけるものを見つけるのです」
"all of us are staying in the non-self"
「私たちはみな非自己の中に留まっている」
"This is how it is, oh Govinda"
「これが現実です、ああゴヴィンダ」
Spoke Govinda, "You say so, oh friend"
ゴヴィンダは言った。「そうおっしゃるのですね、おお友よ」
"and yet you know that Siddhartha is no driver of an ox-cart"
「しかし、シッダールタは牛車の御者ではないことはご存じでしょう」
"and you know a Samana is no drunkard"

「サマナは酔っぱらいではないことはご存じでしょう」
"it's true that a drinker numbs his senses"
「酒を飲むと感覚が麻痺するのは本当だ」
"it's true that he briefly escapes and rests"
「彼が一時的に逃げて休むのは事実だ」
"but he'll return from the delusion and finds everything to be unchanged"
「しかし、彼は妄想から戻り、すべてが変わっていないことに気づくだろう」
"he has not become wiser"
「彼は賢くなっていない」
"he has gathered any enlightenment"
「彼は何らかの悟りを得た」
"he has not risen several steps"
「彼は数段も上がらなかった」
And Siddhartha spoke with a smile
そしてシッダールタは微笑みながら言った
"I do not know, I've never been a drunkard"
「分かりません。私は酒飲みだったことがないんです」
"I know that I find only a short numbing of the senses"
「感覚が一時的に麻痺するだけだとわかっている」
"I find it in my exercises and meditations"
「私はエクササイズと瞑想でそれを見つけます」
"and I find I am just as far removed from wisdom as a child in the mother's womb"
「そして私は、母親の胎内にいる子供のように知恵から遠く離れていることに気づいた」
"this I know, oh Govinda"
「私は知っています、ああゴヴィンダ」

And once again, another time, Siddhartha began to speak
そしてまた、シッダールタは話し始めた
Siddhartha had left the forest, together with Govinda
シッダールタはゴーヴィンダとともに森を去った
they left to beg for some food in the village

彼らは村に食べ物を乞いに出かけた
he said, "What now, oh Govinda?"
彼は言いました。「さて、どうするんだ、ゴヴィンダ？」
"are we on the right path?"
「私たちは正しい道を歩んでいるのだろうか？」
"are we getting closer to enlightenment?"
「私たちは悟りに近づいているのでしょうか？」
"are we getting closer to salvation?"
「私たちは救いに近づいているのでしょうか？」
"Or do we perhaps live in a circle?"
「それとも、私たちは輪になって生きているのでしょうか？」
"we, who have thought we were escaping the cycle"
「この悪循環から抜け出せたと思っていた私たち」
Spoke Govinda, "We have learned a lot"
ゴヴィンダは「私たちは多くのことを学びました」と語った。
"Siddhartha, there is still much to learn"
「シッダールタ、学ぶべきことはまだたくさんある」
"We are not going around in circles"
「私たちは堂々巡りをしているわけではない」
"we are moving up; the circle is a spiral"
「私たちは上昇しています。円は螺旋です」
"we have already ascended many levels"
「私たちはすでに多くのレベルに到達しました」
Siddhartha answered, "How old would you think our oldest Samana is?"
シッダールタは答えました。「私たちの最年長のサマナは何歳だと思いますか？」
"how old is our venerable teacher?"
「私たちの尊敬すべき先生は何歳ですか？」
Spoke Govinda, "Our oldest one might be about sixty years of age"

ゴヴィンダは言った。「うちの最年長者は60歳くらいです」
Spoke Siddhartha, "He has lived for sixty years"
シッダールタは言った。「彼は60年間生きてきた」
"and yet he has not reached the nirvana"
「しかし、彼はまだ涅槃に達していない」
"He'll turn seventy and eighty"
「彼は70歳、80歳になるだろう」
"you and me, we will grow just as old as him"
「あなたも私も、彼と同じくらい年をとるのです」
"and we will do our exercises"
「そして私たちは練習をします」
"and we will fast, and we will meditate"
「そして私たちは断食し、瞑想します」
"But we will not reach the nirvana"
「しかし、私たちは涅槃には到達できないだろう」
"he won't reach nirvana and we won't"
「彼は涅槃に到達できないし、私たちも到達できない」
"there are uncountable Samanas out there"
「そこには数え切れないほどのサマナがいる」
"perhaps not a single one will reach the nirvana"
「おそらく誰一人として涅槃に至らないだろう」
"We find comfort, we find numbness, we learn feats"
「私たちは安らぎを見つけ、無感覚を見つけ、偉業を学ぶ」
"we learn these things to deceive others"
「私たちは他人を騙すためにこれらのことを学ぶのです」
"But the most important thing, the path of paths, we will not find"
「しかし、最も重要なこと、道の中の道は、私たちは見つけられないだろう」
Spoke Govinda "If you only wouldn't speak such terrible words, Siddhartha!"

ゴーヴィンダは言いました。「シッダールタよ、そんなひどい言葉を言わなければいいのに！」

"there are so many learned men"
「学識のある人がたくさんいる」

"how could not one of them not find the path of paths?"
「どうして彼らのうちの一人が道の中の道を見つけられなかったのか？」

"how can so many Brahmans not find it?"
「どうしてそんなに多くのバラモンがそれを見つけられないのか？」

"how can so many austere and venerable Samanas not find it?"
「どうしてこれほど多くの厳格で敬虔なサマナがそれを見つけられないのか？」

"how can all those who are searching not find it?"
「探している人たち全員が、どうして見つけられないのでしょうか？」

"how can the holy men not find it?"
「どうして聖人たちはそれを見つけられないのか？」

But Siddhartha spoke with as much sadness as mockery
しかしシッダールタは嘲笑と同じくらい悲しみを込めて話した

he spoke with a quiet, a slightly sad, a slightly mocking voice
彼は静かで、少し悲しく、少し嘲るような声で話した

"Soon, Govinda, your friend will leave the path of the Samanas"
「ゴヴィンダ、もうすぐあなたの友人はサマナの道を離れるでしょう」

"he has walked along your side for so long"
「彼は長い間あなたのそばを歩いてきました」

"I'm suffering of thirst"
「喉が渇いています」

"on this long path of a Samana, my thirst has remained as strong as ever"

「サマナのこの長い道のりで、私の渇きは相変わらず強いままでした」
"I always thirsted for knowledge"
「私は常に知識を渇望していました」
"I have always been full of questions"
「私はいつも疑問でいっぱいでした」
"I have asked the Brahmans, year after year"
「私は毎年バラモンに尋ねてきました」
"and I have asked the holy Vedas, year after year"
「そして私は聖なるヴェーダに毎年尋ねてきた」
"and I have asked the devoted Samanas, year after year"
「そして私は毎年、敬虔なサマナに尋ねてきました」
"perhaps I could have learned it from the hornbill bird"
「おそらくサイチョウから学んだのかもしれない」
"perhaps I should have asked the chimpanzee"
「チンパンジーに聞いてみればよかったのかもしれない」
"It took me a long time"
「長い時間がかかりました」
"and I am not finished learning this yet"
「そして私はまだこれを学び終えていない」
"oh Govinda, I have learned that there is nothing to be learned!"
「ああ、ゴヴィンダよ、私は学ぶべきことは何もないことを学びました！」
"There is indeed no such thing as learning"
「確かに学習というものは存在しない」
"There is just one knowledge"
「知識はただ一つ」
"this knowledge is everywhere, this is Atman"
「この知識はどこにでもある、これがアートマンだ」
"this knowledge is within me and within you"
「この知識は私の中にあり、あなたの中にもあります」
"and this knowledge is within every creature"
「そしてこの知識はすべての生き物の中にある」

"this knowledge has no worse enemy than the desire to know it"
「この知識にとって、それを知りたいという欲求ほど悪い敵はない」
"that is what I believe"
「それが私の信念です」
At this, Govinda stopped on the path
ゴヴィンダは道の途中で立ち止まった
he rose his hands, and spoke
彼は手を挙げて話した
"If only you would not bother your friend with this kind of talk"
「こんな話で友達を煩わせなければいいのに」
"Truly, your words stir up fear in my heart"
「本当に、あなたの言葉は私の心に恐怖を呼び起こします」
"consider, what would become of the sanctity of prayer?"
「考えてみてください、祈りの神聖さはどうなるのでしょうか？」
"what would become of the venerability of the Brahmans' caste?"
「バラモン階級の尊厳はどうなるのでしょうか？」
"what would happen to the holiness of the Samanas?
「サマナの神聖さはどうなるのでしょうか？
"What would then become of all of that is holy"
「そのすべてがどうなるかは神聖だ」
"what would still be precious?"
「何がまだ貴重なのでしょうか？」
And Govinda mumbled a verse from an Upanishad to himself
そしてゴヴィンダはウパニシャッドの一節をつぶやいた
"He who ponderingly, of a purified spirit, loses himself in the meditation of Atman"
「思索にふけり、清らかな精神でアートマンの瞑想に没頭する者」
"inexpressible by words is the blissfulness of his heart"

「彼の心の至福は言葉では言い表せない」
But Siddhartha remained silent
しかしシッダールタは沈黙を守った
He thought about the words which Govinda had said to him
彼はゴヴィンダが彼に言った言葉について考えた
and he thought the words through to their end
そして彼は言葉を最後まで考え抜いた
he thought about what would remain of all that which seemed holy
彼は神聖に思えるものが何を残すのかを考えた
What remains? What can stand the test?
何が残るでしょうか？何が試練に耐えられるでしょうか？
And he shook his head
そして彼は首を横に振った

the two young men had lived among the Samanas for about three years
二人の若者はサマナ族の間で約3年間暮らしていた。
some news, a rumour, a myth reached them
あるニュース、噂、神話が彼らに届いた
the rumour had been retold many times
その噂は何度も語られていた
A man had appeared, Gotama by name
ゴータマという名の男が現れた
the exalted one, the Buddha
崇高なる者、仏陀
he had overcome the suffering of the world in himself
彼は自分自身で世界の苦しみを克服した
and he had halted the cycle of rebirths
そして彼は再生のサイクルを止めた
He was said to wander through the land, teaching
彼は国中を歩き回り、教えを説いたと言われている
he was said to be surrounded by disciples
彼は弟子たちに囲まれていたと言われている

he was said to be without possession, home, or wife
彼は財産も家も妻も持っていなかったと言われている
he was said to be in just the yellow cloak of an ascetic
彼は修行僧の黄色いマントだけを着ていたと言われている
but he was with a cheerful brow
しかし彼は明るい表情をしていた
and he was said to be a man of bliss
彼は幸福の人と言われていた
Brahmans and princes bowed down before him
バラモンや王子たちは彼の前にひれ伏した
and they became his students
そして彼らは彼の弟子となった
This myth, this rumour, this legend resounded
この神話、この噂、この伝説は響き渡った
its fragrance rose up, here and there, in the towns
その香りは町のあちこちに漂っていた
the Brahmans spoke of this legend
バラモンたちはこの伝説について語った
and in the forest, the Samanas spoke of it
そして森の中でサマナ族はそれを語った
again and again, the name of Gotama the Buddha reached the ears of the young men
ゴータマ・ブッダの名が若者たちの耳に何度も届いた
there was good and bad talk of Gotama
ゴータマについては良い話も悪い話もあった
some praised Gotama, others defamed him
ゴータマを称賛する者もいれば、中傷する者もいた
It was as if the plague had broken out in a country
まるで疫病が国中に蔓延したかのようだった
news had been spreading around that in one or another place there was a man
どこかに男がいるという噂が広まっていた
a wise man, a knowledgeable one
賢い人、知識のある人
a man whose word and breath was enough to heal everyone

彼の言葉と息はすべての人を癒すのに十分なものだった
his presence could heal anyone who had been infected with the pestilence
彼の存在は疫病に感染した者を癒すことができた
such news went through the land, and everyone would talk about it
そのようなニュースが国中に広まり、誰もがそれについて話すだろう
many believed the rumours, many doubted them
多くの人が噂を信じたが、多くの人がそれを疑った。
but many got on their way as soon as possible
しかし、多くの人はできるだけ早く出発した。
they went to seek the wise man, the helper
彼らは賢者、助け手を探しに行った
the wise man of the family of Sakya
釈迦族の賢者
He possessed, so the believers said, the highest enlightenment
信者たちは、彼は最高の悟りを持っていたと言った。
he remembered his previous lives; he had reached the nirvana
彼は前世を思い出し、涅槃に達した。
and he never returned into the cycle
そして彼はそのサイクルに戻ることはなかった
he was never again submerged in the murky river of physical forms
彼は二度と物質的な形の濁った川に沈むことはなかった
Many wonderful and unbelievable things were reported of him
彼については多くの素晴らしい、信じられないようなことが報告された
he had performed miracles
彼は奇跡を起こした
he had overcome the devil
彼は悪魔に打ち勝った
he had spoken to the gods

彼は神々に話しかけた
But his enemies and disbelievers said Gotama was a vain seducer
しかし、彼の敵や不信心者はゴータマは虚栄心の強い誘惑者だと言った
they said he spent his days in luxury
彼は贅沢な日々を送っていたと彼らは言った
they said he scorned the offerings
彼らは彼が供物を軽蔑したと言った
they said he was without learning
彼らは彼が学識がないと言った
they said he knew neither meditative exercises nor self-castigation
彼らは、彼は瞑想の訓練も自己懲罰も知らないと言った
The myth of Buddha sounded sweet
仏陀の神話は甘美に聞こえた
The scent of magic flowed from these reports
これらの報告からは魔法の香りが漂ってきた
After all, the world was sick, and life was hard to bear
結局、世界は病んでいて、人生は耐え難いものだった
and behold, here a source of relief seemed to spring forth
そして、ここに救いの源が湧き出たように思えた
here a messenger seemed to call out
ここで使者が呼びかけているようだ
comforting, mild, full of noble promises
慰め、穏やか、高貴な約束に満ちた
Everywhere where the rumour of Buddha was heard, the young men listened up
仏陀の噂が聞こえる所ではどこでも若者たちは耳を傾けた
everywhere in the lands of India they felt a longing
インドのあらゆる場所で彼らは憧れを感じていた
everywhere where the people searched, they felt hope
人々が探し求めたところどこでも希望を感じた
every pilgrim and stranger was welcome when he brought news of him

彼が彼の知らせを持ってくると、すべての巡礼者や旅人は歓迎された。

the exalted one, the Sakyamuni
崇高なる者、釈迦牟尼

The myth had also reached the Samanas in the forest
この神話は森のサマナ族にも伝わっていた

and Siddhartha and Govinda heard the myth too
シッダールタとゴーヴィンダもその神話を聞いた

slowly, drop by drop, they heard the myth
ゆっくりと、一滴ずつ、彼らは神話を聞いた

every drop was laden with hope
一滴一滴に希望が詰まっていた

every drop was laden with doubt
一滴一滴に疑念が込められていた

They rarely talked about it
彼らはそれについてほとんど話さなかった

because the oldest one of the Samanas did not like this myth
サマナ族の長男はこの神話を好まなかったため

he had heard that this alleged Buddha used to be an ascetic
彼は、この仏陀はかつては苦行者だったと聞いていた

he heard he had lived in the forest
彼は森に住んでいたと聞いた

but he had turned back to luxury and worldly pleasures
しかし彼は贅沢と世俗的な快楽に戻っていた

and he had no high opinion of this Gotama
そして彼はこのゴータマを高く評価していなかった

"Oh Siddhartha," Govinda spoke one day to his friend
「ああ、シッダールタ」ゴーヴィンダはある日友人に言った

"Today, I was in the village"
「今日は村にいました」

"and a Brahman invited me into his house"
「そして、あるバラモンが私を家に招いてくれました」

"and in his house, there was the son of a Brahman from Magadha"
「彼の家にはマガダ出身のバラモンの息子がいた」
"he has seen the Buddha with his own eyes"
「彼は自分の目で仏陀を見た」
"and he has heard him teach"
「そして彼は彼が教えるのを聞いた」
"Verily, this made my chest ache when I breathed"
「本当に、息をするたびに胸が痛くなりました」
"and I thought this to myself:"
「そして私はこう思いました。
"if only we heard the teachings from the mouth of this perfected man!"
「この完成された人の口から教えを聞けたらよかったのに！」
"Speak, friend, wouldn't we want to go there too"
「話してくれ、友よ、私たちもそこに行きたいじゃないか」
"wouldn't it be good to listen to the teachings from the Buddha's mouth?"
「仏陀の口から教えを聞くのは良いことではないでしょうか？」
Spoke Siddhartha, "I had thought you would stay with the Samanas"
シッダールタは言った。「私は、あなたがサマナ族と一緒にいると思っていた」
"I always had believed your goal was to live to be seventy"
「あなたの目標は70歳まで生きることだといつも信じていました」
"I thought you would keep practising those feats and exercises"
「君はこれからもその技や訓練を続けていくと思っていたよ」
"and I thought you would become a Samana"
「そして、あなたはサマナになるだろうと思った」

"But behold, I had not known Govinda well enough"
「しかし、私はゴーヴィンダのことを十分に知らなかったのです」
"I knew little of his heart"
「私は彼の心についてほとんど知らなかった」
"So now you want to take a new path"
「それで、あなたは新しい道を歩みたいのですか？」
"and you want to go there where the Buddha spreads his teachings"
「そしてあなたは仏陀が教えを広めている場所に行きたいのです」
Spoke Govinda, "You're mocking me"
ゴヴィンダは言った。「あなたは私を嘲笑しているわ」
"Mock me if you like, Siddhartha!"
「シッダールタよ、私を嘲笑うのも構わない！」
"But have you not also developed a desire to hear these teachings?"
「しかし、あなたもこれらの教えを聞きたいという欲求を抱いたのではないでしょうか？」
"have you not said you would not walk the path of the Samanas for much longer?"
「あなたは、もう長くはサマナスの道を歩まないと言ったではないか？」
At this, Siddhartha laughed in his very own manner
これを聞いてシッダールタは彼なりのやり方で笑った。
the manner in which his voice assumed a touch of sadness
彼の声に悲しみの色が混じっていた様子
but it still had that touch of mockery
しかし、それはまだ嘲笑の雰囲気があった
Spoke Siddhartha, "Govinda, you've spoken well"
シッダールタは言いました。「ゴーヴィンダ、よく言ったな」
"you've remembered correctly what I said"
「私の言ったことをあなたは正しく覚えていた」

"If only you remembered the other thing you've heard from me"
「私から聞いたもう一つのことを思い出していただければ」
"I have grown distrustful and tired against teachings and learning"
「私は教えや学びに対して不信感と疲れを感じてきました」
"my faith in words, which are brought to us by teachers, is small"
「教師が私たちに伝える言葉に対する私の信頼は小さい」
"But let's do it, my dear"
「でも、やってみましょうよ、愛しい人」
"I am willing to listen to these teachings"
「私はこれらの教えに耳を傾けるつもりです」
"though in my heart I do not have hope"
「心の中では希望がないけれど」
"I believe that we've already tasted the best fruit of these teachings"
「私たちはすでにこの教えの最高の成果を味わっていると信じています」
Spoke Govinda, "Your willingness delights my heart"
ゴヴィンダは言いました。「あなたの意欲は私の心を喜ばせます。」
"But tell me, how should this be possible?"
「しかし、教えてください、どうしてこれが可能なのでしょうか?」
"How can the Gotama's teachings have already revealed their best fruit to us?"
「ゴータマの教えが、どうしてすでにその最高の成果を私たちに示しているのでしょうか?」
"we have not heard his words yet"
「私たちはまだ彼の言葉を聞いていない」
Spoke Siddhartha, "Let us eat this fruit"

シッダールタは言いました。「この果実を食べましょう」
"and let us wait for the rest, oh Govinda!"
「そして残りを待ちましょう、ああゴヴィンダ!」
"But this fruit consists in him calling us away from the Samanas"
「しかし、この果実は、彼が私たちをサマナスから遠ざけることにある」
"and we have already received it thanks to the Gotama!"
「そして私たちはゴータマのおかげですでにそれを受け取りました!」
"Whether he has more, let us await with calm hearts"
「彼がさらに何かを持っているかどうか、私たちは穏やかな心で待ちましょう」

On this very same day Siddhartha spoke to the oldest Samana
まさにこの日、シッダールタは最年長のサマナに話しかけました
he told him of his decision to leaves the Samanas
彼はサマナスを去る決心を彼に伝えた
he informed the oldest one with courtesy and modesty
彼は礼儀正しく謙虚に長男に知らせた
but the Samana became angry that the two young men wanted to leave him
しかしサマナは二人の若者が彼のもとを去ろうとしていることに腹を立てた。
and he talked loudly and used crude words
彼は大声で話し、下品な言葉を使った
Govinda was startled and became embarrassed
ゴヴィンダは驚いて恥ずかしくなった
But Siddhartha put his mouth close to Govinda's ear
しかしシッダールタはゴーヴィンダの耳に口を近づけた
"Now, I want to show the old man what I've learned from him"

「今、私は老人に私が彼から学んだことを見せたいのです」
Siddhartha positioned himself closely in front of the Samana
シッダールタはサマナのすぐ前に陣取った
with a concentrated soul, he captured the old man's glance
彼は集中した心で老人の視線を捉えた
he deprived him of his power and made him mute
彼は彼の権力を剥奪し、口がきけないようにした
he took away his free will
彼は彼の自由意志を奪った
he subdued him under his own will, and commanded him
彼は彼を自分の意志で従わせ、彼に命令した。
his eyes became motionless, and his will was paralysed
彼の目は動かなくなり、意志も麻痺した
his arms were hanging down without power
彼の腕は力なく垂れ下がっていた
he had fallen victim to Siddhartha's spell
彼はシッダールタの呪いの犠牲者となった
Siddhartha's thoughts brought the Samana under their control
シッダールタの思想はサマナを支配下に置いた
he had to carry out what they commanded
彼は彼らの命令を実行しなければならなかった
And thus, the old man made several bows
そして老人は何度もお辞儀をした
he performed gestures of blessing
彼は祝福のしぐさをした
he spoke stammeringly a godly wish for a good journey
彼はどもりながら良い旅を願う神聖な言葉を語った
the young men returned the good wishes with thanks
若者たちは感謝の気持ちを込めて祝福を返した
they went on their way with salutations
彼らは挨拶を交わしながら道を進んだ
On the way, Govinda spoke again

途中でゴヴィンダは再び話した
"Oh Siddhartha, you have learned more from the Samanas than I knew"
「おお、シッダールタよ、あなたは私が知っていた以上に多くのことをサマナから学んだのです」
"It is very hard to cast a spell on an old Samana"
「年老いたサマナに呪文をかけるのは非常に難しい」
"Truly, if you had stayed there, you would soon have learned to walk on water"
「本当に、もしあなたがそこに留まっていたなら、すぐに水の上を歩くことを学んでいたでしょう」
"I do not seek to walk on water" said Siddhartha
「私は水の上を歩くことを望んでいない」とシッダールタは言った
"Let old Samanas be content with such feats!"
「サマナス爺さんはそんな偉業で満足しろ！」

Gotama
ゴータマ

In Savathi, every child knew the name of the exalted Buddha
サヴァティでは、すべての子供が高貴な仏陀の名前を知っていた

every house was prepared for his coming
どの家も彼の来訪に備えていた

each house filled the alms-dishes of Gotama's disciples
各家にはゴータマの弟子たちの施し皿がいっぱいに置かれた

Gotama's disciples were the silently begging ones
ゴータマの弟子たちは黙って懇願していた

Near the town was Gotama's favourite place to stay
町の近くにはゴータマのお気に入りの滞在場所がありました

he stayed in the garden of Jetavana
彼はジェータヴァナの庭に滞在した

the rich merchant Anathapindika had given the garden to Gotama
裕福な商人アナタピンディカはゴータマに庭園を与えた。

he had given it to him as a gift
彼はそれを贈り物として彼に与えた

he was an obedient worshipper of the exalted one
彼は崇高な者への従順な崇拝者であった

the two young ascetics had received tales and answers
二人の若い修行僧は物語と答えを受け取った

all these tales and answers pointed them to Gotama's abode
これらの物語と答えはすべてゴータマの住処へと彼らを導いた

they arrived in the town of Savathi
彼らはサヴァティの町に到着した

they went to the very first door of the town

彼らは町の最初の玄関まで行きました
and they begged for food at the door
そして彼らは玄関先で食べ物を乞うた
a woman offered them food
女性が彼らに食べ物を差し出した
and they accepted the food
そして彼らは食べ物を受け取った
Siddhartha asked the woman
シッダールタは女性に尋ねた
"oh charitable one, where does the Buddha dwell?"
「慈悲深い人よ、仏陀はどこに住まわれるのですか？」
"we are two Samanas from the forest"
「私たちは森から来た二人のサマナです」
"we have come to see the perfected one"
「私たちは完成された者を見るために来た」
"we have come to hear the teachings from his mouth"
「私たちは彼の口から教えを聞くために来ました」
Spoke the woman, "you Samanas from the forest"
女性は言った。「あなた方は森のサマナスよ」
"you have truly come to the right place"
「あなたは本当に正しい場所に来ました」
"you should know, in Jetavana, there is the garden of Anathapindika"
「ジェータヴァナにはアナタピンディカの庭があることを知っておくべきだ」
"that is where the exalted one dwells"
「そこは崇高な者が住む場所である」
"there you pilgrims shall spend the night"
「巡礼者たちはそこで夜を過ごすのだ」
"there is enough space for the innumerable, who flock here"
「ここには数え切れないほどの人々が集まるのに十分なスペースがあります」
"they too come to hear the teachings from his mouth"
「彼らも彼の口から教えを聞きに来る」
This made Govinda happy, and full of joy

ゴヴィンダは喜びにあふれ、
he exclaimed, "we have reached our destination"
彼は「目的地に到着した」と叫んだ。
"our path has come to an end!"
「我々の道は終わりを迎えた！」
"But tell us, oh mother of the pilgrims"
「しかし、教えてください、巡礼者の母よ」
"do you know him, the Buddha?"
「あなたは仏陀をご存知ですか？」
"have you seen him with your own eyes?"
「あなたは彼を自分の目で見ましたか？」
Spoke the woman, "Many times I have seen him, the exalted one"
女性は言った。「私は何度も彼を見た、高貴な方を」
"On many days I have seen him"
「私は何日も彼に会った」
"I have seen him walking through the alleys in silence"
「私は彼が黙って路地を歩いているのを見た」
"I have seen him wearing his yellow cloak"
「私は彼が黄色いマントを着ているのを見た」
"I have seen him presenting his alms-dish in silence"
「私は彼が黙って施しの皿を差し出すのを見た」
"I have seen him at the doors of the houses"
「私は彼が家の玄関にいるのを見た」
"and I have seen him leaving with a filled dish"
「そして私は彼が満杯の皿を持って去っていくのを見た」
Delightedly, Govinda listened to the woman
ゴヴィンダは喜んでその女性の話を聞いた
and he wanted to ask and hear much more
そして彼はもっと多くのことを聞きたいと思った
But Siddhartha urged him to walk on
しかしシッダールタは彼に歩き続けるよう促した
They thanked the woman and left
彼らは女性に感謝し立ち去った

they hardly had to ask for directions
彼らはほとんど道を尋ねる必要がなかった
many pilgrims and monks were on their way to the Jetavana
多くの巡礼者と僧侶がジェータヴァナへ向かっていた。
they reached it at night, so there were constant arrivals
夜に到着したので、到着客が絶え間なくいた。
and those who sought shelter got it
そして避難所を求めた人々はそれを得た
The two Samanas were accustomed to life in the forest
二人のサマナは森での生活に慣れていた
so without making any noise they quickly found a place to stay
それで彼らは音を立てずにすぐに泊まる場所を見つけた
and they rested there until the morning
そして彼らは朝までそこで休んだ

At sunrise, they saw with astonishment the size of the crowd
日の出とともに、彼らは群衆の大きさに驚きました
a great many number of believers had come
非常に多くの信者が来ていた
and a great number of curious people had spent the night here
そして多くの好奇心旺盛な人々がここで夜を過ごしました
On all paths of the marvellous garden, monks walked in yellow robes
素晴らしい庭園の小道では修道士たちが黄色い僧衣を着て歩いていた。
under the trees they sat here and there, in deep contemplation
彼らは木々の下のあちこちに座り、深く考え込んでいた
or they were in a conversation about spiritual matters
あるいは霊的な事柄について話し合っていた
the shady gardens looked like a city
日陰の庭園はまるで街のようだった
a city full of people, bustling like bees

蜂のように賑わう、人でいっぱいの街
The majority of the monks went out with their alms-dish
僧侶の大半は托鉢皿を持って出かけた
they went out to collect food for their lunch
彼らは昼食のための食料を集めに出かけた
this would be their only meal of the day
これが彼らの一日の唯一の食事となる
The Buddha himself, the enlightened one, also begged in the mornings
悟りを開いた仏陀自身も朝に物乞いをしていた
Siddhartha saw him, and he instantly recognised him
シッダールタは彼を見て、すぐに彼だと認識した
he recognised him as if a God had pointed him out
彼は神が彼を指摘したかのように彼を認識した
He saw him, a simple man in a yellow robe
彼は黄色いローブを着た素朴な男を見た
he was bearing the alms-dish in his hand, walking silently
彼は施し皿を手に持ち、黙って歩いていた
"Look here!" Siddhartha said quietly to Govinda
「ここを見てください！」シッダールタはゴヴィンダに静かに言った
"This one is the Buddha"
「これが仏陀だ」
Attentively, Govinda looked at the monk in the yellow robe
ゴヴィンダは注意深く黄色い僧衣を着た僧侶を見つめた
this monk seemed to be in no way different from any of the others
この僧侶は他の僧侶と何ら変わらないようだった
but soon, Govinda also realized that this is the one
しかしすぐにゴヴィンダもこれが
And they followed him and observed him
そして彼らは彼に従い、彼を観察した
The Buddha went on his way, modestly and deep in his thoughts
仏陀は謙虚に、そして深く考えながら道を進みました
his calm face was neither happy nor sad

彼の穏やかな顔は幸せでも悲しくもなかった
his face seemed to smile quietly and inwardly
彼の顔は静かに内心微笑んでいるように見えた
his smile was hidden, quiet and calm
彼の笑顔は隠れていて、静かで穏やかだった
the way the Buddha walked somewhat resembled a healthy child
仏陀の歩き方は健康な子供の歩き方に似ていた
he walked just as all of his monks did
彼は他の修道士たちと同じように歩いた
he placed his feet according to a precise rule
彼は正確な規則に従って足を置いた
his face and his walk, his quietly lowered glance
彼の顔と歩き方、静かに下を向いた視線
his quietly dangling hand, every finger of it
静かに垂れ下がった手、その指の全て
all these things expressed peace
これらすべては平和を表している
all these things expressed perfection
これらすべては完璧さを表現した
he did not search, nor did he imitate
彼は探さなかったし、真似もしなかった
he softly breathed inwardly an unwhithering calm
彼は心の中で静かに息を吸い込み、揺るぎない平穏を保った。
he shone outwardly an unwhithering light
彼は外に向かって揺るぎない光を放っていた
he had about him an untouchable peace
彼は触れることのできない平和を身にまとっていた
the two Samanas recognised him solely by the perfection of his calm
二人のサマナは彼の落ち着きの完璧さだけで彼を認識した。
they recognized him by the quietness of his appearance
彼らは彼の外見の静けさから彼を認識した

the quietness in his appearance in which there was no searching
彼の外見は静かで、探している様子はなかった
there was no desire, nor imitation
欲望も模倣もなかった
there was no effort to be seen
目立つ努力はなかった
only light and peace was to be seen in his appearance
彼の外見には光と平和だけが見られた
"Today, we'll hear the teachings from his mouth" said Govinda
「今日は彼の口から教えを聞きます」とゴヴィンダは言った。
Siddhartha did not answer
シッダールタは答えなかった
He felt little curiosity for the teachings
彼は教えにほとんど興味を示さなかった
he did not believe that they would teach him anything new
彼は彼らが何か新しいことを教えてくれるとは思っていなかった
he had heard the contents of this Buddha's teachings again and again
彼はこの仏陀の教えの内容を何度も聞いていた
but these reports only represented second hand information
しかし、これらの報告は間接的な情報に過ぎなかった
But attentively he looked at Gotama's head
しかし彼は注意深くゴータマの頭を見つめた
his shoulders, his feet, his quietly dangling hand
彼の肩、彼の足、静かに垂れ下がった彼の手
it was as if every finger of this hand was of these teachings
まるでこの手の指の全てがこれらの教えであるかのようでした
his fingers spoke of truth
彼の指は真実を語っていた
his fingers breathed and exhaled the fragrance of truth

彼の指は真実の香りを吸い、吐き出した
his fingers glistened with truth
彼の指は真実で輝いていた
this Buddha was truthful down to the gesture of his last finger
この仏陀は最後の指のしぐさまで真実を語っていた
Siddhartha could see that this man was holy
シッダールタはこの男が聖なる人だと分かった
Never before, Siddhartha had venerated a person so much
シッダールタはかつてこれほど人を崇拝したことはなかった
he had never before loved a person as much as this one
彼はこれまでこれほど人を愛したことはなかった
They both followed the Buddha until they reached the town
二人は町に着くまで仏陀に従いました
and then they returned to their silence
そして彼らは再び沈黙に戻った
they themselves intended to abstain on this day
彼ら自身はこの日は棄権するつもりだった
They saw Gotama returning the food that had been given to him
彼らはゴータマが与えられた食べ物を返すのを見た
what he ate could not even have satisfied a bird's appetite
彼が食べたものは鳥の食欲さえ満たせなかっただろう
and they saw him retiring into the shade of the mango-trees
そして彼らは彼がマンゴーの木陰に退くのを見た

in the evening the heat had cooled down
夕方には暑さが和らいだ
everyone in the camp started to bustle about and gathered around
キャンプの全員が慌ただしく動き回り、集まった。
they heard the Buddha teaching, and his voice
彼らは仏陀の教えを聞き、その声を
and his voice was also perfected

そして彼の声も完璧だった
his voice was of perfect calmness
彼の声は完全に穏やかだった
his voice was full of peace
彼の声は平和に満ちていた
Gotama taught the teachings of suffering
ゴータマは苦しみの教えを説いた
he taught of the origin of suffering
彼は苦しみの起源について教えた
he taught of the way to relieve suffering
彼は苦しみを和らげる方法を教えた
Calmly and clearly his quiet speech flowed on
彼の静かなスピーチは穏やかに、明瞭に流れていった
Suffering was life, and full of suffering was the world
苦しみは人生であり、世界は苦しみに満ちていた
but salvation from suffering had been found
しかし苦しみからの救いは見つかった
salvation was obtained by him who would walk the path of the Buddha
仏の道を歩む者には救済が得られた
With a soft, yet firm voice the exalted one spoke
優しくも力強い声で高貴な方は語った
he taught the four main doctrines
彼は4つの主要な教義を教えた
he taught the eight-fold path
彼は八正道を教えた
patiently he went the usual path of the teachings
彼は辛抱強く教えの道を歩み続けた
his teachings contained the examples
彼の教えには次のような例が含まれていた
his teaching made use of the repetitions
彼の教えは繰り返しを利用した
brightly and quietly his voice hovered over the listeners
彼の声は明るく静かに聴衆の上に響き渡った
his voice was like a light

彼の声は光のようだった
his voice was like a starry sky
彼の声は星空のようだった
When the Buddha ended his speech, many pilgrims stepped forward
仏陀が説教を終えると、多くの巡礼者が前に進み出た。
they asked to be accepted into the community
彼らはコミュニティに受け入れられるよう求めた
they sought refuge in the teachings
彼らは教えに避難所を求めた
And Gotama accepted them by speaking
そしてゴータマはこう言って彼らを受け入れた
"You have heard the teachings well"
「あなたは教えをよく聞きました」
"join us and walk in holiness"
「私たちと一緒に聖なる道を歩んでください」
"put an end to all suffering"
「すべての苦しみを終わらせる」
Behold, then Govinda, the shy one, also stepped forward and spoke
すると、内気なゴヴィンダも前に出て話し始めた。
"I also take my refuge in the exalted one and his teachings"
「私もまた、高貴なる方とその教えに信頼を寄せています」
and he asked to be accepted into the community of his disciples
そして彼は弟子たちのコミュニティに受け入れられるよう求めた
and he was accepted into the community of Gotama's disciples
そして彼はゴータマの弟子のコミュニティに受け入れられた

the Buddha had retired for the night
仏陀は夜のために退いた

Govinda turned to Siddhartha and spoke eagerly
ゴーヴィンダはシッダールタの方を向いて熱心に話した

"Siddhartha, it is not my place to scold you"
「シッダールタ、私があなたを叱る立場ではない」

"We have both heard the exalted one"
「我々は二人とも高貴なる者の言うことを聞きました」

"we have both perceived the teachings"
「私たちは二人とも教えを理解しました」

"Govinda has heard the teachings"
「ゴヴィンダは教えを聞いた」

"he has taken refuge in the teachings"
「彼は教えに帰依した」

"But, my honoured friend, I must ask you"
「しかし、私の尊敬する友人よ、私はあなたに尋ねなければなりません」

"don't you also want to walk the path of salvation?"
「あなたも救いの道を歩みたいと思いませんか？」

"Would you want to hesitate?"
「躊躇したいですか？」

"do you want to wait any longer?"
「もう待ちますか？」

Siddhartha awakened as if he had been asleep
シッダールタは眠っていたかのように目覚めた

For a long time, he looked into Govinda's face
彼は長い間ゴヴィンダの顔を見つめていた

Then he spoke quietly, in a voice without mockery
それから彼は嘲りのない声で静かに話した

"Govinda, my friend, now you have taken this step"
「ゴヴィンダ、友よ、あなたは今この一歩を踏み出したのです」

"now you have chosen this path"
「今、あなたはこの道を選んだのです」

"Always, oh Govinda, you've been my friend"
「ゴヴィンダよ、あなたはいつも私の友達でした」

"you've always walked one step behind me"

「あなたはいつも私の一歩後ろを歩いていた」
"Often I have thought about you"
「私はよくあなたのことを考えていました」
"'Won't Govinda for once also take a step by himself'"
「ゴヴィンダも一度は一人で歩んでみたらどうか」
"'won't Govinda take a step without me?'"
「『ゴヴィンダは私なしで一歩も踏み出せないの？』」
"'won't he take a step driven by his own soul?'"
「彼は自分の魂に導かれて一歩を踏み出すのではないだろうか？」
"Behold, now you've turned into a man"
「見よ、あなたは今や男になったのだ」
"you are choosing your path for yourself"
「あなたは自分の道を選んでいるのです」
"I wish that you would go it up to its end"
「最後までやり遂げてほしい」
"oh my friend, I hope that you shall find salvation!"
「ああ、友よ、あなたが救いを見つけることを願っています！」
Govinda, did not completely understand it yet
ゴヴィンダはまだ完全に理解していなかった
he repeated his question in an impatient tone
彼はいらいらした口調で質問を繰り返した
"Speak up, I beg you, my dear!"
「お願いだから、大きな声で話してください！」
"Tell me, since it could not be any other way"
「他に方法はないのだから、教えてください」
"won't you also take your refuge with the exalted Buddha?"
「あなたも尊い仏陀のもとに帰依しませんか？」
Siddhartha placed his hand on Govinda's shoulder
シッダールタはゴーヴィンダの肩に手を置いた
"You failed to hear my good wish for you"
「あなたは私の願いを聞き入れなかった」
"I'm repeating my wish for you"
「私はあなたに願いを繰り返します」

"I wish that you would go this path"
「この道を進んでほしい」

"I wish that you would go up to this path's end"
「この道の終わりまで行ってほしい」

"I wish that you shall find salvation!"
「あなたが救いを見つけることを願っています！」

In this moment, Govinda realized that his friend had left him
この瞬間、ゴヴィンダは友人が自分のもとを去ったことに気づいた。

when he realized this he started to weep
これに気づいた彼は泣き始めた

"Siddhartha!" he exclaimed lamentingly
「シッダールタ！」彼は嘆き悲しんで叫んだ

Siddhartha kindly spoke to him
シッダールタは優しく彼に話しかけた

"don't forget, Govinda, who you are"
「ゴヴィンダ、あなたが誰であるかを忘れないで」

"you are now one of the Samanas of the Buddha"
「あなたは今や仏陀のサマナの一人です」

"You have renounced your home and your parents"
「あなたは自分の家と両親を捨てたのです」

"you have renounced your birth and possessions"
「あなたは生まれと財産を放棄した」

"you have renounced your free will"
「あなたは自由意志を放棄しました」

"you have renounced all friendship"
「あなたはすべての友情を放棄しました」

"This is what the teachings require"
「これが教えの要求です」

"this is what the exalted one wants"
「これが高貴なる者の望みである」

"This is what you wanted for yourself"
「これはあなたが望んだことだ」

"Tomorrow, oh Govinda, I will leave you"

「明日、ああゴヴィンダよ、私はあなたと別れます」
For a long time, the friends continued walking in the garden
友人たちは長い間庭を歩き続けた
for a long time, they lay there and found no sleep
彼らは長い間そこに横たわり、眠れなかった
And over and over again, Govinda urged his friend
そしてゴヴィンダは何度も友人に促した
"why would you not want to seek refuge in Gotama's teachings?"
「なぜゴータマの教えに帰依したくないのですか？」
"what fault could you find in these teachings?"
「これらの教えにどんな欠点が見つかるでしょうか？」
But Siddhartha turned away from his friend
しかしシッダールタは友人から背を向けた
every time he said, "Be content, Govinda!"
彼はいつもこう言いました。「満足しなさい、ゴヴィンダ！」
"Very good are the teachings of the exalted one"
「高貴なる者の教えは実に素晴らしい」
"how could I find a fault in his teachings?"
「どうして彼の教えに欠点を見つけることができるだろうか？」

it was very early in the morning
それは朝の早い時間でした
one of the oldest monks went through the garden
最年長の修道士の一人が庭を通り抜けた
he called to those who had taken their refuge in the teachings
彼は教えに頼っていた人々に呼びかけた
he called them to dress them up in the yellow robe
彼は彼らに黄色いローブを着せるよう呼びかけた
and he instruct them in the first teachings and duties of their position

そして彼は彼らに彼らの立場における最初の教えと義務を教える。
Govinda once again embraced his childhood friend
ゴヴィンダは再び幼なじみを抱きしめた
and then he left with the novices
そして彼は修行僧たちと一緒に出発した
But Siddhartha walked through the garden, lost in thought
しかしシッダールタは庭を歩きながら考え事をしていた
Then he happened to meet Gotama, the exalted one
そして彼はゴータマという高貴な人に出会ったのです
he greeted him with respect
彼は敬意を持って挨拶した
the Buddha's glance was full of kindness and calm
仏陀の視線は優しさと穏やかさに満ちていた
the young man summoned his courage
若者は勇気を奮い起こした
he asked the venerable one for the permission to talk to him
彼はその尊者に話をする許可を求めた
Silently, the exalted one nodded his approval
黙って高貴な者はうなずいて承認した
Spoke Siddhartha, "Yesterday, oh exalted one"
シッダールタは言った、「昨日、高貴なる者よ」
"I had been privileged to hear your wondrous teachings"
「私はあなたの素晴らしい教えを聞くという特権に恵まれました」
"Together with my friend, I had come from afar, to hear your teachings"
「私は友人と一緒に、あなたの教えを聞くために遠くから来ました」
"And now my friend is going to stay with your people"
「そして今、私の友人はあなたの人々と一緒にいるつもりです」
"he has taken his refuge with you"
「彼はあなたのところに避難した」
"But I will again start on my pilgrimage"

「しかし私は再び巡礼の旅に出ます」

"As you please," the venerable one spoke politely
「お望みどおりに」と、その尊者は丁寧に言った。

"Too bold is my speech," Siddhartha continued
「私の言葉は大胆すぎる」とシッダールタは続けた。

"but I do not want to leave the exalted on this note"
「しかし、私はこのメモで高貴な人々を残したくない」

"I want to share with the most venerable one my honest thoughts"
「私は最も尊敬すべき方と私の正直な思いを共有したい」

"Does it please the venerable one to listen for one moment longer?"
「尊者様はもう少しだけ聞いていただけますか？」

Silently, the Buddha nodded his approval
仏陀は黙ってうなずいて承認した。

Spoke Siddhartha, "oh most venerable one"
シッダールタは言った、「ああ、最も尊い人よ」

"there is one thing I have admired in your teachings most of all"
「あなたの教えの中で私が最も感心したことが一つあります」

"Everything in your teachings is perfectly clear"
「あなたの教えはすべて完全に明確です」

"what you speak of is proven"
「あなたが話していることは証明されています」

"you are presenting the world as a perfect chain"
「あなたは世界を完璧な連鎖として提示しています」

"a chain which is never and nowhere broken"
「決して、どこでも切れることのない鎖」

"an eternal chain the links of which are causes and effects"
「原因と結果が結びついた永遠の鎖」

"Never before, has this been seen so clearly"
「これまでこれほどはっきりと見えたことはなかった」

"never before, has this been presented so irrefutably"

「これまでこれほど反論の余地なく提示されたことはなかった」
"truly, the heart of every Brahman has to beat stronger with love"
「本当に、すべてのブラフマンの心は愛でより強く鼓動しなければなりません」
"he has seen the world through your perfectly connected teachings"
「彼はあなたの完璧に繋がった教えを通して世界を見てきました」
"without gaps, clear as a crystal"
「隙間なく、水晶のように澄んでいる」
"not depending on chance, not depending on Gods"
「偶然に頼らず、神に頼らず」
"he has to accept it whether it may be good or bad"
「それが良いことであろうと悪いことであろうと、彼はそれを受け入れなければならない」
"he has to live by it whether it would be suffering or joy"
「それが苦しみであろうと喜びであろうと、彼はそれに従って生きなければならない」
"but I do not wish to discuss the uniformity of the world"
「しかし私は世界の均一性について議論したいわけではない」
"it is possible that this is not essential"
「これは必須ではない可能性がある」
"everything which happens is connected"
「起こることはすべてつながっている」
"the great and the small things are all encompassed"
「大きなものも小さなものもすべて包含されている」
"they are connected by the same forces of time"
「それらは同じ時間の力によって結びついている」
"they are connected by the same law of causes"
「それらは同じ原因の法則によって結びついている」
"the causes of coming into being and of dying"
「生まれる原因と死ぬ原因」

"this is what shines brightly out of your exalted teachings"
「これがあなたの崇高な教えから輝き出るものです」
"But, according to your very own teachings, there is a small gap"
「しかし、あなた自身の教えによれば、小さな隙間がある」
"this unity and necessary sequence of all things is broken in one place"
「すべてのものの統一性と必然的な順序は、ある場所で破られている」
"this world of unity is invaded by something alien"
「この統一された世界は異質なものに侵略されている」
"there is something new, which had not been there before"
「これまでなかった新しいものがある」
"there is something which cannot be demonstrated"
「証明できないものがある」
"there is something which cannot be proven"
「証明できないことがある」
"these are your teachings of overcoming the world"
「これが世界を克服するためのあなたの教えです」
"these are your teachings of salvation"
「これがあなたの救いの教えです」
"But with this small gap, the eternal breaks apart again"
「しかし、この小さな隙間によって、永遠は再び崩れ去る」
"with this small breach, the law of the world becomes void"
「この小さな違反により、世界の法は無効になる」
"Please forgive me for expressing this objection"
「このような異議を唱えることをお許しください」
Quietly, Gotama had listened to him, unmoved
ゴータマは静かに、動揺することなく彼の話を聞いていた
Now he spoke, the perfected one, with his kind and polite clear voice
完成された彼は、優しくて丁寧な澄んだ声で話した。

"You've heard the teachings, oh son of a Brahman"
「ブラフマンの息子よ、あなたは教えを聞いたことがある」
"and good for you that you've thought about it this deeply"
「そして、あなたがそれについて深く考えてくれたのは素晴らしいことです」
"You've found a gap in my teachings, an error"
「私の教えに欠陥、間違いを見つけた」
"You should think about this further"
「これについてはさらに考えたほうがいい」
"But be warned, oh seeker of knowledge, of the thicket of opinions"
「しかし、知識を求める者よ、意見の藪には注意せよ」
"be warned of arguing about words"
「言葉について議論するのは危険だ」
"There is nothing to opinions"
「意見なんて関係ない」
"they may be beautiful or ugly"
「それらは美しいかもしれないし、醜いかもしれない」
"opinions may be smart or foolish"
「意見は賢明かもしれないし、愚かかもしれない」
"everyone can support opinions, or discard them"
「誰もが意見を支持することも、捨てることもできる」
"But the teachings, you've heard from me, are no opinion"
「しかし、あなたが私から聞いた教えは意見ではありません」
"their goal is not to explain the world to those who seek knowledge"
「彼らの目的は、知識を求める人々に世界を説明することではない」
"They have a different goal"
「彼らの目標は違う」
"their goal is salvation from suffering"
「彼らの目的は苦しみからの救済だ」
"This is what Gotama teaches, nothing else"

「これがゴータマの教えであり、他には何もない」
"I wish that you, oh exalted one, would not be angry with me" said the young man
「ああ、高貴なる者よ、どうか私に怒らないで下さい」と若者は言った。
"I have not spoken to you like this to argue with you"
「私はあなたと議論するためにこのように話したのではない」
"I do not wish to argue about words"
「言葉について議論したいわけではない」
"You are truly right, there is little to opinions"
「あなたは本当に正しい、意見にはほとんど意味がない」
"But let me say one more thing"
「でも、もう一つ言わせて下さい」
"I have not doubted in you for a single moment"
「私はあなたを一瞬たりとも疑ったことはありません」
"I have not doubted for a single moment that you are Buddha"
「私はあなたが仏陀であることを一瞬たりとも疑ったことはありません」
"I have not doubted that you have reached the highest goal"
「あなたが最高の目標に到達したことを私は疑っていません」
"the highest goal towards which so many Brahmans are on their way"
「多くのバラモンが向かっている最高の目標」
"You have found salvation from death"
「あなたは死からの救いを見つけました」
"It has come to you in the course of your own search"
「それはあなた自身の探求の過程であなたにやって来たのです」
"it has come to you on your own path"
「それはあなた自身の道を通ってあなたにやって来たのです」

"it has come to you through thoughts and meditation"
「それは思考と瞑想を通してあなたにもたらされたのです」
"it has come to you through realizations and enlightenment"
「それは悟りと啓蒙を通してあなたにもたらされたのです」
"but it has not come to you by means of teachings!"
「しかし、それは教えによってあなた方に伝わったのではないのです！」
"And this is my thought"
「これが私の考えです」
"nobody will obtain salvation by means of teachings!"
「教えによって救済される者は誰もいない！」
"You will not be able to convey your hour of enlightenment"
「あなたは悟りの時を伝えることができないでしょう」
"words of what has happened to you won't convey the moment!"
「あなたに何が起こったのか言葉では伝えきれない瞬間です！」
"The teachings of the enlightened Buddha contain much"
「悟りを開いた仏陀の教えには多くのことが含まれている」
"it teaches many to live righteously"
「多くの人に正しく生きることを教える」
"it teaches many to avoid evil"
「多くの人に悪を避けるように教える」
"But there is one thing which these teachings do not contain"
「しかし、これらの教えには含まれていないことが一つあります」
"they are clear and venerable, but the teachings miss something"
「それらは明確で尊いものですが、教えには何かが欠けています」
"the teachings do not contain the mystery"
「教えには謎は含まれていない」

"the mystery of what the exalted one has experienced for himself"
「高貴な者が自ら経験したことの神秘」
"among hundreds of thousands, only he experienced it"
「何十万人もの中で、それを経験したのは彼だけだった」
"This is what I have thought and realized, when I heard the teachings"
「これは私が教えを聞いたときに考え、理解したことです」
"This is why I am continuing my travels"
「これが私が旅を続ける理由です」
"this is why I do not to seek other, better teachings"
「これが私が他のより良い教えを求めない理由です」
"I know there are no better teachings"
「これより良い教えはないことは分かっています」
"I leave to depart from all teachings and all teachers"
「私はすべての教えとすべての教師から離れます」
"I leave to reach my goal by myself, or to die"
「私は自分の目標を達成するために出発します、さもなければ死ぬのです」
"But often, I'll think of this day, oh exalted one"
「しかし、私はしばしばこの日のことを思い出すでしょう、高貴なる者よ」
"and I'll think of this hour, when my eyes beheld a holy man"
「そして私は、私の目が聖なる人を見たこの時のことを思い出すだろう」
The Buddha's eyes quietly looked to the ground
仏陀の目は静かに地面を見ていた
quietly, in perfect equanimity, his inscrutable face was smiling
静かに、完全に平静に、彼の不可解な顔は微笑んでいた
the venerable one spoke slowly
尊者はゆっくりと話した

"I wish that your thoughts shall not be in error"
「あなたの考えが間違っていないことを願います」
"I wish that you shall reach the goal!"
「目標達成を祈っています！」
"But there is something I ask you to tell me"
「でも、あなたに教えてほしいことがあります」
"Have you seen the multitude of my Samanas?"
「私のサマナの大群を見たことがありますか？」
"they have taken refuge in the teachings"
「彼らは教えに頼ってきた」
"do you believe it would be better for them to abandon the teachings?"
「彼らにとって教えを放棄する方が良いと思いますか？」
"should they to return into the world of desires?"
「彼らは欲望の世界に戻るべきでしょうか？」
"Far is such a thought from my mind" exclaimed Siddhartha
「そんな考えは私の心にはない」とシッダールタは叫んだ。
"I wish that they shall all stay with the teachings"
「彼ら全員が教えを守ってくれることを願います」
"I wish that they shall reach their goal!"
「彼らが目標を達成することを祈ります！」
"It is not my place to judge another person's life"
「他人の人生を判断するのは私の役目ではない」
"I can only judge my own life"
「私は自分の人生しか判断できない」
"I must decide, I must chose, I must refuse"
「私は決めなければならない、私は選ばなければならない、私は拒否しなければならない」
"Salvation from the self is what we Samanas search for"
「自己からの救済こそが、私たちサマナが求めるものである」
"oh exalted one, if only I were one of your disciples"

「ああ、高貴なる者よ、私があなたの弟子の一人であったなら」
"I'd fear that it might happen to me"
「私にもそんなことが起こるかもしれないと怖い」
"only seemingly, would my self be calm and be redeemed"
「一見すると、私自身は落ち着き、救済されるだろう」
"but in truth it would live on and grow"
「しかし、実際にはそれは生き続け、成長するだろう」
"because then I would replace my self with the teachings"
「そうすると、私は自分自身を教えに置き換えることになるからです」
"my self would be my duty to follow you"
「私はあなたに従う義務があります」
"my self would be my love for you"
「私自身があなたへの愛となるでしょう」
"and my self would be the community of the monks!"
「そして私自身が修道士たちのコミュニティとなるでしょう！」
With half of a smile Gotama looked into the stranger's eyes
ゴータマは半笑いで見知らぬ人の目を見つめた
his eyes were unwaveringly open and kind
彼の目は揺るぎなく開かれ、優しかった
he bid him to leave with a hardly noticeable gesture
彼はほとんど気づかれないような仕草で彼に立ち去るように言った
"You are wise, oh Samana" the venerable one spoke
「あなたは賢明です、サマナ」と尊者は言った
"You know how to talk wisely, my friend"
「あなたは賢く話す方法を知っています、友よ」
"Be aware of too much wisdom!"
「知恵のなさには気をつけろ！」
The Buddha turned away
仏陀は背を向けた
Siddhartha would never forget his glance
シッダールタは彼の視線を決して忘れないだろう

his half smile remained forever etched in Siddhartha's memory
彼の半笑いはシッダールタの記憶に永遠に刻み込まれた。

Siddhartha thought to himself
シッダールタは心の中で思った

"I have never before seen a person glance and smile this way"
「こんなふうにちらっと見て笑う人を私は今まで見たことがない」

"no one else sits and walks like he does"
「彼のように座ったり歩いたりできる人は他にいない」

"truly, I wish to be able to glance and smile this way"
「本当に、こうやって見て微笑んでいられたらいいのに」

"I wish to be able to sit and walk this way, too"
「私もこうやって座ったり歩いたりできるようになりたい」

"liberated, venerable, concealed, open, childlike and mysterious"
「解放された、尊敬に値する、隠された、開かれた、子供っぽい、神秘的な」

"he must have succeeded in reaching the innermost part of his self"
「彼は自分の心の奥底に到達することに成功したに違いない」

"only then can someone glance and walk this way"
「そのとき初めて、誰かがこちらを見て、こちらへ歩いていくことができるのです」

"I will also seek to reach the innermost part of my self"
「私も自分の心の奥底に迫ろうと努めます」

"I saw a man" Siddhartha thought
「私は男を見た」シッダールタは思った

"a single man, before whom I would have to lower my glance"

「私が視線を下げなければならない一人の男」
"I do not want to lower my glance before anyone else"
「誰よりも先に視線を下げたくない」
"No teachings will entice me more anymore"
「どんな教えも私をこれ以上魅了することはない」
"because this man's teachings have not enticed me"
「この男の教えは私を魅了しなかったから」
"I am deprived by the Buddha" thought Siddhartha
「私は仏陀に奪われた」とシッダールタは思った
"I am deprived, although he has given so much"
「彼は多くのものを与えてくれたのに、私は奪われている」
"he has deprived me of my friend"
「彼は私から友人を奪った」
"my friend who had believed in me"
「私を信じてくれた友人」
"my friend who now believes in him"
「今や彼を信じる私の友人」
"my friend who had been my shadow"
「私の影だった友人」
"and now he is Gotama's shadow"
「そして今、彼はゴータマの影である」
"but he has given me Siddhartha"
「しかし彼は私にシッダールタを与えた」
"he has given me myself"
「彼は私に私自身を与えてくれました」

Awakening
目覚め

Siddhartha left the mango grove behind him
シッダールタはマンゴー畑を後にした
but he felt his past life also stayed behind
しかし、彼は過去の人生も残されていると感じていた
the Buddha, the perfected one, stayed behind
完成された仏陀は後に残った
and Govinda stayed behind too
ゴヴィンダも残って
and his past life had parted from him
そして彼の過去の人生は彼から離れてしまった
he pondered as he was walking slowly
彼はゆっくり歩きながら考えていた
he pondered about this sensation, which filled him completely
彼はこの感覚について考えていた。それは彼を完全に満たした。
He pondered deeply, like diving into a deep water
彼は深い水に飛び込むように深く考え込んだ
he let himself sink down to the ground of the sensation
彼は感覚の底に身を沈めた
he let himself sink down to the place where the causes lie
彼は原因がどこにあるかに自らを落とし込んだ
to identify the causes is the very essence of thinking
原因を特定することは思考の本質である
this was how it seemed to him
彼にはそのように思われた
and by this alone, sensations turn into realizations
そしてこれだけで、感覚は実現に変わる
and these sensations are not lost
そしてこれらの感覚は失われない
but the sensations become entities
しかし感覚は実体となる

and the sensations start to emit what is inside of them
そして感覚は内側にあるものを放出し始める
they show their truths like rays of light
彼らは光線のように真実を明かす
Slowly walking along, Siddhartha pondered
ゆっくりと歩きながら、シッダールタは考えていた
He realized that he was no youth any more
彼はもう若くないことに気づいた
he realized that he had turned into a man
彼は自分が人間になったことに気づいた
He realized that something had left him
彼は何かが自分から去ったことに気づいた
the same way a snake is left by its old skin
蛇が古い皮を剥がされるのと同じように
what he had throughout his youth no longer existed in him
彼が若い頃に持っていたものはもう彼の中には存在しなかった
it used to be a part of him; the wish to have teachers
それはかつて彼の一部だった。教師が欲しいという願い
the wish to listen to teachings
教えを聞きたいという願い
He had also left the last teacher who had appeared on his path
彼はまた、彼の道に現れた最後の教師とも別れた。
he had even left the highest and wisest teacher
彼は最高で最も賢明な教師さえも残した
he had left the most holy one, Buddha
彼は最も神聖な仏陀を残した
he had to part with him, unable to accept his teachings
彼は彼の教えを受け入れることができず、彼と別れなければならなかった。
Slower, he walked along in his thoughts
彼はゆっくりと考えながら歩いた
and he asked himself, "But what is this?"

そして彼は自分自身に尋ねました。「しかし、これは何なのだろう？」

"what have you sought to learn from teachings and from teachers?"
「あなたは教えや教師から何を学ぼうとしましたか？」

"and what were they, who have taught you so much?"
「そして、あなたにこれほど多くのことを教えた人たちは何者だったのですか？」

"what are they if they have been unable to teach you?"
「彼らがあなたに教えることができなかったとしたら、彼らは何なのでしょう？」

And he found, "It was the self"
そして彼は「それは自分自身だった」と気づいた

"it was the purpose and essence of which I sought to learn"
「それが私が学ぼうとしていた目的と本質でした」

"It was the self I wanted to free myself from"
「私は自分自身から解放されたかったのです」

"the self which I sought to overcome"
「私が克服しようとした自分」

"But I was not able to overcome it"
「でも、私はそれを乗り越えられなかった」

"I could only deceive it"
「騙すことしかできなかった」

"I could only flee from it"
「私は逃げることしかできなかった」

"I could only hide from it"
「私はそれから隠れることしかできなかった」

"Truly, no thing in this world has kept my thoughts so busy"
「本当に、この世でこれほど私の心を忙しくさせるものはない」

"I have been kept busy by the mystery of me being alive"
「私は自分が生きていることの謎に悩まされてきた」

"the mystery of me being one"
「私が一つであるという謎」

"the mystery if being separated and isolated from all others"

「他のすべてから分離され孤立していることの謎」
"the mystery of me being Siddhartha!"
「私がシッダールタであるという謎！」
"And there is no thing in this world I know less about"
「この世で私が知らないことは何もない」
he had been pondering while slowly walking along
彼はゆっくりと歩きながら考えていた
he stopped as these thoughts caught hold of him
彼はこれらの考えに捕らわれて立ち止まった
and right away another thought sprang forth from these thoughts
そしてすぐに別の考えが浮かび上がった
"there's one reason why I know nothing about myself"
「私が自分自身について何も知らないのには理由が一つある」
"there's one reason why Siddhartha has remained alien to me"
「シッダールタが私にとって異質な存在であり続ける理由は一つある」
"all of this stems from one cause"
「これらすべては一つの原因から生じている」
"I was afraid of myself, and I was fleeing"
「私は自分自身が怖くて逃げていました」
"I have searched for both Atman and Brahman"
「私はアートマンとブラフマンの両方を探しました」
"for this I was willing to dissect my self"
「このために私は自分自身を解剖するつもりでした」
"and I was willing to peel off all of its layers"
「そして私はそのすべての層を剥ぎ取るつもりだった」
"I wanted to find the core of all peels in its unknown interior"
「私は、すべての皮の核となる部分をその未知の内部から見つけたかったのです」
"the Atman, life, the divine part, the ultimate part"
「アートマン、生命、神聖な部分、究極の部分」

"But I have lost myself in the process"
「しかし、その過程で私は自分を見失ってしまった」
Siddhartha opened his eyes and looked around
シッダールタは目を開けて周りを見回した
looking around, a smile filled his face
周りを見回すと、彼の顔には笑みが浮かんでいた
a feeling of awakening from long dreams flowed through him
長い夢から目覚めたような感覚が彼の中に流れ込んだ
the feeling flowed from his head down to his toes
その感情は頭からつま先まで流れ落ちた
And it was not long before he walked again
そして、彼が再び歩くまでにはそう時間はかからなかった
he walked quickly, like a man who knows what he has got to do
彼は、自分が何をすべきかを知っている男のように、足早に歩いた。
"now I will not let Siddhartha escape from me again!"
「もう二度とシッダールタを逃がさないぞ!」
"I no longer want to begin my thoughts and my life with Atman"
「私はもう、アートマンから自分の考えや人生を始めたくありません」
"nor do I want to begin my thoughts with the suffering of the world"
「私は世界の苦しみについて考え始めたくはない」
"I do not want to kill and dissect myself any longer"
「もう自分を殺したり解剖したりしたくない」
"Yoga-Veda shall not teach me anymore"
「ヨガ・ヴェーダはもう私に教えない」
"nor Atharva-Veda, nor the ascetics"
「アタルヴァ・ヴェーダも、苦行者も」
"there will not be any kind of teachings"
「いかなる種類の教えも存在しない」
"I want to learn from myself and be my student"

「自分自身から学び、自分の生徒になりたい」
"I want to get to know myself; the secret of Siddhartha"
「私は自分自身を知りたい。シッダールタの秘密」

He looked around, as if he was seeing the world for the first time
彼はまるで初めて世界を見るかのように辺りを見回した
Beautiful and colourful was the world
世界は美しく色彩豊かだった
strange and mysterious was the world
世界は奇妙で神秘的だった
Here was blue, there was yellow, here was green
ここは青、ここは黄色、ここは緑
the sky and the river flowed
空と川が流れた
the forest and the mountains were rigid
森と山は厳しかった
all of the world was beautiful
世界のすべてが美しかった
all of it was mysterious and magical
すべてが神秘的で魔法のようでした
and in its midst was he, Siddhartha, the awakening one
そしてその中には、目覚めた者、シッダールタがいた
and he was on the path to himself
そして彼は自分自身への道を歩んでいた
all this yellow and blue and river and forest entered Siddhartha
この黄色と青と川と森のすべてがシッダールタの中に入りました
for the first time it entered through the eyes
初めて目から入った
it was no longer a spell of Mara
それはもはやマーラの呪文ではなかった
it was no longer the veil of Maya
それはもはやマヤのベールではなかった

it was no longer a pointless and coincidental
それはもはや無意味な偶然ではなかった
things were not just a diversity of mere appearances
物事は単なる外見の多様性ではなく
appearances despicable to the deeply thinking Brahman
深く考えるブラフマンにとって卑劣な外見
the thinking Brahman scorns diversity, and seeks unity
思考するブラフマンは多様性を軽蔑し、統一を求める
Blue was blue and river was river
青は青、川は川だった
the singular and divine lived hidden in Siddhartha
シッダールタには唯一無二の神聖なものが隠れていた
divinity's way and purpose was to be yellow here, and blue there
神の道と目的は、ここは黄色、あちらは青であることだった
there sky, there forest, and here Siddhartha
そこに空、そこに森、そしてここにシッダールタ
The purpose and essential properties was not somewhere behind the things
目的と本質的な性質は、物事のどこかに隠れているわけではない
the purpose and essential properties was inside of everything
目的と本質的な性質はすべてのものの中にあった
"How deaf and stupid have I been!" he thought
「自分はなんて耳が遠くて、愚かだったんだろう！」と彼は思った
and he walked swiftly along
そして彼は足早に歩き出した
"When someone reads a text he will not scorn the symbols and letters"
「文章を読むとき、人は記号や文字を軽蔑しない」
"he will not call the symbols deceptions or coincidences"
「彼はシンボルを欺瞞や偶然とは呼ばないだろう」
"but he will read them as they were written"

「しかし、彼はそれを書かれたとおりに読むだろう」
"he will study and love them, letter by letter"
「彼は文字ごとに学び、愛するだろう」
"I wanted to read the book of the world and scorned the letters"
「私は世界の本を読みたくて、文字を軽蔑した」
"I wanted to read the book of myself and scorned the symbols"
「私は自分自身の本を読みたかったし、シンボルを軽蔑した」
"I called my eyes and my tongue coincidental"
「私の目と舌は偶然だ」
"I said they were worthless forms without substance"
「私は、それらは実体のない価値のない形式だと言った」
"No, this is over, I have awakened"
「いや、もう終わりだ、目覚めた」
"I have indeed awakened"
「私は確かに目覚めた」
"I had not been born before this very day"
「私は今日まで生まれていなかった」
In thinking these thoughts, Siddhartha suddenly stopped once again
こうした考えを巡らせていたシッダールタは、突然また立ち止まった。
he stopped as if there was a snake lying in front of him
彼はまるで目の前に蛇が横たわっているかのように立ち止まった
suddenly, he had also become aware of something else
突然、彼はまた別のことに気づいた
He was indeed like someone who had just woken up
彼はまさに目覚めたばかりの人のようだった
he was like a new-born baby starting life anew
彼は新たな人生を始める新生児のようだった
and he had to start again at the very beginning

そして彼は最初からやり直さなければならなかった
in the morning he had had very different intentions
朝、彼は全く違う意図を持っていた
he had thought to return to his home and his father
彼は家と父親のところへ戻ることを考えていた
But now he stopped as if a snake was lying on his path
しかし今、彼はまるで蛇が道に横たわっているかのように立ち止まった
he made a realization of where he was
彼は自分がどこにいるのかに気づいた
"I am no longer the one I was"
「私はもう以前の私ではない」
"I am no ascetic anymore"
「私はもう修行僧ではない」
"I am not a priest anymore"
「私はもう司祭ではありません」
"I am no Brahman anymore"
「私はもうブラフマンではない」
"Whatever should I do at my father's place?"
「お父さんのところで何をしたらいいの?」
"Study? Make offerings? Practise meditation?"
「勉強?お供え?瞑想?」
"But all this is over for me"
「でも、私にとってはもう終わりだ」
"all of this is no longer on my path"
「これらすべてはもう私の道ではない」
Motionless, Siddhartha remained standing there
シッダールタは動かずにそこに立ち続けた
and for the time of one moment and breath, his heart felt cold
そして一瞬、息をする間、彼の心は冷たくなりました
he felt a coldness in his chest
彼は胸に冷たさを感じた
the same feeling a small animal feels when it sees how alone it is

小さな動物が孤独を感じた時に感じるのと同じ感情
For many years, he had been without home and had felt nothing
彼は何年も家を失って何も感じていなかった
Now, he felt he had been without a home
今、彼は家を失ったように感じている
Still, even in the deepest meditation, he had been his father's son
それでも、最も深い瞑想の中でも、彼は父親の息子だった
he had been a Brahman, of a high caste
彼は高位カーストのバラモンであった
he had been a cleric
彼は聖職者だった
Now, he was nothing but Siddhartha, the awoken one
今、彼は目覚めた者、シッダールタに他ならない
nothing else was left of him
彼には何も残っていなかった
Deeply, he inhaled and felt cold
彼は深く息を吸い込み、寒さを感じた
a shiver ran through his body
彼の体中に震えが走った
Nobody was as alone as he was
彼ほど孤独な人はいなかった
There was no nobleman who did not belong to the noblemen
貴族に属していない貴族はいなかった
there was no worker that did not belong to the workers
労働者に属していない労働者はいなかった
they had all found refuge among themselves
彼らは皆、自分たちの間で避難所を見つけた
they shared their lives and spoke their languages
彼らは生活を共有し、言語を話した
there are no Brahman who would not be regarded as Brahmans
バラモンとみなされないバラモンは存在しない

and there are no Brahmans that didn't live as Brahmans
バラモンとして生きなかったバラモンはいない
there are no ascetic who could not find refuge with the Samanas
サマナに避難できない修行者はいない
and even the most forlorn hermit in the forest was not alone
森の最も孤独な隠者でさえ孤独ではなかった
he was also surrounded by a place he belonged to
彼はまた、自分が属する場所に囲まれていた
he also belonged to a caste in which he was at home
彼はまた、故郷のカーストに属していた
Govinda had left him and became a monk
ゴヴィンダは彼のもとを去り、僧侶になった
and a thousand monks were his brothers
そして千人の修道士が彼の兄弟であった
they wore the same robe as him
彼らは彼と同じローブを着ていた
they believed in his faith and spoke his language
彼らは彼の信仰を信じ、彼の言語を話した
But he, Siddhartha, where did he belong to?
しかし、彼、シッダールタはどこに属していたのでしょうか？
With whom would he share his life?
彼は誰と人生を共にするのでしょうか？
Whose language would he speak?
彼は誰の言語を話すのでしょうか？
the world melted away all around him
彼の周りの世界は溶けて消え去った
he stood alone like a star in the sky
彼は空の星のように一人で立っていた
cold and despair surrounded him
寒さと絶望が彼を取り囲んだ
but Siddhartha emerged out of this moment
しかしシッダールタはこの瞬間から現れた
Siddhartha emerged more his true self than before

シッダールタは以前よりも本当の自分を見せた
he was more firmly concentrated than he had ever been
彼は今までにないほど集中していた
He felt; "this had been the last tremor of the awakening"
彼は「これは目覚めの最後の震えだった」と感じた。
"the last struggle of this birth"
「この誕生の最後の闘い」
And it was not long until he walked again in long strides
そして、彼が再び大股で歩くようになるまで、そう時間はかからなかった。
he started to proceed swiftly and impatiently
彼は急いで、せっかちに進み始めた
he was no longer going home
彼はもう家に帰らなかった
he was no longer going to his father
彼はもう父親のところへ行かなかった

Part Two
パート2

***

Kamala
カマラ

Siddhartha learned something new on every step of his path
シッダールタは道のあらゆる段階で何か新しいことを学んだ
because the world was transformed and his heart was enchanted
世界は変わり、彼の心は魅了された。
He saw the sun rising over the mountains
彼は山々の向こうに太陽が昇るのを見た
and he saw the sun setting over the distant beach
そして彼は遠くの浜辺に沈む夕日を見た
At night, he saw the stars in the sky in their fixed positions
夜になると、彼は空の星が定まった位置にあるのを見た。
and he saw the crescent of the moon floating like a boat in the blue
そして彼は青い空に船のように浮かぶ三日月を見た
He saw trees, stars, animals, and clouds
彼は木々、星、動物、雲を見た
rainbows, rocks, herbs, flowers, streams and rivers
虹、岩、ハーブ、花、小川、川
he saw the glistening dew in the bushes in the morning
彼は朝、茂みの中の輝く露を見た
he saw distant high mountains which were blue
彼は遠くの青い高い山々を見た
wind blew through the rice-field
風が田んぼを吹き抜けた

all of this, a thousand-fold and colourful, had always been there
これらすべては千倍も多彩で、常にそこにあった
the sun and the moon had always shone
太陽と月はいつも輝いていた
rivers had always roared and bees had always buzzed
川はいつも轟音を立て、蜂はいつもブンブンと鳴いていた
but in former times all of this had been a deceptive veil
しかし、昔はこれらすべてが偽りのベールだった
to him it had been nothing more than fleeting
彼にとってそれはつかの間の出来事に過ぎなかった
it was supposed to be looked upon in distrust
それは不信の目で見られるはずだった
it was destined to be penetrated and destroyed by thought
それは思考によって貫かれ破壊される運命にあった
since it was not the essence of existence
それは存在の本質ではなかったから
since this essence lay beyond, on the other side of, the visible
この本質は目に見えるものの向こう側にあるので
But now, his liberated eyes stayed on this side
しかし今、解放された彼の目はここに留まっていた
he saw and became aware of the visible
彼は目に見えるものを見て気づいた
he sought to be at home in this world
彼はこの世界で居心地のよい場所を求めていた
he did not search for the true essence
彼は真の本質を探さなかった
he did not aim at a world beyond
彼はそれ以上の世界を目指していなかった
this world was beautiful enough for him
この世界は彼にとって十分に美しかった
looking at it like this made everything childlike
こうやって見ると、すべてが子供っぽくなる
Beautiful were the moon and the stars

月と星は美しかった
beautiful was the stream and the banks
川と川岸は美しかった
the forest and the rocks, the goat and the gold-beetle
森と岩、ヤギと金色の甲虫
the flower and the butterfly; beautiful and lovely it was
花と蝶。それは美しく愛らしかった
to walk through the world was childlike again
世界を歩くことは再び子供のようだった
this way he was awoken
こうして彼は目覚めた
this way he was open to what is near
こうして彼は近くにあるものに心を開いていた
this way he was without distrust
こうすれば彼は不信感を抱かなかった
differently the sun burnt the head
太陽が頭を焼いた
differently the shade of the forest cooled him down
森の木陰が彼を涼しくしてくれた
differently the pumpkin and the banana tasted
カボチャとバナナの味が違っていた
Short were the days, short were the nights
日は短かった、夜は短かった
every hour sped swiftly away like a sail on the sea
毎時間が海の帆のようにあっという間に過ぎ去っていく
and under the sail was a ship full of treasures, full of joy
そして帆の下には宝物と喜びに満ちた船があった
Siddhartha saw a group of apes moving through the high canopy
シッダールタは高い樹冠の間を移動する猿の群れを見た
they were high in the branches of the trees
彼らは木の枝の高いところにいた
and he heard their savage, greedy song
そして彼は彼らの野蛮で貪欲な歌を聞いた
Siddhartha saw a male sheep following a female one and mating with her

シッダールタは雄羊が雌羊を追いかけて交尾しているのを見た。
In a lake of reeds, he saw the pike hungrily hunting for its dinner
葦の湖で、彼はカワカマスが空腹で食事を探しているのを見た
young fish were propelling themselves away from the pike
若い魚はカワカマスから逃げようとしていた
they were scared, wiggling and sparkling
彼らは怯え、身をくねらせ、キラキラ輝いていた
the young fish jumped in droves out of the water
若い魚が群れをなして水から飛び出した
the scent of strength and passion came forcefully out of the water
力強さと情熱の香りが水から力強く漂ってきた
and the pike stirred up the scent
そしてカワカマスは匂いをかき立てた
All of this had always existed
これらはすべて常に存在していた
and he had not seen it, nor had he been with it
彼はそれを見たことも、一緒にいたこともなかった
Now he was with it and he was part of it
今、彼はそれと共にあり、その一部となっていた
Light and shadow ran through his eyes
彼の目に光と影が走った
stars and moon ran through his heart
星と月が彼の心を駆け巡った

Siddhartha remembered everything he had experienced in the Garden Jetavana
シッダールタはジェータヴァナの園で経験したことをすべて思い出した。
he remembered the teaching he had heard there from the divine Buddha
彼はそこで神聖な仏陀から聞いた教えを思い出した

he remembered the farewell from Govinda
彼はゴヴィンダとの別れを思い出した
he remembered the conversation with the exalted one
彼は高貴な方との会話を思い出した
Again he remembered his own words that he had spoken to the exalted one
彼は再び、高貴な方に向かって語った自分の言葉を思い出しました
he remembered every word
彼はすべての言葉を覚えていた
he realized he had said things which he had not really known
彼は自分が本当に知らないことを言ってしまったことに気づいた
he astonished himself with what he had said to Gotama
彼はゴータマに言ったことに自分自身驚いた
the Buddha's treasure and secret was not the teachings
仏陀の宝と秘密は教えではなかった
but the secret was the inexpressible and not teachable
しかしその秘密は言葉では言い表せず、教えることもできないものだった
the secret which he had experienced in the hour of his enlightenment
彼が悟りを開いた時に体験した秘密
the secret was nothing but this very thing which he had now gone to experience
その秘密は、彼が今体験しようとしていることそのものである。
the secret was what he now began to experience
その秘密は彼が今体験し始めたものだった
Now he had to experience his self
今、彼は自分自身を体験しなければならなかった
he had already known for a long time that his self was Atman

彼はすでに長い間、自分自身がアートマンであることを知っていた
he knew Atman bore the same eternal characteristics as Brahman
彼はアートマンがブラフマンと同じ永遠の特徴を持っていることを知っていた
But he had never really found this self
しかし彼は、この自分を見つけることができなかった
because he had wanted to capture the self in the net of thought
彼は思考の網の中に自己を捕らえたかったからだ
but the body was not part of the self
しかし、身体は自分自身の一部ではなかった
it was not the spectacle of the senses
それは感覚の光景ではなかった
so it also was not the thought, nor the rational mind
だからそれは思考でも理性的な心でもなかった
it was not the learned wisdom, nor the learned ability
それは学んだ知恵でも、学んだ能力でもなかった
from these things no conclusions could be drawn
これらのことから結論は導き出せない
No, the world of thought was also still on this side
いや、思考の世界もまだこちら側にあった
Both, the thoughts as well as the senses, were pretty things
思考も感覚もどちらも美しいものだった
but the ultimate meaning was hidden behind both of them
しかし、その両方の背後には究極の意味が隠されていた
both had to be listened to and played with
どちらも聴いて、演奏しなければならなかった
neither had to be scorned nor overestimated
軽蔑されることも過大評価されることもなかった
there were secret voices of the innermost truth
そこには心の奥底にある真実の秘密の声があった
these voices had to be attentively perceived
これらの声は注意深く聞き取らなければならなかった

He wanted to strive for nothing else
彼は他の何にも努力したくなかった
he would do what the voice commanded him to do
彼は声が命じたことを実行するだろう
he would dwell where the voices advised him to
彼は声が彼に勧める場所に住むだろう
Why had Gotama sat down under the Bodhi tree?
ゴータマはなぜ菩提樹の下に座ったのでしょうか？
He had heard a voice in his own heart
彼は自分の心の中で声を聞いた
a voice which had commanded him to seek rest under this tree
この木の下で休むように命じた声
he could have gone on to make offerings
彼は供物を捧げ続けたかもしれない
he could have performed his ablutions
彼は身を清めることができたかもしれない
he could have spent that moment in prayer
彼はその瞬間を祈りに費やすことができただろう
he had chosen not to eat or drink
彼は食べも飲みもしないことを選んだ
he had chosen not to sleep or dream
彼は眠ることも夢を見ることもしないことを選んだ
instead, he had obeyed the voice
代わりに彼は声に従った
To obey like this was good
このように従うのは良かった
it was good not to obey to an external command
外部の命令に従わないのは良かった
it was good to obey only the voice
声だけに従うのがよかった
to be ready like this was good and necessary
このように準備しておくことは良いことであり、必要だった
there was nothing else that was necessary

他に必要なものは何もなかった

in the night Siddhartha got to a river
夜、シッダールタは川に着いた
he slept in the straw hut of a ferryman
彼は渡し守の藁小屋で寝た
this night Siddhartha had a dream
その夜、シッダールタは夢を見た
Govinda was standing in front of him
ゴヴィンダは彼の前に立っていた
he was dressed in the yellow robe of an ascetic
彼は修行僧の黄色いローブを着ていた
Sad was how Govinda looked
ゴヴィンダの表情は悲しかった
sadly he asked, "Why have you forsaken me?"
彼は悲しそうに尋ねました。「なぜ私を見捨てたのですか?」
Siddhartha embraced Govinda, and wrapped his arms around him
シッダールタはゴーヴィンダを抱きしめ、両腕で彼を包み込んだ。
he pulled him close to his chest and kissed him
彼は彼を胸に抱き寄せてキスをした
but it was not Govinda anymore, but a woman
しかしそれはもうゴヴィンダではなく、女性だった
a full breast popped out of the woman's dress
女性のドレスから豊かな胸が飛び出していた
Siddhartha lay and drank from the breast
シッダールタは横たわり乳房から飲んだ
sweetly and strongly tasted the milk from this breast
この乳房から出る乳を甘く強く味わった
It tasted of woman and man
それは女と男の味だった
it tasted of sun and forest
太陽と森の味がした

it tasted of animal and flower
動物と花の味がした

it tasted of every fruit and every joyful desire
それはあらゆる果実とあらゆる喜びの欲望の味でした

It intoxicated him and rendered him unconscious
彼は酔って意識を失った。

Siddhartha woke up from the dream
シッダールタは夢から目覚めた

the pale river shimmered through the door of the hut
小屋のドアの向こうに淡い川の水がきらめいていた

a dark call of an owl resounded deeply through the forest
フクロウの暗い鳴き声が森中に深く響き渡った

Siddhartha asked the ferryman to get him across the river
シッダールタは渡し守に川を渡ってもらうよう頼んだ

The ferryman got him across the river on his bamboo-raft
渡し守は竹のいかだで彼を川を渡らせた

the water shimmered reddish in the light of the morning
水は朝の光の中で赤く輝いていた

"This is a beautiful river," he said to his companion
「美しい川だ」と彼は同行者に言った。

"Yes," said the ferryman, "a very beautiful river"
「はい」と渡し守は言った。「とても美しい川です」

"I love it more than anything"
「何よりも大好きです」

"Often I have listened to it"
「よく聴いています」

"often I have looked into its eyes"
「私は何度もその目を見つめてきた」

"and I have always learned from it"
「そして私はいつもそこから学んできました」

"Much can be learned from a river"
「川から多くのことを学べる」

"I thank you, my benefactor" spoke Siddhartha
「恩人に感謝します」とシッダールタは言った。

he disembarked on the other side of the river

彼は川の反対側に降り立った

"I have no gift I could give you for your hospitality, my dear"
「あなたのおもてなしに対して、私には何も贈る物がありません、愛しい人よ」

"and I also have no payment for your work"
「そして私はあなたの仕事に対しても報酬を受け取っていない」

"I am a man without a home"
「私は家のない男だ」

"I am the son of a Brahman and a Samana"
「私はバラモンとサマナの息子です」

"I did see it," spoke the ferryman
「確かに見たよ」と船頭は言った。

"I did not expect any payment from you"
「私はあなたからの支払いを期待していませんでした」

"it is custom for guests to bear a gift"
「客が贈り物を持ってくるのが習慣です」

"but I did not expect this from you either"
「でも、私もあなたにはこんなことは期待していませんでした」

"You will give me the gift another time"
「また別の機会にプレゼントをください」

"Do you think so?" asked Siddhartha, bemusedly
「そう思う？」シッダールタは困惑しながら尋ねた。

"I am sure of it," replied the ferryman
「それは間違いない」と渡し守は答えた。

"This too, I have learned from the river"
「これも川から学んだことだ」

"everything that goes comes back!"
「去ったものはすべて戻ってくる！」

"You too, Samana, will come back"
「サマナ、あなたもまた戻ってくるよ」

"Now farewell! Let your friendship be my reward"

「さようなら！あなたの友情が私のご褒美になりますように」
"Commemorate me, when you make offerings to the gods"
「神々に供物を捧げるときには、私を記念してください」
Smiling, they parted from each other
二人は微笑みながら別れた
Smiling, Siddhartha was happy about the friendship
シッダールタは笑顔で友情を喜んだ
and he was happy about the kindness of the ferryman
そして彼は渡し守の親切さに満足した
"He is like Govinda," he thought with a smile
「彼はゴヴィンダのようだ」と彼は微笑みながら思った。
"all I meet on my path are like Govinda"
「私が道中で出会う人はすべてゴヴィンダのような人です」
"All are thankful for what they have"
「誰もが持っているものに感謝している」
"but they are the ones who would have a right to receive thanks"
「しかし、彼らこそ感謝を受ける権利がある」
"all are submissive and would like to be friends"
「みんな従順で友達になりたいと思っています」
"all like to obey and think little"
「みんな従順であまり考えないことを好む」
"all people are like children"
「人は皆、子供のようだ」

At about noon, he came through a village
正午ごろ、彼は村を通り過ぎた
In front of the mud cottages, children were rolling about in the street
泥造りの小屋の前では、子供たちが道で転げ回っていた
they were playing with pumpkin-seeds and sea-shells

彼らはカボチャの種と貝殻で遊んでいました
they screamed and wrestled with each other
彼らは叫びながら互いに格闘した
but they all timidly fled from the unknown Samana
しかし、彼らは皆、未知のサマナから臆病に逃げた。
In the end of the village, the path led through a stream
村の端には小川を通る道があった
by the side of the stream, a young woman was kneeling
小川のほとりで若い女性がひざまずいていた
she was washing clothes in the stream
彼女は小川で洗濯をしていた
When Siddhartha greeted her, she lifted her head
シッダールタが彼女に挨拶すると、彼女は頭を上げて
and she looked up to him with a smile
そして彼女は微笑みながら彼を見上げた
he could see the white in her eyes glistening
彼は彼女の目の白が光っているのを見た
He called out a blessing to her
彼は彼女に祝福の言葉を叫んだ
this was the custom among travellers
これは旅行者の習慣だった
and he asked how far it was to the large city
そして彼は大きな街までどのくらい遠いのか尋ねた
Then she got up and came to him
それから彼女は立ち上がって彼のところへ行きました
beautifully her wet mouth was shimmering in her young face
彼女の濡れた口が若々しい顔の中で美しく輝いていた
She exchanged humorous banter with him
彼女は彼と面白い会話を交わした
she asked whether he had eaten already
彼女は彼がもう食べたかどうか尋ねた
and she asked curious questions
そして彼女は興味深い質問をした
"is it true that the Samanas slept alone in the forest at night?"

「サマナ族が夜、森の中で一人で眠っていたというのは本当ですか？」
"is it true Samanas are not allowed to have women with them"
「サマナ族は女性を連れて行くことが許されていないというのは本当ですか？」
While talking, she put her left foot on his right one
彼女は話をしながら、彼の右足に左足を乗せた。
the movement of a woman who would want to initiate sexual pleasure
性的快楽を求めようとする女性の動き
the textbooks call this "climbing a tree"
教科書ではこれを「木登り」と呼んでいます
Siddhartha felt his blood heating up
シッダールタは血が熱くなるのを感じた
he had to think of his dream again
彼は再び自分の夢について考えなければならなかった
he bend slightly down to the woman
彼は女性に向かって少し身をかがめた
and he kissed with his lips the brown nipple of her breast
そして彼は彼女の胸の茶色い乳首に唇でキスをした
Looking up, he saw her face smiling
見上げると、彼女の笑顔が見えた
and her eyes were full of lust
彼女の目は欲望に満ちていた
Siddhartha also felt desire for her
シッダールタも彼女への欲望を感じた
he felt the source of his sexuality moving
彼は自分の性的欲求の源が動いているのを感じた
but he had never touched a woman before
しかし彼はこれまで女性に触れたことがなかった
so he hesitated for a moment
そこで彼は一瞬躊躇した
his hands were already prepared to reach out for her
彼の手はすでに彼女に手を伸ばす準備ができていた

but then he heard the voice of his innermost self
しかし、彼は自分の心の奥底からの声を聞いた
he shuddered with awe at his voice
彼はその声に畏怖の念を抱いて震えた
and this voice told him no
そしてこの声は彼にノーと言った
all charms disappeared from the young woman's smiling face
若い女性の笑顔からすべての魅力が消えた
he no longer saw anything else but a damp glance
彼はもう湿った視線以外何も見ていなかった
all he could see was female animal in heat
彼に見えたのは発情期の雌の動物だけだった
Politely, he petted her cheek
彼は丁寧に彼女の頬を撫でた
he turned away from her and disappeared away
彼は彼女から背を向けて姿を消した
he left from the disappointed woman with light steps
彼は軽やかな足取りで失望した女性のもとを去った
and he disappeared into the bamboo-wood
そして彼は竹林の中に姿を消した

he reached the large city before the evening
彼は夕方前に大都市に到着した
and he was happy to have reached the city
そして彼は街に到着して嬉しかった
because he felt the need to be among people
彼は人々の中にいる必要性を感じていたので
or a long time, he had lived in the forests
あるいは長い間、彼は森に住んでいた
for first time in a long time he slept under a roof
彼は久しぶりに屋根の下で眠った
Before the city was a beautifully fenced garden
街が建つ以前は、美しい柵で囲まれた庭園があった
the traveller came across a small group of servants

旅行者は小さな召使いの集団に出会った
the servants were carrying baskets of fruit
召使たちは果物の入った籠を運んでいた
four servants were carrying an ornamental sedan-chair
4人の召使が装飾的な輿を運んでいた
on this chair sat a woman, the mistress
この椅子には女主人が座っていた
she was on red pillows under a colourful canopy
彼女は色鮮やかな天蓋の下の赤い枕の上にいた
Siddhartha stopped at the entrance to the pleasure-garden
シッダールタは遊園地の入り口で立ち止まった
and he watched the parade go by
そして彼はパレードが通り過ぎるのを眺めた
he saw saw the servants and the maids
彼は召使と女中たちを見た
he saw the baskets and the sedan-chair
彼は籠と輿を見た
and he saw the lady on the chair
そして彼は椅子に座っている女性を見た
Under her black hair he saw a very delicate face
彼女の黒い髪の下には、とても繊細な顔が見えた
a bright red mouth, like a freshly cracked fig
割れたてのイチジクのような真っ赤な口
eyebrows which were well tended and painted in a high arch
眉毛はよく手入れされ、高いアーチ状に描かれていた
they were smart and watchful dark eyes
彼らは賢く用心深い黒い目だった
a clear, tall neck rose from a green and golden garment
緑と金色の衣服から、澄んだ長い首が立ち上がった。
her hands were resting, long and thin
彼女の手は長くて細いまま休んでいた
she had wide golden bracelets over her wrists
彼女は手首に幅広の金のブレスレットをしていた
Siddhartha saw how beautiful she was, and his heart rejoiced

シッダールタは彼女の美しさを見て心から喜びました
He bowed deeply, when the sedan-chair came closer
輿が近づくと、彼は深くお辞儀をした。
straightening up again, he looked at the fair, charming face
彼は再び背筋を伸ばし、その美しく魅力的な顔を見た。
he read her smart eyes with the high arcs
彼は彼女の鋭い目を高く見つめて読み取った
he breathed in a fragrance of something he did not know
彼は何か知らない匂いを嗅いだ
With a smile, the beautiful woman nodded for a moment
美しい女性は微笑みながら、しばらくうなずいた。
then she disappeared into the garden
そして彼女は庭に消えていった
and then the servants disappeared as well
そして召使たちも姿を消した
"I am entering this city with a charming omen" Siddhartha thought
「私はこの街に魅力的な前兆を持って入ってきた」シッダールタは思った
He instantly felt drawn into the garden
彼はすぐに庭に引き込まれたように感じた
but he thought about his situation
しかし彼は自分の状況について考えた
he became aware of how the servants and maids had looked at him
彼は召使や女中たちが自分をどう見ていたかに気づいた。
they thought him despicable, distrustful, and rejected him
彼らは彼を卑劣で不信感を抱き、拒絶した。
"I am still a Samana" he thought
「私はまだサマナだ」と彼は思った
"I am still an ascetic and beggar"
「私はまだ苦行者であり、乞食です」
"I must not remain like this"
「このままではいけない」

"I will not be able to enter the garden like this," he laughed
「このままでは庭に入れないだろう」と彼は笑った。
he asked the next person who came along the path about the garden
彼は道に沿って次に来た人に庭について尋ねた
and he asked for the name of the woman
そして彼はその女性の名前を尋ねた
he was told that this was the garden of Kamala, the famous courtesan
彼はここが有名な娼婦カマラの庭だと教えられた
and he was told that she also owned a house in the city
そして彼女は市内に家も所有していると聞かされた
Then, he entered the city with a goal
そして、彼は目標を持って街に入った
Pursuing his goal, he allowed the city to suck him in
彼は目標を追い求め、街に吸い込まれていった
he drifted through the flow of the streets
彼は通りの流れの中を漂っていた
he stood still on the squares in the city
彼は市内の広場に立ち止まった
he rested on the stairs of stone by the river
彼は川沿いの石の階段で休んだ
When the evening came, he made friends with a barber's assistant
夕方になると、彼は理髪店の店員と友達になった
he had seen him working in the shade of an arch
彼はアーチの陰で彼が働いているのを見た
and he found him again praying in a temple of Vishnu
そして彼はヴィシュヌの寺院で祈っている彼を見つけた
he told about stories of Vishnu and the Lakshmi
彼はヴィシュヌとラクシュミの物語を語った
Among the boats by the river, he slept this night
川沿いの船の間で彼はその夜眠った
Siddhartha came to him before the first customers came into his shop

シッダールタは彼の店に最初の客が来る前に彼のもとを訪れた

he had the barber's assistant shave his beard and cut his hair
彼は理髪店の店員にひげを剃ってもらい、髪を切ってもらった。
he combed his hair and anointed it with fine oil
彼は髪をとかし、上等な油を塗った
Then he went to take his bath in the river
それから彼は川で水浴びをしに行きました

late in the afternoon, beautiful Kamala approached her garden
午後遅く、美しいカマラは庭に近づきました
Siddhartha was standing at the entrance again
シッダールタは再び入り口に立っていた
he made a bow and received the courtesan's greeting
彼はお辞儀をして遊女の挨拶を受けた
he got the attention of one of the servant
彼は召使の一人の注意を引いた
he asked him to inform his mistress
彼は愛人に知らせるように頼んだ
"a young Brahman wishes to talk to her"
「若いブラフマンが彼女と話したい」
After a while, the servant returned
しばらくして召使が戻ってきた
the servant asked Siddhartha to follow him
召使いはシッダールタに彼について来るように頼んだ
Siddhartha followed the servant into a pavilion
シッダールタは召使の後を追って東屋に入った
here Kamala was lying on a couch
ここでカマラはソファに横たわっていた
and the servant left him alone with her
そして召使は彼を彼女と二人きりにして
"Weren't you also standing out there yesterday, greeting me?" asked Kamala

「昨日もそこに立って私に挨拶していませんでしたか？」とカマラは尋ねた。

"It's true that I've already seen and greeted you yesterday"
「確かに昨日もお会いしてご挨拶させて頂きました」

"But didn't you yesterday wear a beard, and long hair?"
「でも、昨日はひげを生やして髪も長かったでしょう？」

"and was there not dust in your hair?"
「あなたの髪には埃が付いていませんでしたか？」

"You have observed well, you have seen everything"
「あなたはよく観察しました、あなたはすべてを見ました」

"You have seen Siddhartha, the son of a Brahman"
「あなたはバラモンの息子であるシッダールタを見た」

"the Brahman who has left his home to become a Samana"
「家を離れてサマナになったブラフマン」

"the Brahman who has been a Samana for three years"
「3年間サマナであったブラフマン」

"But now, I have left that path and came into this city"
「しかし今、私はその道を離れ、この街に来たのです」

"and the first one I met, even before I had entered the city, was you"
「そして私が街に入る前に最初に会ったのはあなたでした」

"To say this, I have come to you, oh Kamala!"
「これを言うために、私はあなたのところに来ました、カマラよ！」

"before, Siddhartha addressed all woman with his eyes to the ground"
「以前、シッダールタは地面に目を落としながらすべての女性に話しかけていました」

"You are the first woman whom I address otherwise"
「あなたは私がそう呼んだ最初の女性です」

"Never again do I want to turn my eyes to the ground"
「二度と地面に目を向けたくない」

"I won't turn when I'm coming across a beautiful woman"
「美しい女性に出会ったら振り返らない」
Kamala smiled and played with her fan of peacocks' feathers
カマラは微笑みながら孔雀の羽根の扇子で遊んだ
"And only to tell me this, Siddhartha has come to me?"
「そして、シッダールタは私にこれを告げるためにだけ私のところに来たのですか？」
"To tell you this and to thank you for being so beautiful"
「あなたにこれを伝えて、あなたがこんなに美しいことに感謝するために」
"I would like to ask you to be my friend and teacher"
「私の友達であり先生になってほしい」
"for I know nothing yet of that art which you have mastered"
「あなたが習得したその技術について、私はまだ何も知らないのです」
At this, Kamala laughed aloud
これを聞いてカマラは大声で笑った。
"Never before this has happened to me, my friend"
「こんなことは今まで一度もなかったよ、友よ」
"a Samana from the forest came to me and wanted to learn from me!"
「森のサマナが私のところに来て、私から学びたいと言ってきました！」
"Never before this has happened to me"
「こんなことは今まで一度もなかった」
"a Samana came to me with long hair and an old, torn loincloth!"
「長い髪と、古くて破れた腰布をつけたサマナが私のところにやって来た！」
"Many young men come to me"
「多くの若者が私のところにやって来ます」
"and there are also sons of Brahmans among them"
「彼らの中にはバラモンの子らもいる」
"but they come in beautiful clothes"

「でも彼らは美しい服を着てやって来る」
"they come in fine shoes"
「彼らは良い靴を履いて来ます」
"they have perfume in their hair
「髪に香水をつけている
"and they have money in their pouches"
「そして彼らの財布にはお金が入っている」
"This is how the young men are like, who come to me"
「私のところに来る若者たちはこんな感じです」
Spoke Siddhartha, "Already I am starting to learn from you"
シッダールタは言った、「私はすでにあなたから学び始めています」
"Even yesterday, I was already learning"
「昨日もすでに学んでいた」
"I have already taken off my beard"
「もう髭は剃ったよ」
"I have combed the hair"
「髪をとかしました」
"and I have oil in my hair"
「髪にオイルがついてるよ」
"There is little which is still missing in me"
「私にまだ欠けているものはほとんどありません」
"oh excellent one, fine clothes, fine shoes, money in my pouch"
「ああ、素晴らしい人よ、素敵な服、素敵な靴、そして私の財布にはお金がある」
"You shall know Siddhartha has set harder goals for himself"
「シッダールタは自分自身にさらに厳しい目標を設定したことをあなたは知るだろう」
"and he has reached these goals"
「そして彼はこれらの目標を達成した」
"How shouldn't I reach that goal?"
「どうしてその目標を達成できないのでしょうか？」
"the goal which I have set for myself yesterday"

「昨日私が自分自身に設定した目標」
"to be your friend and to learn the joys of love from you"
「あなたの友達になり、あなたから愛の喜びを学びたい」
"You'll see that I'll learn quickly, Kamala"
「私がすぐに学ぶのがわかるでしょう、カマラ」
"I have already learned harder things than what you're supposed to teach me"
「あなたが私に教えるべきことよりも難しいことを私はすでに学んできました」
"And now let's get to it"
「それでは始めましょう」
"You aren't satisfied with Siddhartha as he is?"
「あなたはシッダールタの現状に満足していないのですか？」
"with oil in his hair, but without clothes"
「髪には油を塗っているが、衣服は着ていない」
"Siddhartha without shoes, without money"
「靴もお金もないシッダールタ」
Laughing, Kamala exclaimed, "No, my dear"
カマラは笑いながら「いいえ、愛しい人よ」と叫んだ。
"he doesn't satisfy me, yet"
「彼はまだ私を満足させていない」
"Clothes are what he must have"
「服は彼にとってなくてはならないものだ」
"pretty clothes, and shoes is what he needs"
「彼にはきれいな服と靴が必要なのです」
"pretty shoes, and lots of money in his pouch"
「かわいい靴と、ポーチにたくさんのお金」
"and he must have gifts for Kamala"
「そして彼はカマラに贈り物を持っているに違いない」
"Do you know it now, Samana from the forest?"
「森のサマナ、もう分かったか？」
"Did you mark my words?"
「私の言葉を覚えていましたか？」

"Yes, I have marked your words," Siddhartha exclaimed
「はい、私はあなたの言葉を覚えました」とシッダールタは叫んだ

"How should I not mark words which are coming from such a mouth!"
「こんな口から出てくる言葉をどうして気に留めずにいられるだろうか！」

"Your mouth is like a freshly cracked fig, Kamala"
「あなたの口は、割ったばかりのイチジクのようだね、カマラ」

"My mouth is red and fresh as well"
「口の中も赤くて爽やかです」

"it will be a suitable match for yours, you'll see"
「きっとあなたのものにぴったり合うはずです」

"But tell me, beautiful Kamala"
「でも、教えてください、美しいカマラ」

"aren't you at all afraid of the Samana from the forest""
「森のサマナが怖くないの？」

"the Samana who has come to learn how to make love"
「愛し合う方法を学びに来たサマナ」

"Whatever for should I be afraid of a Samana?"
「どうしてサマナを恐れなければならないのか？」

"a stupid Samana from the forest"
「森から来た愚かなサマナ」

"a Samana who is coming from the jackals"
「ジャッカルから来たサマナ」

"a Samana who doesn't even know yet what women are?"
「まだ女性が何であるかさえ知らないサマナ？」

"Oh, he's strong, the Samana"
「ああ、サマナは強いな」

"and he isn't afraid of anything"
「そして彼は何も恐れない」

"He could force you, beautiful girl"
「彼はあなたを強制できるかもしれない、美しい娘よ」

"He could kidnap you and hurt you"

「彼はあなたを誘拐して傷つけるかもしれない」
"No, Samana, I am not afraid of this"
「いいえ、サマナ、私はこれを恐れていません」
"Did any Samana or Brahman ever fear someone might come and grab him?"
「サマナやバラモンは、誰かが来て自分を捕まえるかもしれないと恐れたことがありますか?」
"could he fear someone steals his learning?
「誰かが彼の学習を盗むのではないかと恐れているのだろうか?
"could anyone take his religious devotion"
「彼の宗教的信仰を誰かが受け継ぐことができるだろうか」
"is it possible to take his depth of thought?
「彼の思考の深さを捉えることは可能でしょうか?
"No, because these things are his very own"
「いいえ、これらは彼のものだからです」
"he would only give away the knowledge he is willing to give"
「彼は自分が与えたいと思う知識だけを与えるだろう」
"he would only give to those he is willing to give to"
「彼は自分が与えたいと思う人にだけ与えるだろう」
"precisely like this it is also with Kamala"
「カマラの場合もまさに同じです」
"and it is the same way with the pleasures of love"
「そしてそれは愛の喜びでも同じです」
"Beautiful and red is Kamala's mouth," answered Siddhartha
「カマラの口は美しく赤い」とシッダールタは答えた。
"but don't try to kiss it against Kamala's will"
「でも、カマラの意志に反してキスしようとしないで」
"because you will not obtain a single drop of sweetness from it"
「そこからは一滴の甘さも得られないからです」
"You are learning easily, Siddhartha"
「あなたは簡単に学んでいます、シッダールタ」

"you should also learn this"
「これも学ぶべきです」

"love can be obtained by begging, buying"
「愛は物乞いや買い物によって得られる」

"you can receive it as a gift"
「ギフトとして受け取ることができます」

"or you can find it in the street"
「または路上で見つけることもできます」

"but love cannot be stolen"
「しかし愛は盗めない」

"In this, you have come up with the wrong path"
「これであなたは間違った道を選んでしまった」

"it would be a pity if you would want to tackle love in such a wrong manner"
「もしあなたが愛を間違ったやり方で扱おうとするなら残念だ」

Siddhartha bowed with a smile
シッダールタは微笑みながらお辞儀をした

"It would be a pity, Kamala, you are so right"
「それは残念ですね、カマラさん、あなたは本当に正しいです」

"It would be such a great pity"
「それは本当に残念なことだ」

"No, I shall not lose a single drop of sweetness from your mouth"
「いいえ、あなたの口から一滴の甘さも失わせません」

"nor shall you lose sweetness from my mouth"
「わたしの口から甘さが失われることはない」

"So it is agreed. Siddhartha will return"
「それで合意した。シッダールタは戻ってくるだろう」

"Siddhartha will return once he has what he still lacks"
「シッダールタは、まだ足りないものを手に入れたら戻ってくるだろう」

"he will come back with clothes, shoes, and money"
「彼は服と靴とお金を持って戻ってくるだろう」

"But speak, lovely Kamala, couldn't you still give me one small advice?"
「でもね、愛しいカマラ、私に小さなアドバイスを一つだけしてくれませんか？」

"Give you an advice? Why not?"
「アドバイスをしましょうか？なぜダメなの？」

"Who wouldn't like to give advice to a poor, ignorant Samana?"
「貧しく無知なサマナにアドバイスをしたくない人がいるだろうか？」

"Dear Kamala, where I should go to find these three things most quickly?"
「親愛なるカマラ、この3つのものを最も早く見つけるにはどこに行けばいいでしょうか？」

"Friend, many would like to know this"
「友よ、多くの人がこれを知りたいと思うだろう」

"You must do what you've learned and ask for money"
「学んだことを実行し、お金を要求しなければなりません」

"There is no other way for a poor man to obtain money"
「貧しい人がお金を得るには他に方法はない」

"What might you be able to do?"
「あなたに何ができるでしょうか？」

"I can think. I can wait. I can fast" said Siddhartha
「私は考えることができる。私は待つことができる。私は断食することができる」とシッダールタは言った。

"Nothing else?" asked Kamala
「他には何もないの？」とカマラは尋ねた。

"yes, I can also write poetry"
「はい、詩も書けますよ」

"Would you like to give me a kiss for a poem?"
「詩を書いてくれたらキスをしてくれませんか？」

"I would like to, if I like your poem"
「あなたの詩が気に入ったら、そうしたいです」

"What would be its title?"

「タイトルは何でしょうか?」
Siddhartha spoke, after he had thought about it for a moment
シッダールタはしばらく考えた後、こう言った。
"Into her shady garden stepped the pretty Kamala"
「美しいカマラが彼女の木陰の庭に足を踏み入れた」
"At the garden's entrance stood the brown Samana"
「庭の入り口には茶色のサマナが立っていた」
"Deeply, seeing the lotus's blossom, Bowed that man"
「蓮の花を見て、深く頭を下げた」
"and smiling, Kamala thanked him"
「そしてカマラは微笑みながら彼に感謝した」
"More lovely, thought the young man, than offerings for gods"
「神への供物よりも美しい」と若者は思った。
Kamala clapped her hands so loud that the golden bracelets clanged
カマラは金のブレスレットが鳴るほど大きな音で手を叩いた
"Beautiful are your verses, oh brown Samana"
「あなたの詩は美しい、ああ、褐色のサマナよ」
"and truly, I'm losing nothing when I'm giving you a kiss for them"
「そして、本当に、彼らのためにあなたにキスをしても、私は何も失うことはありません」
She beckoned him with her eyes
彼女は目で彼を招いた
he tilted his head so that his face touched hers
彼は彼女の顔に触れるように頭を傾けた
and he placed his mouth on her mouth
そして彼は彼女の口に自分の口を当てた
the mouth which was like a freshly cracked fig
口は割れたてのイチジクのようだった
For a long time, Kamala kissed him
カマラは長い間彼にキスをした

and with a deep astonishment Siddhartha felt how she taught him
そしてシッダールタは深い驚きとともに、彼女が彼に教えたことを感じた
he felt how wise she was
彼は彼女がいかに賢いかを感じた
he felt how she controlled him
彼は彼女が自分を支配していることを感じた
he felt how she rejected him
彼は彼女に拒絶されたと感じた
he felt how she lured him
彼は彼女が彼を誘惑したと感じた
and he felt how there were to be more kisses
そして彼はもっとキスをしたいと思った
every kiss was different from the others
キスはどれも違っていた
he was still, when he received the kisses
彼はキスを受けたとき、じっとしていた
Breathing deeply, he remained standing where he was
深呼吸しながら、彼はその場に立ったままだった
he was astonished like a child about the things worth learning
彼は学ぶ価値のある事柄について子供のように驚いた
the knowledge revealed itself before his eyes
その知識は彼の目の前に現れた
"Very beautiful are your verses" exclaimed Kamala
「あなたの詩はとても美しい」とカマラは叫んだ。
"if I were rich, I would give you pieces of gold for them"
「もし私が金持ちだったら、金貨をあげてもいいのに」
"But it will be difficult for you to earn enough money with verses"
「しかし、詩で十分なお金を稼ぐのは難しいでしょう」
"because you need a lot of money, if you want to be Kamala's friend"
「カマラの友達になりたいなら、たくさんのお金が必要よ」

"The way you're able to kiss, Kamala!" stammered Siddhartha
「カマラ、君がキスできる方法だよ！」シッダールタは口ごもりながら言った。
"Yes, this I am able to do"
「はい、これはできます」
"therefore I do not lack clothes, shoes, bracelets"
「だから私は衣服、靴、ブレスレットに不足していません」
"I have all the beautiful things"
「私は美しいものをすべて持っています」
"But what will become of you?"
「でも、あなたはどうなるんですか？」
"Aren't you able to do anything else?"
「他に何かできないんですか？」
"can you do more than think, fast, and make poetry?"
「考えること、断食すること、詩を作ること以上のことができるか？」
"I also know the sacrificial songs" said Siddhartha
「私は犠牲の歌も知っている」とシッダールタは言った
"but I do not want to sing those songs anymore"
「でももうあの歌は歌いたくない」
"I also know how to make magic spells"
「魔法の呪文の作り方も知っています」
"but I do not want to speak them anymore"
「でももう話したくない」
"I have read the scriptures"
「私は聖典を読みました」
"Stop!" Kamala interrupted him
「やめて！」カマラは彼を遮った
"You're able to read and write?"
「読み書きはできますか？」
"Certainly, I can do this, many people can"
「もちろん、私にはできるし、多くの人にもできる」
"Most people can't," Kamala replied

「ほとんどの人はできない」とカマラは答えた。
"I am also one of those who can't do it"
「私もできない人の一人です」
"It is very good that you're able to read and write"
「読み書きができるのはとても良いことだ」
"you will also find use for the magic spells"
「魔法の呪文も役に立つでしょう」
In this moment, a maid came running in
その時メイドが走って来た
she whispered a message into her mistress's ear
彼女は愛人の耳元でメッセージをささやいた
"There's a visitor for me" exclaimed Kamala
「訪問者が来た」とカマラは叫んだ
"Hurry and get yourself away, Siddhartha"
「急いで立ち去れ、シッダールタ」
"nobody may see you in here, remember this!"
「ここでは誰にも見られていないかもしれない、これを覚えておいて！」
"Tomorrow, I'll see you again"
「明日、また会おうね」
Kamala ordered her maid to give Siddhartha white garments
カマラは侍女にシッダールタに白い衣服を与えるように命じた
and then Siddhartha found himself being dragged away by the maid
そしてシッダールタは侍女に引きずり出されてしまった
he was brought into a garden-house out of sight of any paths
彼は道から見えない庭の家に連れて行かれた
then he was led into the bushes of the garden
それから彼は庭の茂みの中に連れて行かれました
he was urged to get himself out of the garden as soon as possible
彼はできるだけ早く庭から出るように促された
and he was told he must not be seen
そして彼は見られてはいけないと言われた

he did as he had been told
彼は言われた通りにした
he was accustomed to the forest
彼は森に慣れていた
so he managed to get out without making a sound
彼は音を立てずに脱出することができた

he returned to the city carrying the rolled up garments under his arm
彼は丸めた衣服を腕に抱えて町に戻った
At the inn, where travellers stay, he positioned himself by the door
旅人が泊まる宿屋で、彼はドアのそばに立った
without words he asked for food
彼は何も言わずに食べ物を求めた
without a word he accepted a piece of rice-cake
彼は何も言わずに餅を受け取った
he thought about how he had always begged
彼はいつも物乞いをしていたことを思い出した
"Perhaps as soon as tomorrow I will ask no one for food anymore"
「明日から、もう誰にも食べ物を頼まなくなるかもしれない」
Suddenly, pride flared up in him
突然、彼の中にプライドが燃え上がった
He was no Samana any more
彼はもうサマナではなかった
it was no longer appropriate for him to beg for food
食べ物を乞うのはもはや適切ではなかった
he gave the rice-cake to a dog
彼は犬に餅を与えた
and that night he remained without food
そしてその夜、彼は何も食べずに
Siddhartha thought to himself about the city
シッダールタは街について考えた
"Simple is the life which people lead in this world"

「この世の人々の暮らしはシンプルだ」
"this life presents no difficulties"
「この人生には何の困難もない」
"Everything was difficult and toilsome when I was a Samana"
「私がサマナだった頃は、すべてが困難で骨の折れる仕事でした」
"as a Samana everything was hopeless"
「サマナとしてはすべてが絶望的だった」
"but now everything is easy"
「でも今はすべてが簡単です」
"it is easy like the lesson in kissing from Kamala"
「カマラのキスのレッスンのように簡単です」
"I need clothes and money, nothing else"
「必要なのは服とお金、それ以外は何もない」
"these goals are small and achievable"
「これらの目標は小さく、達成可能です」
"such goals won't make a person lose any sleep"
「そのような目標は人を眠れなくさせることはない」

the next day he returned to Kamala's house
翌日彼はカマラの家に戻った
"Things are working out well" she called out to him
「物事はうまくいっているわ」彼女は彼に声をかけた。
"They are expecting you at Kamaswami's"
「カマスワミのところで待っています」
"he is the richest merchant of the city"
「彼は市内で最も裕福な商人だ」
"If he likes you, he'll accept you into his service"
「もし彼があなたを気に入ったら、彼はあなたを彼の部下として受け入れるでしょう」
"but you must be smart, brown Samana"
「でも、あなたは賢くなければなりません、茶色のサマナ」
"I had others tell him about you"

「他の人にあなたについて彼に話してもらった」

"Be polite towards him, he is very powerful"
「彼に対しては礼儀正しく接してください。彼はとても力強いのです」

"But I warn you, don't be too modest!"
「でも、あまり謙虚になりすぎないように注意してください！」

"I do not want you to become his servant"
「私はあなたが彼の召使いになることを望みません」

"you shall become his equal"
「あなたは彼と同等になるだろう」

"or else I won't be satisfied with you"
「そうしないと、私はあなたに満足できないでしょう」

"Kamaswami is starting to get old and lazy"
「カーマスワミは年老いて怠け始めている」

"If he likes you, he'll entrust you with a lot"
「彼があなたを好きなら、彼はあなたに多くのことを託すでしょう」

Siddhartha thanked her and laughed
シッダールタは彼女に感謝して笑った

she found out that he had not eaten
彼女は彼が食べていなかったことを知った

so she sent him bread and fruits
そこで彼女はパンと果物を彼に送りました

"You've been lucky" she said when they parted
「あなたは幸運だったわ」と彼女は別れ際に言った

"I'm opening one door after another for you"
「あなたのために、次々と扉を開けていきます」

"How come? Do you have a spell?"
「どうして？呪文でもあるのか？」

"I told you I knew how to think, to wait, and to fast"
「私は考えること、待つこと、そして断食することを知っていると言った」

"but you thought this was of no use"
「でも、これは無駄だと思ったのね」

"But it is useful for many things"
「でも、それはいろいろなことに役立ちます」
"Kamala, you'll see that the stupid Samanas are good at learning"
「カマラ、バカなサマナたちが学習能力に優れていることがわかるだろう」
"you'll see they are able to do many pretty things in the forest"
「森の中で彼らがたくさんの素敵なことをできるのがわかるでしょう」
"things which the likes of you aren't capable of"
「あなたのような人間にはできないこと」
"The day before yesterday, I was still a shaggy beggar"
「一昨日、私はまだ毛むくじゃらの乞食だった」
"as recently as yesterday I have kissed Kamala"
「つい昨日もカマラにキスしたのに」
"and soon I'll be a merchant and have money"
「そしてすぐに商人になってお金持ちになるよ」
"and I'll have all those things you insist upon"
「そして私はあなたが主張するものをすべて手に入れます」
"Well yes," she admitted, "but where would you be without me?"
「ええ、そうです」と彼女は認めた。「でも、私がいなかったらあなたはどうするの？」
"What would you be, if Kamala wasn't helping you?"
「もしカマラがあなたを助けてくれなかったら、あなたはどうなっていたでしょう？」
"Dear Kamala" said Siddhartha
「親愛なるカマラ」とシッダールタは言った
and he straightened up to his full height
そして彼は背筋を伸ばして
"when I came to you into your garden, I did the first step"
「あなたの庭に来たとき、私は最初の一歩を踏み出しました」

"It was my resolution to learn love from this most beautiful woman"
「この最も美しい女性から愛を学ぶことが私の決意でした」
"that moment I had made this resolution"
「その瞬間、私はこの決意をしました」
"and I knew I would carry it out"
「そして私はそれを実行できると分かっていました」
"I knew that you would help me"
「あなたが助けてくれると分かっていました」
"at your first glance at the entrance of the garden I already knew it"
「庭の入り口を一目見ただけで、私はすでにそれを知っていました」
"But what if I hadn't been willing?" asked Kamala
「でも、もし私がその気でなかったらどうなっていたの?」とカマラは尋ねた。
"You were willing" replied Siddhartha
「あなたは喜んでそうしました」とシッダールタは答えた。
"When you throw a rock into water, it takes the fastest course to the bottom"
「石を水に投げ込むと、最も速く底まで落ちていきます。」
"This is how it is when Siddhartha has a goal"
「シッダールタが目標を持っているとき、それはこのようになる」
"Siddhartha does nothing; he waits, he thinks, he fasts"
「シッダールタは何もしない。待つ、考える、断食する。」
"but he passes through the things of the world like a rock through water"
「しかし彼は、水の中の岩のように、この世の物事を通り抜けます」
"he passed through the water without doing anything"

「彼は何もせずに水を通過した」
"he is drawn to the bottom of the water"
「彼は水の底に引き寄せられる」
"he lets himself fall to the bottom of the water"
「彼は水の底に落ちた」
"His goal attracts him towards it"
「彼の目標は彼をそこに引き寄せる」
"he doesn't let anything enter his soul which might oppose the goal"
「彼は目標に反するかもしれないものを自分の心の中に入れない」
"This is what Siddhartha has learned among the Samanas"
「これがシッダールタがサマナの中で学んだことである」
"This is what fools call magic"
「これが愚か者が魔法と呼ぶものだ」
"they think it is done by daemons"
「彼らはそれが悪魔によって行われたと考えている」
"but nothing is done by daemons"
「しかしデーモンは何もしない」
"there are no daemons in this world"
「この世に悪魔は存在しない」
"Everyone can perform magic, should they choose to"
「誰でも魔法を使うことができます、望めば」
"everyone can reach his goals if he is able to think"
「考えることができれば、誰でも目標を達成できる」
"everyone can reach his goals if he is able to wait"
「待つことができれば、誰でも目標を達成できる」
"everyone can reach his goals if he is able to fast"
「断食できれば誰でも目標を達成できる」
Kamala listened to him; she loved his voice
カマラは彼の話を聞いた。彼女は彼の声が大好きだった。
she loved the look from his eyes
彼女は彼の目つきが好きだった

"Perhaps it is as you say, friend"
「あなたの言う通りかもしれませんね、友よ」

"But perhaps there is another explanation"
「しかし、別の説明もあるかもしれない」

"Siddhartha is a handsome man"
「シッダールタはハンサムな男だ」

"his glance pleases the women"
「彼の視線は女性たちを喜ばせる」

"good fortune comes towards him because of this"
「このおかげで彼には幸運が訪れる」

With one kiss, Siddhartha bid his farewell
シッダールタはキス一つで別れを告げた

"I wish that it should be this way, my teacher"
「先生、こうなればいいなと思います」

"I wish that my glance shall please you"
「私の視線があなたを喜ばせることを願っています」

"I wish that that you always bring me good fortune"
「いつも私に幸運をもたらしてくれることを祈ります」

With the Childlike People
子供のような人々とともに

Siddhartha went to Kamaswami the merchant
シッダールタは商人のカマスワミのところへ行き
he was directed into a rich house
彼は裕福な家に導かれた
servants led him between precious carpets into a chamber
召使たちは彼を高価な絨毯の間を通って部屋へと案内した
in the chamber was where he awaited the master of the house
その部屋は彼が家の主人を待つ場所だった
Kamaswami entered swiftly into the room
カマスワミは素早く部屋に入ってきた
he was a smoothly moving man
彼はスムーズに動く男だった
he had very gray hair and very intelligent, cautious eyes
彼は白髪で、とても知的で用心深い目をしていた
and he had a greedy mouth
彼は貪欲な口を持っていた
Politely, the host and the guest greeted one another
ホストとゲストは丁寧に挨拶を交わした
"I have been told that you were a Brahman" the merchant began
「あなたはバラモンだと聞いています」と商人は話し始めた。
"I have been told that you are a learned man"
「あなたは学識のある人だと聞いています」
"and I have also been told something else"
「そして、私はまた別のことを言われました」
"you seek to be in the service of a merchant"
「あなたは商人に仕えることを望んでいる」
"Might you have become destitute, Brahman, so that you seek to serve?"

「ブラフマンよ、あなたは奉仕を求めるほどに貧しくなったのでしょうか？」

"No," said Siddhartha, "I have not become destitute"
「いいえ」シッダールタは言った。「私は貧困にはなっていません」

"nor have I ever been destitute" added Siddhartha
「私は一度も貧困に陥ったことがない」とシッダールタは付け加えた。

"You should know that I'm coming from the Samanas"
「私がサマナスから来たことを知っておくべきだ」

"I have lived with them for a long time"
「私は彼らと長い間一緒に暮らしてきました」

"you are coming from the Samanas"
「あなたはサマナスから来ています」

"how could you be anything but destitute?"
「どうしてあなたは貧困でないと言えるのですか？」

"Aren't the Samanas entirely without possessions?"
「サマナ族は何も所有していないのではないですか？」

"I am without possessions, if that is what you mean" said Siddhartha
「もしそれがあなたの言うことなら、私には何もないのです」とシッダールタは言った。

"But I am without possessions voluntarily"
「しかし私は自発的に所有物を持たないのです」

"and therefore I am not destitute"
「だから私は貧困ではない」

"But what are you planning to live from, being without possessions?"
「しかし、何も持たずに何で生きていくつもりですか？」

"I haven't thought of this yet, sir"
「まだ考えていません」

"For more than three years, I have been without possessions"
「3年以上、私は何も所有していませんでした」

"and I have never thought about of what I should live"

「そして私は自分がどう生きるべきかについて考えたことがなかった」
"So you've lived of the possessions of others"
「つまり、あなたは他人の所有物で生きてきたのですね」
"Presumable, this is how it is?"
「おそらく、こんな感じでしょうか？」
"Well, merchants also live of what other people own"
「まあ、商人も他人の所有物で生活しているんだ」
"Well said," granted the merchant
「よく言った」と商人は認めた。
"But he wouldn't take anything from another person for nothing"
「しかし彼は他人から何も無償で受け取ることはなかった」
"he would give his merchandise in return" said Kamaswami
「彼は代わりに商品をくれるだろう」とカマスワミは言った。
"So it seems to be indeed"
「確かにそうみたいですね」
"Everyone takes, everyone gives, such is life"
「誰もが受け取り、誰もが与える、それが人生だ」
"But if you don't mind me asking, I have a question"
「でも、もしよろしければ、質問があるんです」
"being without possessions, what would you like to give?"
「何も持っていないのに、何をあげたいですか？」
"Everyone gives what he has"
「誰もが持っているものを与える」
"The warrior gives strength"
「戦士は力を与える」
"the merchant gives merchandise"
「商人は商品を与える」
"the teacher gives teachings"
「先生は教えを与える」
"the farmer gives rice"

「農家は米を与える」
"the fisher gives fish"
「漁師は魚を与える」
"Yes indeed. And what is it that you've got to give?"
「はい、その通りです。それで、あなたが差し出すものは何ですか？」
"What is it that you've learned?"
「何を学んだのですか？」
"what you're able to do?"
「あなたに何ができるの？」
"I can think. I can wait. I can fast"
「私は考えることができる。私は待つことができる。私は断食することができる」
"That's everything?" asked Kamaswami
「それで全部？」とカマスワミは尋ねた。
"I believe that is everything there is!"
「それがすべてだと信じています！」
"And what's the use of that?"
「それで何の役に立つの？」
"For example; fasting. What is it good for?"
「例えば、断食。それは何に良いのでしょうか？」
"It is very good, sir"
「とてもよかったです、先生」
"there are times a person has nothing to eat"
「人は食べるものがない時もある」
"then fasting is the smartest thing he can do"
「それなら断食するのが彼にとって最も賢いことだ」
"there was a time where Siddhartha hadn't learned to fast"
「シッダールタが断食を学んでいなかった時代があった」
"in this time he had to accept any kind of service"
「この時期、彼はどんな奉仕も受け入れなければならなかった」
"because hunger would force him to accept the service"
「空腹のため、彼は奉仕を受け入れざるを得なかった」

"But like this, Siddhartha can wait calmly"
「しかし、こうすればシッダールタは静かに待つことができる」
"he knows no impatience, he knows no emergency"
「彼は焦りを知らず、緊急事態を知らない」
"for a long time he can allow hunger to besiege him"
「彼は長い間、飢えに苦しむことになるだろう」
"and he can laugh about the hunger"
「そして彼は飢えを笑うことができる」
"This, sir, is what fasting is good for"
「これが断食の良いところなのです」
"You're right, Samana" acknowledged Kamaswami
「サマナ、その通りだ」とカマスワミは認めた。
"Wait for a moment" he asked of his guest
「ちょっと待ってください」と彼は客に尋ねた。
Kamaswami left the room and returned with a scroll
カマスワミは部屋を出て巻物を持って戻ってきた
he handed Siddhartha the scroll and asked him to read it
彼はシッダールタに巻物を手渡し、それを読むように頼んだ。
Siddhartha looked at the scroll handed to him
シッダールタは手渡された巻物を見て
on the scroll a sales-contract had been written
巻物には売買契約書が書かれていた
he began to read out the scroll's contents
彼は巻物の内容を読み始めた
Kamaswami was very pleased with Siddhartha
カマスワミはシッダールタにとても満足していた
"would you write something for me on this piece of paper?"
「この紙に何か書いてもらえますか？」
He handed him a piece of paper and a pen
彼は紙とペンを手渡した
Siddhartha wrote, and returned the paper
シッダールタは手紙を書いて返した
Kamaswami read, "Writing is good, thinking is better"

カマスワミは「書くことは良いが、考えることはもっと良い」と読んだ。

"Being smart is good, being patient is better"
「賢いのは良いことだが、忍耐強いのはもっと良いことだ」

"It is excellent how you're able to write" the merchant praised him
「あなたの文章力は素晴らしいですね」と商人は彼を褒めた。

"Many a thing we will still have to discuss with one another"
「私たちはまだ互いに話し合うべきことがたくさんある」

"For today, I'm asking you to be my guest"
「今日は、私のゲストになってください」

"please come to live in this house"
「この家に住んでください」

Siddhartha thanked Kamaswami and accepted his offer
シッダールタはカーマスワミに感謝し、彼の申し出を受け入れた。

he lived in the dealer's house from now on
彼はこれからディーラーの家に住むことになる

Clothes were brought to him, and shoes
衣服や靴が彼のところに運ばれてきた

and every day, a servant prepared a bath for him
そして毎日召使いが彼のために風呂を用意した

Twice a day, a plentiful meal was served
一日二回、たっぷりの食事が提供された

but Siddhartha only ate once a day
しかしシッダールタは一日に一回しか食べなかった

and he ate neither meat, nor did he drink wine
彼は肉も食べず、ワインも飲まなかった

Kamaswami told him about his trade
カマスワミは彼に自分の商売について話した

he showed him the merchandise and storage-rooms

彼は商品と倉庫を見せた
he showed him how the calculations were done
彼は計算がどのように行われるかを示した
Siddhartha got to know many new things
シッダールタは多くの新しいことを知りました
he heard a lot and spoke little
彼はよく聞き、あまり話さなかった
but he did not forget Kamala's words
しかし彼はカマラの言葉を忘れなかった
so he was never subservient to the merchant
だから彼は決して商人に従属しなかった
he forced him to treat him as an equal
彼は彼を平等に扱うよう強制した
perhaps he forced him to treat him as even more than an equal
おそらく彼は彼を同等以上の存在として扱うよう強制したのだろう
Kamaswami conducted his business with care
カマスワミは慎重に事業を運営した
and he was very passionate about his business
彼は自分のビジネスにとても熱心でした
but Siddhartha looked upon all of this as if it was a game
しかしシッダールタはこれをすべてゲームのように考えていた
he tried hard to learn the rules of the game precisely
彼はゲームのルールを正確に学ぼうと一生懸命努力した
but the contents of the game did not touch his heart
しかし、試合の内容は彼の心には響かなかった
He had not been in Kamaswami's house for long
彼はカマスワミの家に長くいなかった
but soon he took part in his landlord's business
しかしすぐに彼は地主の事業に参加するようになった

every day he visited beautiful Kamala
彼は毎日美しいカマラを訪れた

Kamala had an hour appointed for their meetings
カマラは会合のために1時間を設けた
she was wearing pretty clothes and fine shoes
彼女はきれいな服と素敵な靴を履いていた
and soon he brought her gifts as well
そしてすぐに彼は彼女にも贈り物を持ってきました
Much he learned from her red, smart mouth
彼は彼女の赤くて口の悪い口から多くのことを学んだ
Much he learned from her tender, supple hand
彼は彼女の優しくしなやかな手から多くのことを学んだ
regarding love, Siddhartha was still a boy
愛に関しては、シッダールタはまだ少年だった
and he had a tendency to plunge into love blindly
彼は盲目的に恋に落ちる傾向があった
he fell into lust like into a bottomless pit
彼は底なしの穴のような欲望に陥った
she taught him thoroughly, starting with the basics
彼女は基礎から徹底的に教えた
pleasure cannot be taken without giving pleasure
喜びを与えずに喜びを得ることはできない
every gesture, every caress, every touch, every look
あらゆる仕草、あらゆる愛撫、あらゆる接触、あらゆる表情
every spot of the body, however small it was, had its secret
体のあらゆる部分には、どんなに小さなものであっても、秘密がある
the secrets would bring happiness to those who know them
その秘密はそれを知る人々に幸福をもたらすだろう
lovers must not part from one another after celebrating love
恋人たちは愛を祝った後、別れてはならない
they must not part without one admiring the other
お互いを尊敬し合うことなく別れてはならない
they must be as defeated as they have been victorious
彼らは勝利したのと同じくらい敗北したに違いない
neither lover should start feeling fed up or bored

どちらの恋人もうんざりしたり退屈したりし始めるべきではない
they should not get the evil feeling of having been abusive
虐待をしたという嫌な気持ちを抱くべきではない
and they should not feel like they have been abused
そして彼らは虐待を受けたと感じるべきではない
Wonderful hours he spent with the beautiful and smart artist
美しくて賢いアーティストと過ごした素晴らしい時間
he became her student, her lover, her friend
彼は彼女の生徒となり、恋人となり、友人となった
Here with Kamala was the worth and purpose of his present life
カマラの今生の価値と目的はここにあった
his purpose was not with the business of Kamaswami
彼の目的はカマスワミの事業ではなかった

Siddhartha received important letters and contracts
シッダールタは重要な手紙や契約書を受け取った
Kamaswami began discussing all important affairs with him
カマスワミは彼とあらゆる重要な事柄について話し合い始めた
He soon saw that Siddhartha knew little about rice and wool
彼はすぐにシッダールタが米と羊毛についてほとんど知らないことに気づいた。
but he saw that he acted in a fortunate manner
しかし彼は幸運な行動をとったことに気づいた
and Siddhartha surpassed him in calmness and equanimity
シッダールタは平静さと冷静さにおいて彼を上回った
he surpassed him in the art of understanding previously unknown people
彼は、それまで知られていなかった人々を理解する技術において彼を凌駕した。
Kamaswami spoke about Siddhartha to a friend
カマスワミは友人にシッダールタについて話した

"This Brahman is no proper merchant"
「このブラフマンはまともな商人ではない」
"he will never be a merchant"
「彼は決して商人にはなれないだろう」
"for business there is never any passion in his soul"
「彼の魂にはビジネスに対する情熱がまったくない」
"But he has a mysterious quality about him"
「しかし、彼には神秘的な性質がある」
"this quality brings success about all by itself"
「この性質はそれ自体で成功をもたらす」
"it could be from a good Star of his birth"
「それは彼の誕生のよい星から来ているのかもしれない」
"or it could be something he has learned among Samanas"
「あるいは、サマナの間で学んだことかもしれない」
"He always seems to be merely playing with our business-affairs"
「彼はいつも私たちのビジネス上の事柄を弄んでいるだけのようだ」
"his business never fully becomes a part of him"
「彼のビジネスは決して完全に彼の一部にはならない」
"his business never rules over him"
「彼の仕事が彼を支配することは決してない」
"he is never afraid of failure"
「彼は決して失敗を恐れない」
"he is never upset by a loss"
「彼は負けても決して落ち込まない」
The friend advised the merchant
友人は商人にアドバイスした
"Give him a third of the profits he makes for you"
「彼があなたのために稼いだ利益の3分の1を彼にあげなさい」
"but let him also be liable when there are losses"
「しかし、損失があった場合には、彼も責任を負うことになる」

"Then, he'll become more zealous"
「そうすれば、彼はもっと熱心になるだろう」
Kamaswami was curious, and followed the advice
カマスワミは興味を持ち、アドバイスに従った。
But Siddhartha cared little about loses or profits
しかしシッダールタは損失や利益をあまり気にしていなかった
When he made a profit, he accepted it with equanimity
彼は利益が出ると平静にそれを受け入れた
when he made losses, he laughed it off
彼は損失を出してもそれを笑い飛ばした
It seemed indeed, as if he did not care about the business
彼は確かにビジネスに興味がなかったようだ
At one time, he travelled to a village
ある時、彼は村を旅した
he went there to buy a large harvest of rice
彼は大量の米を買うためにそこへ行った
But when he got there, the rice had already been sold
しかし、彼がそこに着いたとき、米はすでに売り切れていた
another merchant had gotten to the village before him
彼より先に別の商人が村に到着していた
Nevertheless, Siddhartha stayed for several days in that village
それにもかかわらず、シッダールタはその村に数日間滞在した。
he treated the farmers for a drink
彼は農民たちに酒を振る舞った
he gave copper-coins to their children
彼は子供たちに銅貨を与えた
he joined in the celebration of a wedding
彼は結婚式の祝賀会に参加した
and he returned extremely satisfied from his trip
そして彼は旅行から非常に満足して帰ってきた

Kamaswami was angry that Siddhartha had wasted time and money
カマスワミはシッダールタが時間とお金を無駄にしたことに怒っていた

Siddhartha answered "Stop scolding, dear friend!"
シッダールタは答えました。「叱るのはやめなさい、親愛なる友よ！」

"Nothing was ever achieved by scolding"
「叱っても何も達成されない」

"If a loss has occurred, let me bear that loss"
「損失が発生した場合、その損失を私が負担します」

"I am very satisfied with this trip"
「この旅行にとても満足しています」

"I have gotten to know many kinds of people"
「いろいろな人と知り合うことができました」

"a Brahman has become my friend"
「ブラフマンが私の友達になった」

"children have sat on my knees"
「子供たちが私の膝の上に座った」

"farmers have shown me their fields"
「農家の人たちが畑を見せてくれた」

"nobody knew that I was a merchant"
「私が商人だなんて誰も知らなかった」

"That's all very nice," exclaimed Kamaswami indignantly
「それはとても素晴らしいことだ」とカマスワミは憤慨して叫んだ。

"but in fact, you are a merchant after all"
「でも実際、あなたは商人なんですよ」

"Or did you have only travel for your amusement?"
「それとも、単に楽しみのために旅行したのですか？」

"of course I have travelled for my amusement" Siddhartha laughed
「もちろん私は楽しみのために旅をしてきた」シッダールタは笑った

"For what else would I have travelled?"

「他に何のために旅をしたというのか？」
"I have gotten to know people and places"
「人々や場所を知るようになりました」
"I have received kindness and trust"
「優しさと信頼をいただきました」
"I have found friendships in this village"
「私はこの村で友情を見つけました」
"if I had been Kamaswami, I would have travelled back annoyed"
「もし私がカマスワミだったら、腹を立てて帰っただろう」
"I would have been in hurry as soon as my purchase failed"
「購入に失敗したらすぐに急いでいただろう」
"and time and money would indeed have been lost"
「そして時間とお金は確かに無駄になっていただろう」
"But like this, I've had a few good days"
「でも、こんな感じで、良い日も何日かあったよ」
"I've learned from my time there"
「私はそこで過ごした時間から学びました」
"and I have had joy from the experience"
「そして私はその経験から喜びを得ました」
"I've neither harmed myself nor others by annoyance and hastiness"
「私はイライラや性急さによって自分自身や他人を傷つけたことはありません」
"if I ever return friendly people will welcome me"
「もし私が戻ってきたら、友好的な人々が私を歓迎してくれるだろう」
"if I return to do business friendly people will welcome me too"
「ビジネスのために戻っても、友好的な人々は私を歓迎してくれるだろう」
"I praise myself for not showing any hurry or displeasure"
「私は、急いだり、不満を漏らしたりしなかったことを自分自身に褒めています」

"So, leave it as it is, my friend"
「だから、そのままにしておけよ、友よ」
"and don't harm yourself by scolding"
「叱ることで自分自身を傷つけないでください」
"If you see Siddhartha harming himself, then speak with me".
「シッダールタが自分を傷つけているのを見たら、私に話してください」
"and Siddhartha will go on his own path"
「そしてシッダールタは自らの道を歩むだろう」
"But until then, let's be satisfied with one another"
「でもそれまではお互い満足しましょう」
the merchant's attempts to convince Siddhartha were futile
商人がシッダールタを説得しようとした試みは無駄だった
he could not make Siddhartha eat his bread
彼はシッダールタに自分のパンを食べさせることができなかった
Siddhartha ate his own bread
シッダールタは自分のパンを食べた
or rather, they both ate other people's bread
むしろ、彼らは他人のパンを食べた
Siddhartha never listened to Kamaswami's worries
シッダールタはカマスワミの心配を決して聞かなかった
and Kamaswami had many worries he wanted to share
カマスワミは多くの悩みを共有したいと思っていた
there were business-deals going on in danger of failing
失敗する危険のある商取引が進行中であった
shipments of merchandise seemed to have been lost
商品の出荷は紛失したようだ
debtors seemed to be unable to pay
債務者は支払いができないようだ
Kamaswami could never convince Siddhartha to utter words of worry

カマスワミはシッダールタに心配の言葉を言わせることはできなかった
Kamaswami could not make Siddhartha feel anger towards business
カマスワミはシッダールタにビジネスに対する怒りを感じさせることはできなかった
he could not get him to to have wrinkles on the forehead
彼は額にシワを寄せることができなかった
he could not make Siddhartha sleep badly
彼はシッダールタを眠らせることができなかった

one day, Kamaswami tried to speak with Siddhartha
ある日、カーマスワミはシッダールタと話をしようとした
"Siddhartha, you have failed to learn anything new"
「シッダールタ、あなたは何も新しいことを学ぶことができませんでした」
but again, Siddhartha laughed at this
しかし、シッダールタはこれに対してまた笑った
"Would you please not kid me with such jokes"
「そんな冗談で私をからかわないで下さい」
"What I've learned from you is how much a basket of fish costs"
「あなたから学んだのは、魚の入った籠がいくらするかということだ」
"and I learned how much interest may be charged on loaned money"
「そして、貸したお金にどのくらいの利息がかかるかを学びました」
"These are your areas of expertise"
「これらはあなたの専門分野です」
"I haven't learned to think from you, my dear Kamaswami"
「私はあなたから考えることを学んでいません、私の愛しいカマスワミ」
"you ought to be the one seeking to learn from me"

「あなたは私から学ぶことを求める人であるべきだ」
Indeed his soul was not with the trade
確かに彼の魂は商売には向いていなかった
The business was good enough to provide him with money for Kamala
そのビジネスはカマラに資金を提供するのに十分なほど成功していた
and it earned him much more than he needed
そしてそれは彼が必要とする以上のものを稼いだ
Besides Kamala, Siddhartha's curiosity was with the people
カマラ以外にも、シッダールタの好奇心は人々に向けられていた
their businesses, crafts, worries, and pleasures
彼らのビジネス、工芸、悩み、そして楽しみ
all these things used to be alien to him
これらすべてのことは彼にとって異質なものだった
their acts of foolishness used to be as distant as the moon
彼らの愚かな行為はかつては月のように遠いものだった
he easily succeeded in talking to all of them
彼は彼ら全員と簡単に話をすることに成功した
he could live with all of them
彼は彼ら全員と一緒に暮らすことができた
and he could continue to learn from all of them
そして彼は彼ら全員から学び続けることができた
but there was something which separated him from them
しかし、彼と彼らとの間には隔たりがあった
he could feel a divide between him and the people
彼は自分と国民の間に溝を感じていた
this separating factor was him being a Samana
この決定的な要因は彼がサマナだったことだ
He saw mankind going through life in a childlike manner
彼は人類が子供のように人生を歩んでいるのを見た
in many ways they were living the way animals live
多くの点で彼らは動物と同じように暮らしていた
he loved and also despised their way of life

彼は彼らの生き方を愛し、また軽蔑した
He saw them toiling and suffering
彼らが苦労し苦しんでいるのを見た
they were becoming gray for things unworthy of this price
彼らはこの値段に値しない物のために灰色になっていった
they did things for money and little pleasures
彼らはお金とちょっとした楽しみのために何かをした
they did things for being slightly honoured
彼らは少し名誉を得るために何かをした
he saw them scolding and insulting each other
彼は彼らがお互いを叱り、侮辱し合っているのを見た
he saw them complaining about pain
彼は彼らが痛みを訴えているのを見た
pains at which a Samana would only smile
サマナが微笑むだけの苦痛
and he saw them suffering from deprivations
そして彼は彼らが貧困に苦しんでいるのを見た
deprivations which a Samana would not feel
サマナが感じないであろう欠乏
He was open to everything these people brought his way
彼は人々がもたらすあらゆるものに対してオープンだった
welcome was the merchant who offered him linen for sale
リネンを売りに出した商人は歓迎した
welcome was the debtor who sought another loan
新たな融資を求める債務者を歓迎した
welcome was the beggar who told him the story of his poverty
彼に貧困の話をしてくれた乞食は歓迎された
the beggar who was not half as poor as any Samana
サマナの半分も貧しくない乞食
He did not treat the rich merchant and his servant different
彼は裕福な商人とその召使を区別しなかった
he let street-vendor cheat him when buying bananas

彼はバナナを買うときに露天商に騙された
Kamaswami would often complain to him about his worries
カマスワミはよく彼の悩みについて愚痴をこぼしていた。
or he would reproach him about his business
あるいは彼の仕事について非難するだろう
he listened curiously and happily
彼は興味深く、そして楽しそうに聞いていた
but he was puzzled by his friend
しかし彼は友人に困惑した
he tried to understand him
彼は彼を理解しようとした
and he admitted he was right, up to a certain point
そして彼は、ある点までは自分が正しかったと認めた。
there were many who asked for Siddhartha
シッダールタを求める人はたくさんいた
many wanted to do business with him
多くの人が彼とビジネスをしたいと思った
there were many who wanted to cheat him
彼を騙そうとする者が多かった
many wanted to draw some secret out of him
多くの人が彼から何か秘密を聞き出そうとした
many wanted to appeal to his sympathy
多くの人が彼の同情に訴えたかった
many wanted to get his advice
多くの人が彼のアドバイスを聞きたがった
He gave advice to those who wanted it
彼は望む人々にアドバイスを与えた
he pitied those who needed pity
彼は同情を必要とする人々を同情した
he made gifts to those who liked presents
彼はプレゼントが好きな人に贈り物をした
he let some cheat him a bit
彼は誰かに騙された
this game which all people played occupied his thoughts

誰もがプレイするこのゲームは彼の心を占めていた
he thought about this game just as much as he had about the Gods
彼は神々について考えるのと同じくらいこのゲームについても考えていた
deep in his chest he felt a dying voice
彼は胸の奥底で死にゆく声を感じた
this voice admonished him quietly
この声は静かに彼を戒めた
and he hardly perceived the voice inside of himself
そして彼は自分の内なる声をほとんど感じなかった
And then, for an hour, he became aware of something
そして、1時間ほど経って、彼はあることに気づいた。
he became aware of the strange life he was leading
彼は自分が奇妙な生活を送っていることに気づいた
he realized this life was only a game
彼はこの人生が単なるゲームに過ぎないことに気づいた
at times he would feel happiness and joy
時々彼は幸せと喜びを感じた
but real life was still passing him by
しかし現実の生活は彼を通り過ぎていった
and it was passing by without touching him
そしてそれは彼に触れることなく通り過ぎていった
Siddhartha played with his business-deals
シッダールタは商取引で遊んだ
Siddhartha found amusement in the people around him
シッダールタは周囲の人々に面白さを感じた
but regarding his heart, he was not with them
しかし、心に関しては、彼は彼らと共にいなかった
The source ran somewhere, far away from him
情報源は彼から遠く離れたどこかへ走った
it ran and ran invisibly
それは目に見えないまま走り続けた
it had nothing to do with his life any more
それはもう彼の人生とは何の関係もなかった

at several times he became scared on account of such thoughts
彼は何度かそのような考えから怖くなった
he wished he could participate in all of these childlike games
彼はこれらの子供っぽいゲームすべてに参加できたらよかったのにと思った
he wanted to really live
彼は本当に生きたかった
he wanted to really act in their theatre
彼は本当に彼らの劇場で演技したかった
he wanted to really enjoy their pleasures
彼は彼らの喜びを本当に楽しみたかった
and he wanted to live, instead of just standing by as a spectator
そして彼は傍観者としてただ立っているのではなく、生きたいと思ったのです

But again and again, he came back to beautiful Kamala
しかし、彼は何度も美しいカマラに戻ってきた
he learned the art of love
彼は愛の芸術を学んだ
and he practised the cult of lust
そして彼は欲望の崇拝を実践した
lust, in which giving and taking becomes one
与えることと受け取ることが一体となる欲望
he chatted with her and learned from her
彼は彼女と会話をし、彼女から学んだ
he gave her advice, and he received her advice
彼は彼女にアドバイスを与え、そして彼女のアドバイスを受け取った
She understood him better than Govinda used to understand him
彼女はゴヴィンダが彼を理解していた以上に彼を理解していた

she was more similar to him than Govinda had been
彼女はゴヴィンダよりも彼に似ていた
"You are like me," he said to her
「君は僕と同じだ」と彼は彼女に言った
"you are different from most people"
「あなたはほとんどの人とは違います」
"You are Kamala, nothing else"
「あなたはカマラ、それ以外に何もありません」
"and inside of you, there is a peace and refuge"
「そしてあなたの中には平和と避難所がある」
"a refuge to which you can go at every hour of the day"
「一日中いつでも行ける避難所」
"you can be at home with yourself"
「あなたは自分自身とくつろげる」
"I can do this too"
「私にもできるよ」
"Few people have this place"
「この場所を持っている人はほとんどいません」
"and yet all of them could have it"
「それでも彼ら全員がそれを手に入れることができた」
"Not all people are smart" said Kamala
「すべての人が賢いわけではない」とカマラは言った
"No," said Siddhartha, "that's not the reason why"
「いいえ」シッダールタは言った。「それが理由ではありません」
"Kamaswami is just as smart as I am"
「カマスワミは私と同じくらい賢い」
"but he has no refuge in himself"
「しかし、彼は自分自身の中に避難所を持っていない」
"Others have it, although they have the minds of children"
「他の人は子供の心を持っていても、それを持っています」
"Most people, Kamala, are like a falling leaf"
「ほとんどの人は、カマラ、落ち葉のようなものだ」

"a leaf which is blown and is turning around through the air"
「風に吹かれて空中を回転する葉」
"a leaf which wavers, and tumbles to the ground"
「揺れて地面に落ちる葉」
"But others, a few, are like stars"
「しかし、他の少数の人々は星のようだ」
"they go on a fixed course"
「彼らは決まったコースを進む」
"no wind reaches them"
「風は届かない」
"in themselves they have their law and their course"
「彼ら自身の中に彼らの法則と彼らの道筋がある」
"Among all the learned men I have met, there was one of this kind"
「私が会ったすべての学者の中に、このような人が一人いた」
"he was a truly perfected one"
「彼は本当に完璧な人でした」
"I'll never be able to forget him"
「私は彼を決して忘れることはできない」
"It is that Gotama, the exalted one"
「それはゴータマ、崇高なる者です」
"Thousands of followers are listening to his teachings every day"
「毎日何千人もの信者が彼の教えを聞いています」
"they follow his instructions every hour"
「彼らは毎時間彼の指示に従います」
"but they are all falling leaves"
「でも、それらはすべて落ち葉です」
"not in themselves they have teachings and a law"
「彼ら自身には教えや律法があるわけではない」
Kamala looked at him with a smile
カマラは微笑みながら彼を見た
"Again, you're talking about him," she said
「また、彼のことを話しているのね」と彼女は言った。

"again, you're having a Samana's thoughts"
「また、サマナの考えを抱いている」
Siddhartha said nothing, and they played the game of love
シッダールタは何も言わず、二人は愛のゲームを続けた
one of the thirty or forty different games Kamala knew
カマラが知っていた30～40種類のゲームのうちの1つ
Her body was flexible like that of a jaguar
彼女の体はジャガーのように柔軟だった
flexible like the bow of a hunter
ハンターの弓のように柔軟
he who had learned from her how to make love
彼女から愛し合う方法を学んだ彼は
he was knowledgeable of many forms of lust
彼は多くの形の欲望について知識があった
he that learned from her knew many secrets
彼女から学んだ者は多くの秘密を知った
For a long time, she played with Siddhartha
彼女は長い間シッダールタと遊んだ
she enticed him and rejected him
彼女は彼を誘惑して拒絶した
she forced him and embraced him
彼女は彼を強引に抱きしめた
she enjoyed his masterful skills
彼女は彼の優れた技術を楽しんだ
until he was defeated and rested exhausted by her side
彼が敗北し、疲れ果てて彼女の傍らで休むまで
The courtesan bent over him
娼婦は彼の上にかがんだ
she took a long look at his face
彼女は彼の顔をじっと見つめた
she looked at his eyes, which had grown tired
彼女は疲れた彼の目を見つめた
"You are the best lover I have ever seen" she said
thoughtfully

「あなたは私が今まで見た中で最高の恋人よ」と彼女は思慮深く言った

"You're stronger than others, more supple, more willing"
「あなたは他の人よりも強く、より柔軟で、より意欲的です」

"You've learned my art well, Siddhartha"
「シッダールタよ、私の術をよく学んだな」

"At some time, when I'll be older, I'd want to bear your child"
「いつか、私がもっと大きくなったら、あなたの子供を産みたいわ」

"And yet, my dear, you've remained a Samana"
「それでも、あなたはサマナのままです」

"and despite this, you do not love me"
「それにもかかわらず、あなたは私を愛していない」

"there is nobody that you love"
「あなたが愛する人は誰もいない」

"Isn't it so?" asked Kamala
「そうじゃないの？」とカマラは尋ねた。

"It might very well be so," Siddhartha said tiredly
「それはそうかもしれない」シッダールタは疲れた声で言った。

"I am like you, because you also do not love"
「私もあなたと同じです。あなたも愛さないからです」

"how else could you practise love as a craft?"
「他にどうやって愛を技術として実践できるだろうか？」

"Perhaps, people of our kind can't love"
「もしかしたら、私たちのような人間は愛することができないのかもしれない」

"The childlike people can love, that's their secret"
「子供のような人は愛することができる、それが彼らの秘密だ」

Sansara
サンサーラ

For a long time, Siddhartha had lived in the world and lust
シッダールタは長い間、世俗と欲望の中で生きてきた
he lived this way though, without being a part of it
彼はその一部にならずにこのように生きてきた
he had killed this off when he had been a Samana
彼はサマナだったときにこれを殺した
but now they had awoken again
しかし今、彼らは再び目覚めた
he had tasted riches, lust, and power
彼は富、欲望、権力を味わった
for a long time he had remained a Samana in his heart
彼は長い間心の中でサマナであり続けた
Kamala, being smart, had realized this quite right
カマラは賢いので、このことに正しく気づいていた。
thinking, waiting, and fasting still guided his life
考えること、待つこと、断食することが彼の人生を導いた
the childlike people remained alien to him
子供のような人々は彼にとって異質なままだった
and he remained alien to the childlike people
そして彼は子供のような人々にとって異質な存在であり続けた
Years passed by; surrounded by the good life
年月が経ち、豊かな生活に囲まれて
Siddhartha hardly felt the years fading away
シッダールタは年月が過ぎ去っていくことをほとんど感じなかった
He had become rich and possessed a house of his own
彼は金持ちになり、自分の家を持っていた
he even had his own servants
彼には召使いもいた
he had a garden before the city, by the river

彼は街の前に川沿いに庭を持っていた
The people liked him and came to him for money or advice
人々は彼を好み、金銭やアドバイスを求めて彼のもとに来た。
but there was nobody close to him, except Kamala
しかし、カマラ以外には彼の近くには誰もいなかった
the bright state of being awake
目覚めている明るい状態
the feeling which he had experienced at the height of his youth
彼が青春の絶頂期に経験した感情
in those days after Gotama's sermon
ゴータマの説教の後のその日々
after the separation from Govinda
ゴヴィンダとの別れの後
the tense expectation of life
人生に対する緊張した期待
the proud state of standing alone
一人で立っているという誇りある状態
being without teachings or teachers
教えや教師がいない
the supple willingness to listen to the divine voice in his own heart
自分の心の中の神の声に耳を傾ける柔軟な意志
all these things had slowly become a memory
これらすべてはゆっくりと思い出となっていった
the memory had been fleeting, distant, and quiet
その記憶はつかの間で、遠くで、静かだった
the holy source, which used to be near, now only murmured
かつては近くにあった聖なる源は、今はただ囁くだけ
the holy source, which used to murmur within himself
彼自身の中にささやいていた聖なる源泉
Nevertheless, many things he had learned from the Samanas
それでも、彼はサマナから多くのことを学んだ。
he had learned from Gotama

彼はゴータマから学んだ
he had learned from his father the Brahman
彼は父からブラフマンを学んだ
his father had remained within his being for a long time
彼の父親は長い間彼の中に留まっていた
moderate living, the joy of thinking, hours of meditation
節度ある生活、考える喜び、瞑想の時間
the secret knowledge of the self; his eternal entity
自己の秘密の知識、彼の永遠の実体
the self which is neither body nor consciousness
肉体でも意識でもない自己
Many a part of this he still had
彼はまだこの多くを保有していた
but one part after another had been submerged
しかし、次々と水没していった
and eventually each part gathered dust
そして最終的に各部品は埃をかぶるようになった
a potter's wheel, once in motion, will turn for a long time
ろくろは一度動き出すと長い間回り続ける
it loses its vigour only slowly
活力はゆっくりと失われる
and it comes to a stop only after time
そして時間が経つと止まる
Siddhartha's soul had kept on turning the wheel of asceticism
シッダールタの魂は苦行の輪を回し続けた
the wheel of thinking had kept turning for a long time
思考の車輪は長い間回り続けていた
the wheel of differentiation had still turned for a long time
差別化の車輪は長い間回り続けていた
but it turned slowly and hesitantly
しかしそれはゆっくりとためらいながら向きを変えた
and it was close to coming to a standstill
そしてそれは停止状態に近づきました
Slowly, like humidity entering the dying stem of a tree

枯れゆく木の幹に湿気がゆっくりと入り込むように
filling the stem slowly and making it rot
茎をゆっくりと満たし、腐らせる
the world and sloth had entered Siddhartha's soul
世俗と怠惰がシッダールタの魂に入り込んだ
slowly it filled his soul and made it heavy
それはゆっくりと彼の魂を満たし、重くした
it made his soul tired and put it to sleep
それは彼の魂を疲れさせ、眠らせた
On the other hand, his senses had become alive
一方、彼の感覚は生き生きとしていた
there was much his senses had learned
彼の感覚は多くのことを学んだ
there was much his senses had experienced
彼の感覚は多くのことを経験していた
Siddhartha had learned to trade
シッダールタは商売を学んだ
he had learned how to use his power over people
彼は人々に対する権力の使い方を学んだ
he had learned how to enjoy himself with a woman
彼は女性と楽しく過ごす方法を学んだ
he had learned how to wear beautiful clothes
彼は美しい服を着る方法を学んだ
he had learned how to give orders to servants
彼は召使に命令する方法を学んだ
he had learned how to bathe in perfumed waters
彼は香りのよい水で入浴する方法を学んだ
He had learned how to eat tenderly and carefully prepared food
彼は優しく丁寧に調理された食べ物を食べる方法を学んだ。
he even ate fish, meat, and poultry
彼は魚、肉、鶏肉も食べた
spices and sweets and wine, which causes sloth and forgetfulness

スパイスやお菓子、ワインは怠惰と忘却を引き起こす
He had learned to play with dice and on a chess-board
彼はサイコロやチェス盤で遊ぶことを学んだ
he had learned to watch dancing girls
彼は踊っている女の子たちを観察することを学んだ
he learned to have himself carried about in a sedan-chair
彼は輿に乗って移動することを学んだ
he learned to sleep on a soft bed
彼は柔らかいベッドで眠ることを学んだ
But still he felt different from others
しかし、彼はまだ他の人とは違うと感じていた
he still felt superior to the others
彼はまだ他の人より優れていると感じていた
he always watched them with some mockery
彼はいつも彼らを嘲笑しながら見ていた
there was always some mocking disdain to how he felt about them
彼はいつも彼らに対して軽蔑的な態度をとっていた
the same disdain a Samana feels for the people of the world
サマナが世界の人々に対して抱くのと同じ軽蔑

Kamaswami was ailing and felt annoyed
カマスワミは病気でイライラしていた
he felt insulted by Siddhartha
彼はシッダールタに侮辱されたと感じた
and he was vexed by his worries as a merchant
彼は商人としての悩みに悩まされていた
Siddhartha had always watched these things with mockery
シッダールタはこれらのことを常に嘲笑しながら見ていた
but his mockery had become more tired
しかし彼の嘲笑はますます疲れてきた
his superiority had become more quiet
彼の優位性はより静かになった
as slowly imperceptible as the rainy season passing by

雨季がゆっくりと過ぎていくように、気づかないうちに
slowly, Siddhartha had assumed something of the childlike people's ways
徐々に、シッダールタは子供っぽい人々のやり方を身につけていった
he had gained some of their childishness
彼は彼らの子供っぽさを少し受け継いでいた
and he had gained some of their fearfulness
そして彼は彼らの恐怖心の一部を獲得した
And yet, the more be become like them the more he envied them
しかし、彼らに似てくるほど、彼は彼らを羨ましがるようになった。
He envied them for the one thing that was missing from him
彼は自分に欠けているものの一つを羨ましく思っていた
the importance they were able to attach to their lives
彼らが自分たちの人生にどれほどの重要性を感じていたか
the amount of passion in their joys and fears
喜びと恐怖の情熱の大きさ
the fearful but sweet happiness of being constantly in love
常に恋をしているという恐ろしくも甘い幸福
These people were in love with themselves all of the time
これらの人々は常に自分自身を愛していた
women loved their children, with honours or money
女性は名誉やお金よりも子供を愛した
the men loved themselves with plans or hopes
男たちは計画や希望をもって自分自身を愛した
But he did not learn this from them
しかし彼は彼らからこれを学んだわけではない
he did not learn the joy of children
彼は子供の喜びを学ばなかった
and he did not learn their foolishness
そして彼は彼らの愚かさを学ばなかった
what he mostly learned were their unpleasant things

彼が学んだのは主に彼らの不快なことだった
and he despised these things
そして彼はこれらのことを軽蔑した
in the morning, after having had company
朝、お客さんが来た後
more and more he stayed in bed for a long time
彼はますます長い時間ベッドで過ごすようになった
he felt unable to think, and was tired
彼は考えることができないと感じ、疲れていた
he became angry and impatient when Kamaswami bored him with his worries
カマスワミが彼の悩みを退屈に話すと、彼は怒り、イライラした。
he laughed just too loud when he lost a game of dice
彼はサイコロゲームに負けたとき、大声で笑った。
His face was still smarter and more spiritual than others
彼の顔は他の人たちよりも賢く、精神的に優れていた
but his face rarely laughed anymore
しかし彼の顔はもうほとんど笑わなくなった
slowly, his face assumed other features
ゆっくりと、彼の顔は別の特徴を帯びてきた
the features often found in the faces of rich people
金持ちの人の顔によく見られる特徴
features of discontent, of sickliness, of ill-humour
不満、病気、不機嫌の特徴
features of sloth, and of a lack of love
怠惰と愛情の欠如の特徴
the disease of the soul which rich people have
金持ちが患う魂の病
Slowly, this disease grabbed hold of him
ゆっくりと、この病気は彼を捕らえました
like a thin mist, tiredness came over Siddhartha
薄い霧のように、疲労がシッダールタを襲った
slowly, this mist got a bit denser every day
ゆっくりと、この霧は日に日に濃くなっていった

it got a bit murkier every month
毎月少しずつ曖昧になっていった
and every year it got a bit heavier
そして毎年少しずつ重くなっていきました
dresses become old with time
ドレスは時とともに古くなる
clothes lose their beautiful colour over time
衣服は時間の経過とともに美しい色を失う
they get stains, wrinkles, worn off at the seams
シミやシワができたり、縫い目が擦り切れたりする
they start to show threadbare spots here and there
あちこちに擦り切れた部分が見え始める
this is how Siddhartha's new life was
これがシッダールタの新しい人生でした
the life which he had started after his separation from Govinda
ゴヴィンダとの別れの後に彼が始めた生活
his life had grown old and lost colour
彼の人生は老いて色彩を失っていた
there was less splendour to it as the years passed by
年月が経つにつれてその素晴らしさは薄れていった
his life was gathering wrinkles and stains
彼の人生はしわと汚れを集めていた
and hidden at bottom, disappointment and disgust were waiting
そしてその底には失望と嫌悪が隠れていた
they were showing their ugliness
彼らは醜さを見せていた
Siddhartha did not notice these things
シッダールタはこれらのことに気づかなかった
he remembered the bright and reliable voice inside of him
彼は自分の中の明るく頼もしい声を思い出した
he noticed the voice had become silent
彼は声が静かになったことに気づいた
the voice which had awoken in him at that time
その時彼の中で目覚めた声

the voice that had guided him in his best times
最高の時に彼を導いてくれた声
he had been captured by the world
彼は世界に捕らわれていた
he had been captured by lust, covetousness, sloth
彼は欲望、貪欲、怠惰にとらわれていた
and finally he had been captured by his most despised vice
そしてついに彼は最も嫌悪していた悪徳に捕らわれてしまった
the vice which he mocked the most
彼が最も嘲笑した悪徳
the most foolish one of all vices
あらゆる悪徳の中で最も愚かなもの
he had let greed into his heart
彼は心の中に貪欲を抱いた
Property, possessions, and riches also had finally captured him
財産、所有物、富もついに彼を捕らえた
having things was no longer a game to him
物を持つことは彼にとってもはやゲームではなかった
his possessions had become a shackle and a burden
彼の所有物は足かせとなり重荷となっていた
It had happened in a strange and devious way
それは奇妙で邪悪な方法で起こった
Siddhartha had gotten this vice from the game of dice
シッダールタはこの悪癖をサイコロ遊びから得た
he had stopped being a Samana in his heart
彼は心の中でサマナであることをやめていた
and then he began to play the game for money
そして彼はお金のためにゲームをし始めた
first he joined the game with a smile
彼はまず笑顔でゲームに参加した
at this time he only played casually
当時彼はただカジュアルにプレーしていただけだった
he wanted to join the customs of the childlike people

彼は子供のような人々の習慣に参加したかった
but now he played with an increasing rage and passion
しかし今、彼は怒りと情熱を増してプレーしている
He was a feared gambler among the other merchants
彼は他の商人の間では恐れられるギャンブラーだった
his stakes were so audacious that few dared to take him on
彼の賭けは非常に大胆だったので、彼に挑もうとする者はほとんどいなかった。
He played the game due to a pain of his heart
彼は心の痛みのためにそのゲームをプレイした
losing and wasting his wretched money brought him an angry joy
お金を無駄にし浪費することは彼に怒りの喜びをもたらした
he could demonstrate his disdain for wealth in no other way
彼は他の方法では富に対する軽蔑を示すことができなかった
he could not mock the merchants' false god in a better way
彼は商人たちの偽りの神をもっと良い方法で嘲笑することはできなかった
so he gambled with high stakes
そこで彼は高額の賭け金を賭けた
he mercilessly hated himself and mocked himself
彼は容赦なく自分自身を憎み、嘲笑した
he won thousands, threw away thousands
彼は何千も勝ち、何千も失った
he lost money, jewellery, a house in the country
彼はお金、宝石、田舎の家を失った
he won it again, and then he lost again
彼はまた勝ったが、また負けた
he loved the fear he felt while he was rolling the dice
彼はサイコロを振っているときに感じる恐怖を愛していた
he loved feeling worried about losing what he gambled

彼は賭けたものを失うかもしれないという不安を感じるのが好きだった
he always wanted to get this fear to a slightly higher level
彼は常にこの恐怖を少し高めたいと思っていた
he only felt something like happiness when he felt this fear
彼はこの恐怖を感じたときだけ幸福のようなものを感じた
it was something like an intoxication
それはまるで酔いのようなものだった
something like an elevated form of life
生命の高次の形態のようなもの
something brighter in the midst of his dull life
退屈な生活の中で何か明るいものを見つけた
And after each big loss, his mind was set on new riches
そして大きな損失を被るたびに、彼は新たな富を得ることに心を定めた
he pursued the trade more zealously
彼はより熱心に商売に取り組んだ
he forced his debtors more strictly to pay
彼は債務者に対し、より厳しく支払いを強制した。
because he wanted to continue gambling
彼はギャンブルを続けたかったから
he wanted to continue squandering
彼は浪費を続けたかった
he wanted to continue demonstrating his disdain of wealth
彼は富に対する軽蔑を示し続けたかった
Siddhartha lost his calmness when losses occurred
シッダールタは損失が発生すると冷静さを失った
he lost his patience when he was not paid on time
彼は期日までに給料が支払われなかったため我慢できなくなった
he lost his kindness towards beggars
彼は物乞いに対する優しさを失った
He gambled away tens of thousands at one roll of the dice
彼はサイコロを一振りして何万ものお金を賭けた

he became more strict and more petty in his business
彼は仕事においてより厳しく、よりけちになった
occasionally, he was dreaming at night about money!
彼は時々、夜にお金の夢を見ていました。
whenever he woke up from this ugly spell, he continued fleeing
彼はこの醜い呪いから目覚めるたびに逃げ続けた
whenever he found his face in the mirror to have aged, he found a new game
鏡に映る自分の顔が老けていることに気づくたびに、彼は新しいゲームを見つけた
whenever embarrassment and disgust came over him, he numbed his mind
恥ずかしさや嫌悪感が襲ってくると、彼は心を麻痺させた。
he numbed his mind with sex and wine
彼はセックスとワインで心を麻痺させた
and from there he fled back into the urge to pile up and obtain possessions
そしてそこから彼は財産を積み上げ、手に入れたいという衝動に逃げ込んだ。
In this pointless cycle he ran
この無意味なサイクルの中で彼は
from his life he grow tired, old, and ill
彼は人生で疲れ、老い、病気になる

Then the time came when a dream warned him
そして、夢が彼に警告した時が来た
He had spent the hours of the evening with Kamala
彼はカマラと夕方の時間を過ごした
he had been in her beautiful pleasure-garden
彼は彼女の美しい遊園地にいた
They had been sitting under the trees, talking
彼らは木の下に座って話をしていた
and Kamala had said thoughtful words

カマラは思慮深い言葉を言った
words behind which a sadness and tiredness lay hidden
言葉の裏には悲しみと疲れが隠されていた
She had asked him to tell her about Gotama
彼女はゴータマについて話すように彼に頼んだ
she could not hear enough of him
彼女は彼の話を聞き飽きた
she loved how clear his eyes were
彼女は彼の澄んだ目が大好きだった
she loved how still and beautiful his mouth was
彼女は彼の口元が静かで美しいのが好きだった
she loved the kindness of his smile
彼女は彼の笑顔の優しさを愛した
she loved how peaceful his walk had been
彼女は彼の散歩がとても穏やかだったことを喜んだ
For a long time, he had to tell her about the exalted Buddha
彼は長い間、彼女に高貴な仏陀について語らなければならなかった
and Kamala had sighed, and spoke
カマラはため息をついて言った
"One day, perhaps soon, I'll also follow that Buddha"
「いつか、もしかしたら近いうちに、私もあの仏陀に従うだろう」
"I'll give him my pleasure-garden for a gift"
「私は彼に私の遊園地をプレゼントします」
"and I will take my refuge in his teachings"
「そして私は彼の教えに頼ります」
But after this, she had aroused him
しかしその後、彼女は彼を興奮させた
she had tied him to her in the act of making love
彼女は愛し合う行為の中で彼を自分に縛り付けていた
with painful fervour, biting and in tears
痛ましい熱情と、噛みつきと、涙と
it was as if she wanted to squeeze the last sweet drop out of this wine

まるで彼女はこのワインから最後の一滴まで絞り出そうとしているかのようだった

Never before had it become so strangely clear to Siddhartha
シッダールタにとって、これほど奇妙に明らかになったことはなかった。

he felt how close lust was akin to death
彼は欲望が死にどれほど近いかを感じた

he laid by her side, and Kamala's face was close to him
彼は彼女の横に横たわり、カマラの顔は彼の近くにあった

under her eyes and next to the corners of her mouth
目の下と口角の横

it was as clear as never before
これまでにないほど明確だった

there read a fearful inscription
そこには恐ろしい碑文が書かれていた

an inscription of small lines and slight grooves
細い線とわずかな溝の刻印

an inscription reminiscent of autumn and old age
秋と老年を思わせる碑文

here and there, gray hairs among his black ones
黒い髪の間に白髪がちらほら

Siddhartha himself, who was only in his forties, noticed the same thing
40代だったシッダールタ自身も同じことに気づいていた。

Tiredness was written on Kamala's beautiful face
カマラの美しい顔には疲れが表れていた

tiredness from walking a long path
長い道を歩いて疲れた

a path which has no happy destination
幸せな結末のない道

tiredness and the beginning of withering
疲労と衰えの始まり

fear of old age, autumn, and having to die

老い、衰え、そして死への恐怖
With a sigh, he had bid his farewell to her
彼はため息をつきながら彼女に別れを告げた
the soul full of reluctance, and full of concealed anxiety
心はためらいに満ち、隠れた不安に満ちている

Siddhartha had spent the night in his house with dancing girls
シッダールタは踊り子たちと彼の家で夜を過ごした
he acted as if he was superior to them
彼はまるで彼らより優れているかのように振舞った
he acted superior towards the fellow-members of his caste
彼は同じカーストの仲間に対して優越感を持って行動した
but this was no longer true
しかし、これはもはや真実ではなかった
he had drunk much wine that night
彼はその夜ワインをたくさん飲んだ
and he went to bed a long time after midnight
そして彼は夜中過ぎに寝た
tired and yet excited, close to weeping and despair
疲れているが興奮していて、泣きそうで絶望している
for a long time he sought to sleep, but it was in vain
彼は長い間眠ろうとしたが、それは無駄だった
his heart was full of misery
彼の心は悲しみに満ちていた
he thought he could not bear any longer
彼はもうこれ以上耐えられないと思った
he was full of a disgust, which he felt penetrating his entire body
彼は嫌悪感でいっぱいで、それが全身に浸透していくのを感じた。
like the lukewarm repulsive taste of the wine
ワインの生ぬるい不快な味のように
the dull music was a little too happy

退屈な音楽は少し楽しすぎた
the smile of the dancing girls was a little too soft
踊っている女の子たちの笑顔は少し優しすぎた
the scent of their hair and breasts was a little too sweet
髪と胸の香りがちょっと甘すぎた
But more than by anything else, he was disgusted by himself
しかし、何よりも彼は自分自身に嫌悪感を抱いていた
he was disgusted by his perfumed hair
彼は香水のついた髪に嫌悪感を抱いていた
he was disgusted by the smell of wine from his mouth
彼は口から漂うワインの匂いに嫌悪感を覚えた
he was disgusted by the listlessness of his skin
彼は自分の肌の無気力さに嫌悪感を覚えた
Like when someone who has eaten and drunk far too much
食べ過ぎたり飲み過ぎたりした人のように
they vomit it back up again with agonising pain
彼らは苦痛を伴い再びそれを吐き出す
but they feel relieved by the vomiting
しかし、彼らは嘔吐によって安心している
this sleepless man wished to free himself of these pleasures
この眠れない男はこれらの快楽から解放されたいと願った
he wanted to be rid of these habits
彼はこれらの習慣から抜け出したいと思った
he wanted to escape all of this pointless life
彼はこの無意味な人生から逃げたかった
and he wanted to escape from himself
そして彼は自分自身から逃げたかった
it wasn't until the light of the morning when he had slightly fallen sleep
朝の光が差し込む頃、彼は少し眠りに落ちた。
the first activities in the street were already beginning
路上での最初の活動はすでに始まっていた
for a few moments he had found a hint of sleep

しばらく彼は眠気を感じた
In those moments, he had a dream
その瞬間、彼は夢を見た
Kamala owned a small, rare singing bird in a golden cage
カマラは金色の鳥かごの中に小さくて珍しい鳴鳥を飼っていた
it always sung to him in the morning
朝になるといつも歌われていた
but then he dreamt this bird had become mute
しかし、彼はその鳥が口をきかなくなった夢を見た
since this arose his attention, he stepped in front of the cage
彼はこれに気付き、ケージの前に立ちました
he looked at the bird inside the cage
彼は鳥かごの中の鳥を見た
the small bird was dead, and lay stiff on the ground
小鳥は死んで地面に硬直していた
He took the dead bird out of its cage
彼は死んだ鳥をケージから取り出した
he took a moment to weigh the dead bird in his hand
彼は死んだ鳥を手の中で計量するのに少し時間をかけた
and then threw it away, out in the street
そしてそれを道端に捨てた
in the same moment he felt terribly shocked
同時に彼はひどくショックを受けた
his heart hurt as if he had thrown away all value
彼はすべての価値を捨てたかのように心を痛めた
everything good had been inside of this dead bird
この死んだ鳥の中には良いものがすべてあった
Starting up from this dream, he felt encompassed by a deep sadness
この夢から始まった彼は深い悲しみに包まれた
everything seemed worthless to him
彼にとってすべてが無価値に思えた
worthless and pointless was the way he had been going through life

彼の生き方は無価値で無意味だった
nothing which was alive was left in his hands
彼の手には生きたものは何も残っていなかった
nothing which was in some way delicious could be kept
おいしいものは保存できない
nothing worth keeping would stay
残しておく価値のあるものは何も残らない
alone he stood there, empty like a castaway on the shore
彼は一人、岸に漂着した人のように空虚に立っていた

With a gloomy mind, Siddhartha went to his pleasure-garden
シッダールタは暗い気持ちで遊園地へ向かった
he locked the gate and sat down under a mango-tree
彼は門を閉めてマンゴーの木の下に座った
he felt death in his heart and horror in his chest
彼は心の中に死を感じ、胸の中に恐怖を感じた
he sensed how everything died and withered in him
彼は自分の中ですべてが死に枯れていくのを感じた
By and by, he gathered his thoughts in his mind
やがて彼は心の中で考えをまとめた
once again, he went through the entire path of his life
彼は再び人生の道を歩み始めた
he started with the first days he could remember
彼は覚えている限りの最初の日から始めた
When was there ever a time when he had felt a true bliss?
彼が真の至福を感じた時があっただろうか？
Oh yes, several times he had experienced such a thing
ああ、彼は何度かそのようなことを経験していた
In his years as a boy he had had a taste of bliss
少年時代、彼は至福の時を味わった
he had felt happiness in his heart when he obtained praise from the Brahmans
彼はバラモンから賞賛を受けたとき、心から幸福を感じた。

"There is a path in front of the one who has distinguished himself"
「優れた才能を持つ者の前には道がある」
he had felt bliss reciting the holy verses
彼は聖なる詩を朗読して至福を感じていた
he had felt bliss disputing with the learned ones
彼は学者と議論することで至福を感じていた
he had felt bliss when he was an assistant in the offerings
彼は供物の助手をしていたときに至福を感じていた
Then, he had felt it in his heart
そして、彼は心の中でそれを感じた
"There is a path in front of you"
「あなたの前に道がある」
"you are destined for this path"
「あなたはこの道を歩む運命にある」
"the gods are awaiting you"
「神々があなたを待っています」
And again, as a young man, he had felt bliss
そしてまた、若い頃、彼は至福を感じていた
when his thoughts separated him from those thinking on the same things
彼の考えが同じことを考えている人々から彼を引き離したとき
when he wrestled in pain for the purpose of Brahman
ブラフマンのために苦しみながら格闘したとき
when every obtained knowledge only kindled new thirst in him
得た知識はどれも彼の中に新たな渇きをかき立てるだけだった
in the midst of the pain he felt this very same thing
痛みの中で彼はまさに同じことを感じていた
"Go on! You are called upon!"
「さあ！君が呼ばれたぞ！」
He had heard this voice when he had left his home
彼は家を出た時にこの声を聞いた。

he heard heard this voice when he had chosen the life of a Samana
彼はサマナの人生を選んだときにこの声を聞いた
and again he heard this voice when left the Samanas
そしてサマナスを去ったとき、彼は再びこの声を聞いた
he had heard the voice when he went to see the perfected one
彼は完成した者に会いに行ったときに声を聞いた
and when he had gone away from the perfected one, he had heard the voice
そして彼が完成された者から去ったとき、彼は声を聞いた
he had heard the voice when he went into the uncertain
彼は不確かな世界に入ったときに声を聞いた
For how long had he not heard this voice anymore?
彼はどれくらいこの声を聞かなくなっていたのだろうか？
for how long had he reached no height anymore?
彼はどれくらいの間、高みに到達できなかったのだろうか？
how even and dull was the manner in which he went through life?
彼の人生の生き方はどれほど平坦で退屈なものだっただろうか？
for many long years without a high goal
高い目標を持たずに長年
he had been without thirst or elevation
彼は渇きも高揚も感じていなかった
he had been content with small lustful pleasures
彼は小さな好色な快楽に満足していた
and yet he was never satisfied!
しかし、彼は決して満足しませんでした。
For all of these years he had tried hard to become like the others

彼は長年、他の人たちと同じようになろうと努力してきた

he longed to be one of the childlike people
彼は子供のような人間になりたいと願っていた

but he didn't know that that was what he really wanted
しかし彼はそれが本当に望んでいたことだとは知らなかった

his life had been much more miserable and poorer than theirs
彼の人生は彼らよりもずっと悲惨で貧しかった

because their goals and worries were not his
彼らの目標や悩みは彼のものではないから

the entire world of the Kamaswami-people had only been a game to him
カマスワミ族の世界全体が彼にとって単なるゲームに過ぎなかった

their lives were a dance he would watch
彼らの人生は彼が見守るダンスだった

they performed a comedy he could amuse himself with
彼らは彼が楽しめるコメディを演じた

Only Kamala had been dear and valuable to him
カマラだけが彼にとって大切で価値あるものだった

but was she still valuable to him?
しかし、彼女は彼にとってまだ価値のある存在だったのだろうか？

Did he still need her?
彼はまだ彼女を必要としていたのだろうか？

Or did she still need him?
それとも彼女はまだ彼を必要としていたのでしょうか？

Did they not play a game without an ending?
彼らは終わりのないゲームをプレイしたのではないですか？

Was it necessary to live for this?
そのために生きる必要があったのだろうか？

No, it was not necessary!

いいえ、必要ありませんでした！
The name of this game was Sansara
このゲームの名前はサンサーラでした
a game for children which was perhaps enjoyable to play once
かつては楽しかったかもしれない子供向けのゲーム
maybe it could be played twice
2回プレイできるかもしれない
perhaps you could play it ten times
10回くらいプレイできるかもしれない
but should you play it for ever and ever?
しかし、永遠にプレイし続けるべきでしょうか？
Then, Siddhartha knew that the game was over
そしてシッダールタはゲームが終わったことを知った
he knew that he could not play it any more
彼はもうそれを演奏できないことを知っていた
Shivers ran over his body and inside of him
震えが彼の体中を駆け巡った
he felt that something had died
彼は何かが死んだと感じた

That entire day, he sat under the mango-tree
その日、彼はマンゴーの木の下に座っていた
he was thinking of his father
彼は父親のことを考えていた
he was thinking of Govinda
彼はゴヴィンダのことを考えていた
and he was thinking of Gotama
そして彼はゴータマのことを考えていた
Did he have to leave them to become a Kamaswami?
カマスワミになるために、彼は彼らを捨てなければならなかったのでしょうか？
He was still sitting there when the night had fallen
夜になっても彼はそこに座っていた
he caught sight of the stars, and thought to himself

彼は星を見て、心の中で思った。
"Here I'm sitting under my mango-tree in my pleasure-garden"
「私は今、私の庭のマンゴーの木の下に座っている」
He smiled a little to himself
彼は少し微笑んだ
was it really necessary to own a garden?
本当に庭を持つ必要があったのでしょうか？
was it not a foolish game?
それは愚かなゲームではなかったのか？
did he need to own a mango-tree?
彼はマンゴーの木を所有する必要があったのでしょうか？
He also put an end to this
彼はこれに終止符を打った
this also died in him
これも彼の中で死んだ
He rose and bid his farewell to the mango-tree
彼は立ち上がり、マンゴーの木に別れを告げた。
he bid his farewell to the pleasure-garden
彼は遊園地に別れを告げた
Since he had been without food this day, he felt strong hunger
この日は何も食べていなかったので、彼は強い空腹を感じた。
and he thought of his house in the city
そして彼は街の家のことを思い浮かべた
he thought of his chamber and bed
彼は自分の部屋とベッドのことを考えた
he thought of the table with the meals on it
彼は食事が置かれたテーブルを思い浮かべた
He smiled tiredly, shook himself, and bid his farewell to these things
彼は疲れたように微笑み、体を震わせ、これらのものに別れを告げた。

In the same hour of the night, Siddhartha left his garden
夜の同じ時間に、シッダールタは庭を出て
he left the city and never came back
彼は街を出て二度と戻ってこなかった

For a long time, Kamaswami had people look for him
長い間、カマスワミは人々に捜索されていた
they thought he had fallen into the hands of robbers
彼らは彼が強盗の手に落ちたと思った
Kamala had no one look for him
カマラは誰も彼を探さなかった
she was not astonished by his disappearance
彼女は彼の失踪に驚かなかった
Did she not always expect it?
彼女はいつもそれを期待していなかったのでしょうか？
Was he not a Samana?
彼はサマナではなかったのか？
a man who was at home nowhere, a pilgrim
どこにも帰らない男、巡礼者
she had felt this the last time they had been together
彼女は前回一緒にいた時にこれを感じていた
she was happy despite all the pain of the loss
彼女は喪失の痛みにもかかわらず幸せだった
she was happy she had been with him one last time
彼女は最後にもう一度彼と一緒にいられて幸せだった
she was happy she had pulled him so affectionately to her heart
彼女は彼をこんなにも愛情深く自分の心の中に引き寄せることができて幸せだった
she was happy she had felt completely possessed and penetrated by him
彼女は彼に完全に支配され、貫かれたと感じて幸せだった
When she received the news, she went to the window
彼女はその知らせを受けて窓へ行き

at the window she held a rare singing bird
彼女は窓辺で珍しい鳴鳥を抱いていた
the bird was held captive in a golden cage
その鳥は金色の檻の中に閉じ込められていた
She opened the door of the cage
彼女は檻の扉を開けた
she took the bird out and let it fly
彼女は鳥を連れ出し飛ばした
For a long time, she gazed after it
彼女は長い間それを見つめていた
From this day on, she received no more visitors
この日から彼女はもう訪問客を受けなくなった
and she kept her house locked
そして彼女は家に鍵をかけた
But after some time, she became aware that she was pregnant
しかししばらくして彼女は自分が妊娠していることに気づいた
she was pregnant from the last time she was with Siddhartha
彼女はシッダールタと最後に会った時から妊娠していた

By the River
川沿いで

Siddhartha walked through the forest
シッダールタは森の中を歩いた
he was already far from the city
彼はすでに街から遠く離れていた
and he knew nothing but one thing
そして彼はただ一つのことだけを知っていた
there was no going back for him
彼には後戻りはできなかった
the life that he had lived for many years was over
彼が長年生きてきた人生は終わった
he had tasted all of this life
彼は人生のすべてを味わった
he had sucked everything out of this life
彼はこの人生からすべてを吸い取った
until he was disgusted with it
彼はそれにうんざりするまで
the singing bird he had dreamt of was dead
彼が夢に見た歌う鳥は死んでいた
and the bird in his heart was dead too
そして彼の心の中の鳥も死んでいた
he had been deeply entangled in Sansara
彼はサンサーラに深く巻き込まれていた
he had sucked up disgust and death into his body
彼は嫌悪と死を体内に吸収していた
like a sponge sucks up water until it is full
スポンジがいっぱいになるまで水を吸い上げるように
he was full of misery and death
彼は悲惨と死に満ちていた
there was nothing left in this world which could have attracted him
この世に彼を惹きつけるものは何も残っていなかった
nothing could have given him joy or comfort

彼に喜びや慰めを与えるものは何もなかった
he passionately wished to know nothing about himself anymore
彼は自分自身についてもう何も知りたくないと強く願った
he wanted to have rest and be dead
彼は休んで死にたかった
he wished there was a lightning-bolt to strike him dead!
彼は、自分を打って死なせる雷があればいいのにと思った。
If there only was a tiger to devour him!
彼を食い尽くす虎がいたらいいのに！
If there only was a poisonous wine which would numb his senses
彼の感覚を麻痺させる毒入りのワインがあればいいのに
a wine which brought him forgetfulness and sleep
彼に忘却と眠りをもたらしたワイン
a wine from which he wouldn't awake from
目覚めることのできないワイン
Was there still any kind of filth he had not soiled himself with?
彼がまだ汚していない汚物が何かあったのだろうか？
was there a sin or foolish act he had not committed?
彼が犯さなかった罪や愚かな行為はあったのだろうか？
was there a dreariness of the soul he didn't know?
彼が知らない魂の陰鬱さがあったのだろうか？
was there anything he had not brought upon himself?
彼が自ら招かなかったことは何かあっただろうか？
Was it still at all possible to be alive?
まだ生きていくことは可能だったのだろうか？
Was it possible to breathe in again and again?
何度も息を吸うことは可能でしたか？
Could he still breathe out?
彼はまだ息を吐くことができるだろうか？
was he able to bear hunger?

彼は飢えに耐えることができたでしょうか？
was there any way to eat again?
もう一度食べる方法はありましたか？
was it possible to sleep again?
もう一度眠ることはできましたか？
could he sleep with a woman again?
彼はまた女性と寝ることができるだろうか？
had this cycle not exhausted itself?
このサイクルは尽き果てていなかったのだろうか？
were things not brought to their conclusion?
物事は終結しなかったのですか？

Siddhartha reached the large river in the forest
シッダールタは森の中の大きな川に到着した
it was the same river he crossed when he had still been a young man
それは彼がまだ若い頃に渡ったのと同じ川だった
it was the same river he crossed from the town of Gotama
それはゴータマの町から彼が渡ったのと同じ川だった
he remembered a ferryman who had taken him over the river
彼は川を渡った渡し守のことを思い出した
By this river he stopped, and hesitantly he stood at the bank
彼はこの川のそばで立ち止まり、ためらいながら川岸に立った。
Tiredness and hunger had weakened him
疲労と空腹で彼は衰弱していた
"what should I walk on for?"
「何を歩けばいいの？」
"to what goal was there left to go?"
「あと何の目標が残っていたのか？」
No, there were no more goals
いいえ、それ以上のゴールはありませんでした
there was nothing left but a painful yearning to shake off this dream

この夢を振り払いたいという苦しい思いだけが残った
he yearned to spit out this stale wine
彼はこの古くなったワインを吐き出したいと思った
he wanted to put an end to this miserable and shameful life
彼はこの惨めで恥ずべき人生に終止符を打ちたかった
a coconut-tree bent over the bank of the river
川岸に曲がったココナッツの木
Siddhartha leaned against its trunk with his shoulder
シッダールタは肩を幹に寄りかかって
he embraced the trunk with one arm
彼は片腕で幹を抱きしめた
and he looked down into the green water
そして彼は緑色の水を見下ろした
the water ran under him
水が彼の下を流れた
he looked down and found himself to be entirely filled with the wish to let go
彼は下を向いて、手放したいという願望で満たされていることに気づいた。
he wanted to drown in these waters
彼はこの水に溺れたかった
the water reflected a frightening emptiness back at him
水は恐ろしい空虚さを彼に映し返した
the water answered to the terrible emptiness in his soul
水は彼の魂のひどい空虚に応えた
Yes, he had reached the end
そう、彼は終わりに達した
There was nothing left for him, except to annihilate himself
彼には自分自身を滅ぼす以外に何も残されていなかった
he wanted to smash the failure into which he had shaped his life
彼は自分の人生を形作った失敗を打ち砕きたかった
he wanted to throw his life before the feet of mockingly laughing gods

彼は嘲笑う神々の足元に自分の命を投げ出したいと思った

This was the great vomiting he had longed for; death
これは彼が望んでいた大嘔吐であり、死であった。
the smashing to bits of the form he hated
彼が嫌っていたフォームを粉々に粉砕
Let him be food for fishes and crocodiles
彼を魚やワニの餌食にしよう
Siddhartha the dog, a lunatic
狂人である犬のシッダールタ
a depraved and rotten body; a weakened and abused soul!
堕落し、腐った肉体、弱り、虐待された魂！
let him be chopped to bits by the daemons
悪魔に切り刻まれろ
With a distorted face, he stared into the water
彼は顔をゆがめて水を見つめた
he saw the reflection of his face and spat at it
彼は自分の顔が映っているのを見て、それに唾を吐いた。
In deep tiredness, he took his arm away from the trunk of the tree
ひどく疲れた彼は木の幹から腕を離した。
he turned a bit, in order to let himself fall straight down
彼は少し向きを変えて、まっすぐ下に落ちようとした
in order to finally drown in the river
最終的に川で溺死するために
With his eyes closed, he slipped towards death
目を閉じて彼は死へと向かっていった
Then, out of remote areas of his soul, a sound stirred up
すると、彼の心の奥底から、音が響き渡った。
a sound stirred up out of past times of his now weary life
疲れ果てた彼の人生の過去から呼び起こされた音
It was a singular word, a single syllable
それは一語一音節の単語だった
without thinking he spoke the voice to himself

彼は何も考えずに自分自身に声をかけた
he slurred the beginning and the end of all prayers of the Brahmans
彼はバラモンの祈りの始めと終わりをろれつが回らないように発音した。
he spoke the holy Om
彼は神聖なオームを唱えた
"that what is perfect" or "the completion"
「完璧なもの」または「完成」
And in the moment he realized the foolishness of his actions
そしてその瞬間、彼は自分の行動の愚かさに気づいた
the sound of Om touched Siddhartha's ear
オームの音がシッダールタの耳に届いた
his dormant spirit suddenly woke up
彼の眠っていた魂が突然目覚めた
Siddhartha was deeply shocked
シッダールタは深くショックを受けた
he saw this was how things were with him
彼はこれが自分の状況だと気づいた
he was so doomed that he had been able to seek death
彼は死を求めるほど運命づけられていた
he had lost his way so much that he wished the end
彼は道に迷い、終わりを願った。
the wish of a child had been able to grow in him
子供の願いが彼の中に育まれていた
he had wished to find rest by annihilating his body!
彼は自分の肉体を消滅させることで安息を得たいと望んでいたのです！
all the agony of recent times
最近のあらゆる苦悩
all sobering realizations that his life had created
彼の人生が生み出したすべての厳粛な認識
all the desperation that he had felt
彼が感じていた絶望感は
these things did not bring about this moment

これらのことがこの瞬間をもたらしたのではない
when the Om entered his consciousness he became aware of himself
オームが彼の意識に入ったとき、彼は自分自身に気づいた
he realized his misery and his error
彼は自分の惨めさと過ちに気づいた
Om! he spoke to himself
オーム！彼は独り言を言った
Om! and again he knew about Brahman
オーム！そして彼は再びブラフマンについて知った
Om! he knew about the indestructibility of life
オーム！彼は生命の不滅性を知っていた
Om! he knew about all that is divine, which he had forgotten
オーム！彼は忘れていた神聖なものすべてを知っていた
But this was only a moment that flashed before him
しかし、これは彼の前に一瞬現れたに過ぎなかった
By the foot of the coconut-tree, Siddhartha collapsed
ココナッツの木の根元でシッダールタは倒れた
he was struck down by tiredness
彼は疲労に襲われた
mumbling "Om", he placed his head on the root of the tree
「オーム」とつぶやきながら、彼は木の根元に頭を置いた。
and he fell into a deep sleep
そして彼は深い眠りに落ちた
Deep was his sleep, and without dreams
彼は深い眠りについたが、夢も見なかった
for a long time he had not known such a sleep any more
彼は長い間、そのような眠りを知らなかった

When he woke up after many hours, he felt as if ten years had passed

何時間も経って目が覚めたとき、彼はまるで10年が経過したように感じた。
he heard the water quietly flowing
彼は静かに水が流れる音を聞いた
he did not know where he was
彼は自分がどこにいるか知らなかった
and he did not know who had brought him here
そして誰が彼をここに連れてきたのかは知らなかった
he opened his eyes and looked with astonishment
彼は目を開けて驚いて見た
there were trees and the sky above him
彼の上には木々や空があった
he remembered where he was and how he got here
彼は自分がどこにいて、どうやってここに来たのかを思い出した
But it took him a long while for this
しかし、これには長い時間がかかりました
the past seemed to him as if it had been covered by a veil
彼にとって過去はまるでベールに覆われているかのように思えた
infinitely distant, infinitely far away, infinitely meaningless
限りなく遠い、限りなく遠い、限りなく無意味
He only knew that his previous life had been abandoned
彼は自分の以前の人生が捨てられたことだけを知っていた
this past life seemed to him like a very old, previous incarnation
この過去の人生は彼にとって非常に古い、前世のように思えた
this past life felt like a pre-birth of his present self
この過去の人生は、今の自分の誕生前のように感じられた
full of disgust and wretchedness, he had intended to throw his life away

彼は嫌悪感と惨めさでいっぱいで、自分の人生を捨てるつもりだった

he had come to his senses by a river, under a coconut-tree
彼は川のほとりのココナッツの木の下で正気を取り戻した

the holy word "Om" was on his lips
彼の唇には神聖な言葉「オーム」があった

he had fallen asleep and had now woken up
彼は眠りに落ち、そして今目覚めた

he was looking at the world as a new man
彼は新しい人間として世界を見ていた

Quietly, he spoke the word "Om" to himself
彼は静かに「オーム」という言葉を自分に唱えた

the "Om" he was speaking when he had fallen asleep
彼が眠りに落ちたときに発していた「オーム」

his sleep felt like nothing more than a long meditative recitation of "Om"
彼の睡眠は、まるで「オーム」という長い瞑想の朗読のようだった。

all his sleep had been a thinking of "Om"
彼はずっと「オーム」と唱えながら眠っていた

a submergence and complete entering into "Om"
「オーム」への沈静と完全な入魂

a going into the perfected and completed
完成され、完了したものへと進む

What a wonderful sleep this had been!
なんと素晴らしい睡眠だったことか!

he had never before been so refreshed by sleep
彼はこれまで睡眠によってこれほどリフレッシュしたことはなかった

Perhaps, he really had died
おそらく彼は本当に死んだのだろう

maybe he had drowned and was reborn in a new body?
もしかしたら溺れて新しい体で生まれ変わったのかもしれない。

But no, he knew himself and who he was
しかし、彼は自分自身と自分が何者であるかを知っていた
he knew his hands and his feet
彼は自分の手と足を知っていた
he knew the place where he lay
彼は自分が横たわっている場所を知っていた
he knew this self in his chest
彼は自分の胸の中にこの自分を知っていた
Siddhartha the eccentric, the weird one
風変わりなシッダールタ
but this Siddhartha was nevertheless transformed
しかし、このシッダールタは変容した
he was strangely well rested and awake
彼は不思議なことによく休んでいて目が覚めていた
and he was joyful and curious
彼は喜びと好奇心にあふれていた

Siddhartha straightened up and looked around
シッダールタは立ち上がって周りを見回した
then he saw a person sitting opposite to him
すると彼は向かいに座っている人を見た
a monk in a yellow robe with a shaven head
頭を剃り、黄色い僧衣を着た僧侶
he was sitting in the position of pondering
彼は考え込んでいる姿勢で座っていた
He observed the man, who had neither hair on his head nor a beard
彼は、頭髪も髭もない男を観察した。
he had not observed him for long when he recognised this monk
彼はこの僧侶に気づいたとき、あまり長く観察していなかった。
it was Govinda, the friend of his youth
それは彼の若い頃の友人であるゴヴィンダだった

Govinda, who had taken his refuge with the exalted Buddha
ゴーヴィンダは高貴な仏陀のもとに帰依した
Like Siddhartha, Govinda had also aged
シッダールタ同様、ゴーヴィンダも年老いていた
but his face still bore the same features
しかし彼の顔には依然として同じ特徴があった
his face still expressed zeal and faithfulness
彼の顔には依然として熱意と誠実さが表れていた
you could see he was still searching, but timidly
彼がまだ探し回っているのがわかったが、恐る恐る
Govinda sensed his gaze, opened his eyes, and looked at him
ゴヴィンダは彼の視線を感じて目を開け、彼を見た。
Siddhartha saw that Govinda did not recognise him
シッダールタはゴーヴィンダが自分を認識していないことに気づいた
Govinda was happy to find him awake
ゴヴィンダは彼が目を覚ましていることに喜びを感じた
apparently, he had been sitting here for a long time
どうやら彼は長い間ここに座っていたようだ
he had been waiting for him to wake up
彼は彼が目を覚ますのを待っていた
he waited, although he did not know him
彼は彼を知らなかったが、待っていた
"I have been sleeping" said Siddhartha
「私は眠っていた」とシッダールタは言った
"How did you get here?"
「どうやってここに来たの？」
"You have been sleeping" answered Govinda
「あなたは眠っていたのよ」とゴヴィンダは答えた。
"It is not good to be sleeping in such places"
「こんなところで寝るのはよくない」
"snakes and the animals of the forest have their paths here"
「蛇や森の動物たちはここに道を持っている」
"I, oh sir, am a follower of the exalted Gotama"

「私は、ゴータマの信奉者です」
"I was on a pilgrimage on this path"
「私はこの道を巡礼していた」
"I saw you lying and sleeping in a place where it is dangerous to sleep"
「あなたが危険な場所で横になって眠っているのを見ました」
"Therefore, I sought to wake you up"
「だから、私はあなたを起こそうとしたのです」
"but I saw that your sleep was very deep"
「しかし、私はあなたの眠りがとても深いのを見ました」
"so I stayed behind from my group"
「だから私はグループから外れました」
"and I sat with you until you woke up"
「そして私はあなたが目を覚ますまで一緒に座っていました」
"And then, so it seems, I have fallen asleep myself"
「そして、どうやら私自身も眠りに落ちてしまったようだ」
"I, who wanted to guard your sleep, fell asleep"
「あなたの眠りを守りたかった私は眠りに落ちた」
"Badly, I have served you"
「ひどい仕打ちをしました」
"tiredness had overwhelmed me"
「疲労が私を圧倒した」
"But since you're awake, let me go to catch up with my brothers"
「でも、あなたが目覚めたのなら、兄弟たちに会いに行かせてください」
"I thank you, Samana, for watching out over my sleep" spoke Siddhartha
「サマナよ、私の眠りを守ってくれてありがとう」とシッダールタは言った。
"You're friendly, you followers of the exalted one"

「あなた方は友好的ですね、崇高なる者の信奉者たちよ」

"Now you may go to them"
「さあ、彼らのところへ行ってください」

"I'm going, sir. May you always be in good health"
「行ってきます。ご健康をお祈りします」

"I thank you, Samana"
「ありがとう、サマナ」

Govinda made the gesture of a salutation and said "Farewell"
ゴヴィンダは挨拶のジェスチャーをして「さようなら」と言った。

"Farewell, Govinda" said Siddhartha
「さようなら、ゴーヴィンダ」とシッダールタは言った。

The monk stopped as if struck by lightning
僧侶は雷に打たれたかのように立ち止まった

"Permit me to ask, sir, from where do you know my name?"
「お尋ねしますが、私の名前をどこでご存知ですか？」

Siddhartha smiled, "I know you, oh Govinda, from your father's hut"
シッダールタは微笑んだ。「ゴーヴィンダよ、私はあなたの父親の小屋であなたを知っています」

"and I know you from the school of the Brahmans"
「私はあなたをバラモンの学校で知っています」

"and I know you from the offerings"
「そして私は供物からあなたを知っています」

"and I know you from our walk to the Samanas"
「サマナスへの散歩であなたを知りました」

"and I know you from when you took refuge with the exalted one"
「そして私はあなたが高貴なる者のもとに避難した時からあなたを知っている」

"You're Siddhartha," Govinda exclaimed loudly, "Now, I recognise you"

「あなたはシッダールタよ」とゴヴィンダは大声で叫んだ。「今、私はあなたが誰であるか分かりました」
"I don't comprehend how I couldn't recognise you right away"
「どうしてすぐにあなたを認識できなかったのか理解できません」
"Siddhartha, my joy is great to see you again"
「シッダールタ、またお会いできて嬉しいです」
"It also gives me joy, to see you again" spoke Siddhartha
「あなたにまた会えることは私にとっても嬉しいことだ」とシッダールタは言った。
"You've been the guard of my sleep"
「あなたは私の眠りを守ってくれました」
"again, I thank you for this"
「改めて、感謝します」
"but I wouldn't have required any guard"
「しかし、私は警備を必要としなかっただろう」
"Where are you going to, oh friend?"
「おお、友よ、どこへ行くの？」
"I'm going nowhere," answered Govinda
「私はどこにも行きません」とゴヴィンダは答えた。
"We monks are always travelling"
「私たち僧侶はいつも旅をしています」
"whenever it is not the rainy season, we move from one place to another"
「雨季以外は、私たちはある場所から別の場所へ移動します」
"we live according to the rules of the teachings passed on to us"
「私たちは受け継がれた教えのルールに従って生きています」
"we accept alms, and then we move on"
「私たちは施しを受け取って、それから先へ進みます」
"It is always like this"
「いつもこうだ」

"But you, Siddhartha, where are you going to?"
「しかし、シッダールタよ、あなたはどこへ行くのですか?」
"for me it is as it is with you"
「私にとってもそれはあなたと同じです」
"I'm going nowhere; I'm just travelling"
「私はどこにも行かない、ただ旅をしているだけ」
"I'm also on a pilgrimage"
「私も巡礼の旅に出ています」
Govinda spoke "You say you're on a pilgrimage, and I believe you"
ゴヴィンダはこう言った。「あなたは巡礼の旅をしているとおっしゃいますが、私はそれを信じます」
"But, forgive me, oh Siddhartha, you do not look like a pilgrim"
「しかし、お許しください、シッダールタよ、あなたは巡礼者には見えません」
"You're wearing a rich man's garments"
「あなたは金持ちの服を着ている」
"you're wearing the shoes of a distinguished gentleman"
「あなたは高貴な紳士の靴を履いている」
"and your hair, with the fragrance of perfume, is not a pilgrim's hair"
「そしてあなたの髪は香水の香りが漂い、巡礼者の髪ではない」
"you do not have the hair of a Samana"
「あなたはサマナの髪を持っていません」
"you are right, my dear"
「君の言う通りだよ」
"you have observed things well"
「あなたは物事をよく観察しました」
"your keen eyes see everything"
「あなたの鋭い目はすべてを見通す」
"But I haven't said to you that I was a Samana"
「しかし、私はサマナだと言ったことはありません」

"I said I'm on a pilgrimage"
「巡礼の旅だと言ったのに」
"And so it is, I'm on a pilgrimage"
「そう、私は巡礼の旅をしているのです」
"You're on a pilgrimage" said Govinda
「あなたは巡礼の旅をしているのよ」とゴヴィンダは言った
"But few would go on a pilgrimage in such clothes"
「しかし、そんな服装で巡礼に行く人はほとんどいないだろう」
"few would pilger in such shoes"
「そんな靴で巡礼する人はほとんどいない」
"and few pilgrims have such hair"
「そして、そのような髪を持つ巡礼者はほとんどいない」
"I have never met such a pilgrim"
「こんな巡礼者に会ったことがない」
"and I have been a pilgrim for many years"
「私は長年巡礼をしてきました」
"I believe you, my dear Govinda"
「私はあなたを信じています、愛しいゴヴィンダ」
"But now, today, you've met a pilgrim just like this"
「しかし今日、あなたはこのような巡礼者に出会ったのです」
"a pilgrim wearing these kinds of shoes and garment"
「このような靴と衣服を身に着けている巡礼者」
"Remember, my dear, the world of appearances is not eternal"
「覚えておいて下さい、私の愛しい人よ、外見の世界は永遠ではないのです」
"our shoes and garments are anything but eternal"
「私たちの靴や衣服は決して永遠ではない」
"our hair and bodies are not eternal either"
「私たちの髪や体も永遠ではない」
I'm wearing a rich man's clothes"

私は金持ちの服を着ている」
"you've seen this quite right"
「あなたはこれを正しく見ました」
"I'm wearing them, because I have been a rich man"
「私は金持ちだったからこれを着ているんです」
"and I'm wearing my hair like the worldly and lustful people"
「そして私は世俗的で好色な人々と同じように髪を結んでいる」
"because I have been one of them"
「私も彼らの一人だったから」
"And what are you now, Siddhartha?" Govinda asked
「それで、シッダールタ、あなたは今どうしているのですか？」ゴーヴィンダは尋ねた
"I don't know it, just like you"
「私もあなたと同じように知らない」
"I was a rich man, and now I am not a rich man anymore"
「私はかつて金持ちだったが、今はもう金持ちではない」
"and what I'll be tomorrow, I don't know"
「明日はどうなるか分からない」
"You've lost your riches?" asked Govinda
「財産を失ったのですか？」とゴヴィンダは尋ねた。
"I've lost my riches, or they have lost me"
「私は富を失った、あるいは彼らは私を失った」
"My riches somehow happened to slip away from me"
「私の富はどういうわけか私から逃げ去ってしまった」
"The wheel of physical manifestations is turning quickly, Govinda"
「物理的な顕現の輪は急速に回転しています、ゴヴィンダ」
"Where is Siddhartha the Brahman?"
「ブラフマン・シッダールタはどこにいるのか？」
"Where is Siddhartha the Samana?"
「サマナ・シッダールタはどこにいますか？」

"Where is Siddhartha the rich man?"
「金持ちのシッダールタはどこにいる？」
"Non-eternal things change quickly, Govinda, you know it"
「永遠ではないものはすぐに変わる、ゴヴィンダ、あなたも知っているでしょう」
Govinda looked at the friend of his youth for a long time
ゴヴィンダは長い間、幼なじみの友人を見つめていた
he looked at him with doubt in his eyes
彼は疑いの目で彼を見た
After that, he gave him the salutation which one would use on a gentleman
その後、彼は紳士に使う挨拶をした。
and he went on his way, and continued his pilgrimage
そして彼は旅を続け、巡礼を続けた。
With a smiling face, Siddhartha watched him leave
シッダールタは微笑みながら彼が去るのを見守った
he loved him still, this faithful, fearful man
彼はまだこの忠実で恐れ多い男を愛していた
how could he not have loved everybody and everything in this moment?
この瞬間に、どうして彼はすべての人やすべてのものを愛さずにいられようか？
in the glorious hour after his wonderful sleep, filled with Om!
素晴らしい眠りの後の栄光の時間に、オーム！で満たされました。
The enchantment, which had happened inside of him in his sleep
眠っている間に彼の中に起こった魔法
this enchantment was everything that he loved
この魔法は彼が愛したものすべてでした
he was full of joyful love for everything he saw
彼は見たものすべてに喜びと愛に満ちていた
exactly this had been his sickness before
まさにこれが彼の以前の病気だった
he had not been able to love anybody or anything

彼は誰も何も愛することができなかった
With a smiling face, Siddhartha watched the leaving monk
シッダールタは微笑みながら、去っていく僧侶を見守った。

The sleep had strengthened him a lot
睡眠は彼を大いに元気にさせた
but hunger gave him great pain
しかし飢えは彼に大きな苦痛を与えた
by now he had not eaten for two days
彼はすでに2日間何も食べていなかった
the times were long past when he could resist such hunger
彼がそのような飢えに耐えられる時代はとうに過ぎ去っていた
With sadness, and yet also with a smile, he thought of that time
彼は悲しみと微笑みを抱きながら、その時のことを思い返した。
In those days, so he remembered, he had boasted of three things to Kamala
当時、彼はカマラに3つのことを自慢していたと記憶している。
he had been able to do three noble and undefeatable feats
彼は3つの高貴で無敵の偉業を成し遂げた
he was able to fast, wait, and think
彼は断食し、待ち、そして考えることができた
These had been his possessions; his power and strength
これらは彼の所有物であり、彼の力と強さであった
in the busy, laborious years of his youth, he had learned these three feats
忙しくて苦労した若い頃に、彼はこれらの3つの技を習得した。
And now, his feats had abandoned him
そして今、彼の偉業は彼から去った
none of his feats were his any more

彼の偉業はもはや彼のものではない
neither fasting, nor waiting, nor thinking
断食もせず、待つこともせず、考えることもせず
he had given them up for the most wretched things
彼は最も悲惨なことのためにそれらを放棄した
what is it that fades most quickly?
最も早く消えてしまうものは何ですか?
sensual lust, the good life, and riches!
官能的な欲望、豊かな生活、そして富!
His life had indeed been strange
彼の人生は実に奇妙だった
And now, so it seemed, he had really become a childlike person
そして今、彼は本当に子供のような人間になったようだ
Siddhartha thought about his situation
シッダールタは自分の状況について考えた
Thinking was hard for him now
考えることは彼にとって困難だった
he did not really feel like thinking
彼は本当に考える気がなかった
but he forced himself to think
しかし彼は考えようとした
"all these most easily perishing things have slipped from me"
「これらの最も簡単に滅びるものはすべて私から逃げ去った」
"again, now I'm standing here under the sun"
「また、今私は太陽の下に立っている」
"I am standing here just like a little child"
「私は小さな子供のようにここに立っています」
"nothing is mine, I have no abilities"
「何も私のものではない、私には能力がない」
"there is nothing I could bring about"
「私が成し遂げられることは何もない」
"I have learned nothing from my life"

「私は人生から何も学んでいない」
"How wondrous all of this is!"
「これはすべて何と素晴らしいことなのでしょう！」
"it's wondrous that I'm no longer young"
「もう若くないなんて不思議だ」
"my hair is already half gray and my strength is fading"
「私の髪はすでに半分白髪になり、体力も衰えています」
"and now I'm starting again at the beginning, as a child!"
「そして今、私は子供のころからもう一度始めています！」
Again, he had to smile to himself
彼はまたもや自分自身に微笑みかけた
Yes, his fate had been strange!
そう、彼の運命は奇妙なものだったのです！
Things were going downhill with him
彼の状況は悪化の一途をたどっていた
and now he was again facing the world naked and stupid
そして今、彼は再び裸で愚かな世界に直面していた
But he could not feel sad about this
しかし彼はこれについて悲しむことはできなかった
no, he even felt a great urge to laugh
いや、彼は笑いたくなる衝動さえ感じた
he felt an urge to laugh about himself
彼は自分自身について笑いたくなった
he felt an urge to laugh about this strange, foolish world
彼はこの奇妙で愚かな世界を笑いたくなった
"Things are going downhill with you!" he said to himself
「君の状況は悪化している！」と彼は自分に言い聞かせた
and he laughed about his situation
そして彼は自分の状況を笑い飛ばした
as he was saying it he happened to glance at the river
彼がそう言いながら、偶然川に目をやった。
and he also saw the river going downhill

そして彼は川が下り坂になっているのも見た
it was singing and being happy about everything
歌ったり、何でも喜んでいたり
He liked this, and kindly he smiled at the river
彼はこれを気に入り、優しく川に向かって微笑んだ
Was this not the river in which he had intended to drown himself?
これは彼が自らを溺れさせようとした川ではなかったのか？
in past times, a hundred years ago
昔、100年前に
or had he dreamed this?
それとも彼はこれを夢見ていたのだろうか？
"Wondrous indeed was my life" he thought
「私の人生は本当に素晴らしかった」と彼は思った
"my life has taken wondrous detours"
「私の人生は驚くべき回り道をしてきました」
"As a boy, I only dealt with gods and offerings"
「少年の頃、私は神と供物だけを扱っていました」
"As a youth, I only dealt with asceticism"
「若い頃は、私はただ苦行だけをやっていました」
"I spent my time in thinking and meditation"
「私は考え、瞑想しながら時間を過ごしました」
"I was searching for Brahman
「私はブラフマンを探していた
"and I worshipped the eternal in the Atman"
「そして私はアートマンの永遠を崇拝した」
"But as a young man, I followed the penitents"
「しかし、若い頃、私は悔悛者たちに従いました」
"I lived in the forest and suffered heat and frost"
「私は森に住んでいて、暑さと寒さに苦しみました」
"there I learned how to overcome hunger"
「そこで私は飢えを克服する方法を学びました」
"and I taught my body to become dead"
「そして私は自分の体を死なせるように教えた」

"Wonderfully, soon afterwards, insight came towards me"
「素晴らしいことに、その後すぐに、私に洞察力が湧いてきました」

"insight in the form of the great Buddha's teachings"
「偉大な仏陀の教えの形をとった洞察」

"I felt the knowledge of the oneness of the world"
「私は世界の一体性を知りました」

"I felt it circling in me like my own blood"
「自分の血のように体内を巡っているのを感じました」

"But I also had to leave Buddha and the great knowledge"
「しかし、私は仏陀と偉大な知識も捨てなければなりませんでした」

"I went and learned the art of love with Kamala"
「私はカマラと一緒に愛の芸術を学びに行きました」

"I learned trading and business with Kamaswami"
「私はカマスワミから貿易とビジネスを学びました」

"I piled up money, and wasted it again"
「お金を貯めて、また無駄にした」

"I learned to love my stomach and please my senses"
「私は自分の胃を愛し、自分の感覚を満足させることを学びました」

"I had to spend many years losing my spirit"
「私は何年もの間、自分の精神を失っていました」

"and I had to unlearn thinking again"
「そして私は再び考え方を忘れなければならなかった」

"there I had forgotten the oneness"
「そこで私は一体感を忘れていた」

"Isn't it just as if I had turned slowly from a man into a child"?
「まるで僕がゆっくりと大人から子供に変わってしまったかのようではないか」

"from a thinker into a childlike person"
「思想家から子供のような人間へ」

"And yet, this path has been very good"
「それでも、この道は非常に良かった」

"and yet, the bird in my chest has not died"
「それでも、私の胸の中の鳥は死んでいない」
"what a path has this been!"
「これは何という道だったのだろう!」
"I had to pass through so much stupidity"
「私はたくさんの愚かなことを乗り越えなければならなかった」
"I had to pass through so much vice"
「私は多くの悪徳を経験しなければならなかった」
"I had to make so many errors"
「私はたくさんの間違いを犯しました」
"I had to feel so much disgust and disappointment"
「私はとても嫌悪感と失望を感じました」
"I had to do all this to become a child again"
「もう一度子供になるために、私はこれらすべてをしなければならなかった」
"and then I could start over again"
「そしてまたやり直すことができる」
"But it was the right way to do it"
「でも、それが正しいやり方だった」
"my heart says yes to it and my eyes smile to it"
「私の心はそれに賛成し、私の目はそれに微笑む」
"I've had to experience despair"
「絶望を経験しなければならなかった」
"I've had to sink down to the most foolish of all thoughts"
「私は最も愚かな考えに陥らざるを得なかった」
"I've had to think to the thoughts of suicide"
「自殺を考えなければならなかった」
"only then would I be able to experience divine grace"
「そうして初めて私は神の恵みを体験できるのです」
"only then could I hear Om again"
「そのとき初めて、私は再びオームを聞くことができたのです」
"only then would I be able to sleep properly and awake again"

「そうして初めて、私はきちんと眠り、また目覚めることができるのです」
"I had to become a fool, to find Atman in me again"
「私は愚か者になって、再び私の中にアートマンを見つけなければなりませんでした」
"I had to sin, to be able to live again"
「再び生きるためには罪を犯さなければならなかった」
"Where else might my path lead me to?"
「私の道は他にどこへ導くのだろうか？」
"It is foolish, this path, it moves in loops"
「この道は愚かだ、ループしている」
"perhaps it is going around in a circle"
「おそらくそれはぐるぐる回っている」
"Let this path go where it likes"
「この道が望むところへ行かせてあげよう」
"where ever this path goes, I want to follow it"
「この道がどこへ向かうにせよ、私はそれを辿りたい」
he felt joy rolling like waves in his chest
彼は胸に喜びの波が押し寄せるのを感じた
he asked his heart, "from where did you get this happiness?"
彼は自分の心に尋ねました。「この幸せはどこから来たの？」
"does it perhaps come from that long, good sleep?"
「それは長くて良い睡眠から来るのでしょうか？」
"the sleep which has done me so much good"
「私にとってとても良い睡眠」
"or does it come from the word Om, which I said?"
「それとも、それは私が言った Om という言葉から来ているのでしょうか？」
"Or does it come from the fact that I have escaped?"
「それとも、私が逃げ出したからでしょうか？」
"does this happiness come from standing like a child under the sky?"
「この幸せは、空の下で子供のように立っていることから来るのでしょうか？」

"Oh how good is it to have fled"
「ああ、逃げられてよかった」
"it is great to have become free!"
「自由になってよかった！」
"How clean and beautiful the air here is"
「ここの空気はなんてきれいで美しいんだろう」
"the air is good to breath"
「空気は呼吸するのに良い」
"where I ran away from everything smelled of ointments"
「私が逃げた場所は、すべて軟膏の匂いがした」
"spices, wine, excess, sloth"
「スパイス、ワイン、過剰、怠惰」
"How I hated this world of the rich"
「私はこの金持ちの世界をどれほど嫌っていたか」
"I hated those who revel in fine food and the gamblers!"
「私は、おいしい食べ物を食って楽しむ人や、ギャンブラーを憎みました！」
"I hated myself for staying in this terrible world for so long!
「こんなに長い間、このひどい世界に留まっていた自分を憎みました！
"I have deprived, poisoned, and tortured myself"
「私は自分自身を奪い、毒を盛って、苦しめてきた」
"I have made myself old and evil!"
「私は自分自身を老いて邪悪なものにしてしまった！」
"No, I will never again do the things I liked doing so much"
「いや、あんなに好きだったことを二度とやらないよ」
"I won't delude myself into thinking that Siddhartha was wise!"
「私はシッダールタが賢いなどと自分を欺くつもりはない！」
"But this one thing I have done well"
「しかし、この一つのことはうまくやった」
"this I like, this I must praise"
「これは好きだ、これは賞賛しなければならない」
"I like that there is now an end to that hatred against myself"

「自分に対する憎しみが終わったことが嬉しい」
"there is an end to that foolish and dreary life!"
「その愚かで退屈な人生に終わりが来た！」
"I praise you, Siddhartha, after so many years of foolishness"
「シッダールタよ、長年の愚かな行為の後、私はあなたを讃えます」
"you have once again had an idea"
「またアイデアが浮かんだね」
"you have heard the bird in your chest singing"
「胸の中の鳥が歌うのを聞いたことがあるでしょう」
"and you followed the song of the bird!"
「そしてあなたは鳥の歌を追ったのです！」
with these thoughts he praised himself
彼はこう考えながら自分を褒めた

he had found joy in himself again
彼は再び自分自身に喜びを見出した

he listened curiously to his stomach rumbling with hunger
彼は空腹でゴロゴロ鳴るお腹の音を興味深く聞いていた

he had tasted and spat out a piece of suffering and misery
彼は苦しみと悲惨の一部を味わい、吐き出した

in these recent times and days, this is how he felt
最近の日々、彼はこう感じていた

he had devoured it up to the point of desperation and death
彼は絶望と死に至るまでそれを貪り食った

how everything had happened was good
すべてがうまくいった

he could have stayed with Kamaswami for much longer
彼はカマスワミともっと長く一緒にいられたかもしれない

he could have made more money, and then wasted it
彼はもっとお金を稼いでそれを無駄にしていたかもしれない

he could have filled his stomach and let his soul die of thirst
彼はお腹を満たして魂を渇きで死なせることもできた

he could have lived in this soft upholstered hell much longer
彼はこの柔らかく覆われた地獄でもっと長く生きられたかもしれない

if this had not happened, he would have continued this life
もしこれが起こらなかったら、彼はこの人生を続けていただろう

the moment of complete hopelessness and despair
完全な絶望と絶望の瞬間

the most extreme moment when he hung over the rushing waters
彼が急流の上にぶら下がった最も極端な瞬間

the moment he was ready to destroy himself
彼が自らを破滅させる覚悟をした瞬間

the moment he had felt this despair and deep disgust
彼がこの絶望と深い嫌悪感を感じた瞬間

he had not succumbed to it
彼はそれに屈しなかった

the bird was still alive after all
結局その鳥はまだ生きていた

this was why he felt joy and laughed
だから彼は喜びを感じて笑った

this was why his face was smiling brightly under his hair
だから彼の顔は髪の下で明るく笑っていた

his hair which had now turned gray
彼の髪は今では白髪になっていた

"It is good," he thought, "to get a taste of everything for oneself"
「すべてを自分で味わってみるのもいいことだ」と彼は思った。

"everything which one needs to know"
「知る必要のあるすべてのこと」

"lust for the world and riches do not belong to the good things"
「世俗と富への欲望は善いことに属するものではない」

"I have already learned this as a child"

「私は子供の頃にこれをすでに学んでいました」
"I have known it for a long time"
「ずっと前から知ってたよ」
"but I hadn't experienced it until now"
「でも今まで経験したことがなかった」
"And now that I I've experienced it I know it"
「そして今、私はそれを経験して、それを知っています」
"I don't just know it in my memory, but in my eyes, heart, and stomach"
「記憶だけでなく、目、心、そして胃袋で知っている」
"it is good for me to know this!"
「これを知れてよかった！」

For a long time, he pondered his transformation
彼は長い間、自分の変容について考えていた
he listened to the bird, as it sang for joy
彼は鳥が喜びの歌を歌うのを聞いた
Had this bird not died in him?
この鳥は彼の中で死んでいなかったのだろうか？
had he not felt this bird's death?
彼はこの鳥の死を感じなかったのだろうか？
No, something else from within him had died
いや、彼の中で何かが死んでしまったのだ
something which yearned to die had died
死にたいと思っていたものが死んだ
Was it not this that he used to intend to kill?
彼が殺そうとしていたのはこれではなかったのか？
Was it not his his small, frightened, and proud self that had died?
死んだのは、彼の小さくて怯えていて、誇り高き自己ではなかったのか？
he had wrestled with his self for so many years
彼は長年自分自身と格闘していた
the self which had defeated him again and again

何度も彼を打ち負かしてきた自己
the self which was back again after every killing
殺すたびに再び戻ってくる自分
the self which prohibited joy and felt fear?
喜びを禁じ、恐怖を感じていた自分？
Was it not this self which today had finally come to its death?
今日、ついに死を迎えたのは、この自己ではなかったか。
here in the forest, by this lovely river
この森の、この美しい川のそばで
Was it not due to this death, that he was now like a child?
彼が今や子供のようになってしまったのは、この死のせいではなかったのか？
so full of trust and joy, without fear
信頼と喜びに満ち、恐れることなく
Now Siddhartha also got some idea of why he had fought this self in vain
シッダールタは、なぜ自分がこの自己と戦って無駄だったのかをある程度理解した。
he knew why he couldn't fight his self as a Brahman
彼はなぜブラフマンとして自分自身と戦うことができないのかを知っていた
Too much knowledge had held him back
知識が多すぎるために彼は足かせになっていた
too many holy verses, sacrificial rules, and self-castigation
聖句、犠牲の規則、自己懲罰が多すぎる
all these things held him back
これらすべてが彼を妨げた
so much doing and striving for that goal!
その目標のために、たくさんのことを実行し、努力しました！
he had been full of arrogance
彼は傲慢さに満ちていた
he was always the smartest

彼はいつも一番賢かった
he was always working the most
彼はいつも一番働いていた
he had always been one step ahead of all others
彼は常に他の誰よりも一歩先を進んでいた
he was always the knowing and spiritual one
彼は常に知識が豊富で精神的な人でした
he was always considered the priest or wise one
彼は常に司祭または賢者とみなされていた
his self had retreated into being a priest, arrogance, and spirituality
彼の自己は司祭、傲慢、そして霊性へと退却した
there it sat firmly and grew all this time
そこにしっかりと座り、ずっと成長してきた
and he had thought he could kill it by fasting
そして彼は断食でそれを殺せると考えていた
Now he saw his life as it had become
今、彼は自分の人生がどうなったかを知った
he saw that the secret voice had been right
彼は秘密の声が正しかったことを知った
no teacher would ever have been able to bring about his salvation
いかなる教師も彼の救済をもたらすことはできなかっただろう
Therefore, he had to go out into the world
だから彼は世界へ出て行かなければならなかった
he had to lose himself to lust and power
彼は欲望と権力に身を委ねなければならなかった
he had to lose himself to women and money
彼は女性と金に身を委ねなければならなかった
he had to become a merchant, a dice-gambler, a drinker
彼は商人、サイコロ賭博師、酒飲みにならなければならなかった
and he had to become a greedy person
そして彼は貪欲な人間にならなければならなかった

he had to do this until the priest and Samana in him was dead
彼は司祭とサマナが死ぬまでこれをしなければならなかった
Therefore, he had to continue bearing these ugly years
そのため、彼はこの醜い年月に耐え続けなければならなかった
he had to bear the disgust and the teachings
彼は嫌悪感と教えに耐えなければならなかった
he had to bear the pointlessness of a dreary and wasted life
彼は退屈で無駄な人生の無意味さに耐えなければならなかった
he had to conclude it up to its bitter end
彼は最後までそれを終わらせなければならなかった
he had to do this until Siddhartha the lustful could also die
彼は好色なシッダールタが死ぬまでこれを続けなければならなかった
He had died and a new Siddhartha had woken up from the sleep
彼は亡くなり、新たなシッダールタが眠りから目覚めた
this new Siddhartha would also grow old
この新しいシッダールタもまた年老いていくだろう
he would also have to die eventually
彼も最終的には死ななければならないだろう
Siddhartha was still mortal, as is every physical form
シッダールタは、他の肉体と同じように、死すべき存在であった。
But today he was young and a child and full of joy
しかし、今日彼は若く、子供で、喜びに満ちていた
He thought these thoughts to himself
彼は心の中でこう考えた
he listened with a smile to his stomach
彼はお腹に微笑みながら聞いた
he listened gratefully to a buzzing bee
彼はブンブンという蜂の音をありがたく聞いた

Cheerfully, he looked into the rushing river
彼は楽しそうに川の流れを眺めた
he had never before liked a water as much as this one
彼はこれまでこれほど水を好きになったことはなかった
he had never before perceived the voice so stronger
彼はその声をこれほど強く感じたことはなかった
he had never understood the parable of the moving water so strongly
彼は動く水のたとえ話をこれほど強く理解したことはなかった
he had never before noticed how beautifully the river moved
彼はこれまで川がこんなに美しく流れることに気づいていなかった
It seemed to him, as if the river had something special to tell him
川は彼に何か特別なことを伝えているように思えた
something he did not know yet, which was still awaiting him
彼がまだ知らない何かが彼を待っていた
In this river, Siddhartha had intended to drown himself
この川でシッダールタは溺死するつもりだった
in this river the old, tired, desperate Siddhartha had drowned today
この川で老いて疲れ果てた絶望したシッダールタは今日溺死した
But the new Siddhartha felt a deep love for this rushing water
しかし、新しいシッダールタはこの流れ落ちる水に深い愛を感じた
and he decided for himself, not to leave it very soon
そして彼はすぐにはそこを離れないことを決意した

The Ferryman
渡し守

"By this river I want to stay," thought Siddhartha
「この川のそばに留まりたい」とシッダールタは思った
"it is the same river which I have crossed a long time ago"
「それは私がずっと昔に渡ったのと同じ川です」
"I was on my way to the childlike people"
「私は子供のような人々のところへ向かっていました」
"a friendly ferryman had guided me across the river"
「親切な船頭が私を川を渡らせてくれた」
"he is the one I want to go to"
「私が行きたいのは彼だ」
"starting out from his hut, my path led me to a new life"
「彼の小屋から出発して、私の道は新しい人生へと導いた」
"a path which had grown old and is now dead"
「古くなって今は死んでしまった道」
"my present path shall also take its start there!"
「私の現在の道もそこから始まるのです！」
Tenderly, he looked into the rushing water
彼は優しく流れ落ちる水を見つめた

he looked into the transparent green lines the water drew
彼は水が描く透明な緑の線を見つめた

the crystal lines of water were rich in secrets
水の結晶線には秘密が詰まっていた

he saw bright pearls rising from the deep
彼は深海から輝く真珠が浮かび上がるのを見た

quiet bubbles of air floating on the reflecting surface
反射面に浮かぶ静かな空気の泡

the blue of the sky depicted in the bubbles
泡に描かれた空の青

the river looked at him with a thousand eyes
川は千の目で彼を見つめた

the river had green eyes and white eyes

川には緑の目と白い目があった
the river had crystal eyes and sky-blue eyes
川には水晶の目と空色の目があった
he loved this water very much, it delighted him
彼はこの水がとても好きで、喜んでいた。
he was grateful to the water
彼は水に感謝していた
In his heart he heard the voice talking
彼は心の中で声が聞こえた
"Love this water! Stay near it!"
「この水が大好き！近くにいてください！」
"Learn from the water!" his voice commanded him
「水から学べ！」彼の声は彼に命じた
Oh yes, he wanted to learn from it
ああ、彼はそこから学びたかった
he wanted to listen to the water
彼は水の音を聞きたかった
He who would understand this water's secrets
この水の秘密を理解しようとする者は
he would also understand many other things
彼は他の多くのことも理解するだろう
this is how it seemed to him
彼にはそのように見えた
But out of all secrets of the river, today he only saw one
しかし、川のあらゆる秘密のうち、今日彼が見たのはたった一つだけだった
this secret touched his soul
この秘密は彼の心に触れた
this water ran and ran, incessantly
この水は絶え間なく流れ続けた
the water ran, but nevertheless it was always there
水は流れていたが、それでも常にそこにあった
the water always, at all times, was the same
水はいつも、いつでも同じだった
and at the same time it was new in every moment

そして同時に、それは常に新しいものだった
he who could grasp this would be great
これを理解できる人は偉大だろう
but he didn't understand or grasp it
しかし彼はそれを理解したり把握したりしなかった
he only felt some idea of it stirring
彼はそれが動き出すというアイデアだけを感じた
it was like a distant memory, a divine voices
それは遠い記憶のようで、神の声のようでした

Siddhartha rose as the workings of hunger in his body became unbearable
シッダールタは、体内の飢餓が耐え難いものとなり立ち上がった。
In a daze he walked further away from the city
彼はぼんやりしながら街からさらに離れていった
he walked up the river along the path by the bank
彼は川岸の小道に沿って川を上って歩いた
he listened to the current of the water
彼は水の流れに耳を傾けた
he listened to the rumbling hunger in his body
彼は体内で鳴り響く空腹感に耳を傾けた
When he reached the ferry, the boat was just arriving
彼がフェリーに着いたとき、ちょうど船が到着したところだった
the same ferryman who had once transported the young Samana across the river
かつて若いサマナを川の向こう岸に運んだ渡し守と同じ人物
he stood in the boat and Siddhartha recognised him
彼はボートの中に立っていた、そしてシッダールタは彼を認識した
he had also aged very much
彼もかなり老けていた

the ferryman was astonished to see such an elegant man walking on foot
渡し守は、このような優雅な男が歩いているのを見て驚いた。

"Would you like to ferry me over?" he asked
「私を乗せて運んでくれませんか？」と彼は尋ねた

he took him into his boat and pushed it off the bank
彼は彼をボートに乗せて岸から押し出した

"It's a beautiful life you have chosen for yourself" the passenger spoke
「あなたが自分で選んだ人生は美しい」と乗客は言った

"It must be beautiful to live by this water every day"
「毎日この水のそばで暮らすのは美しいことだろう」

"and it must be beautiful to cruise on it on the river"
「川をクルーズするのはきっと美しいでしょうね」

With a smile, the man at the oar moved from side to side
笑顔で、オールを漕いでいた男は左右に動いた。

"It is as beautiful as you say, sir"
「おっしゃる通り、とても美しいです」

"But isn't every life and all work beautiful?"
「しかし、すべての人生とすべての仕事は美しいのではないですか？」

"This may be true" replied Siddhartha
「それは本当かもしれない」とシッダールタは答えた。

"But I envy you for your life"
「でも、あなたの人生が羨ましいです」

"Ah, you would soon stop enjoying it"
「ああ、すぐに楽しめなくなってしまうよ」

"This is no work for people wearing fine clothes"
「これは、立派な服を着ている人がする仕事ではない」

Siddhartha laughed at the observation
シッダールタはその観察に笑った

"Once before, I have been looked upon today because of my clothes"
「以前、私は服装のせいで今日も見られました」

"I have been looked upon with distrust"

「私は不信感を持たれてきました」
"they are a nuisance to me"
「彼らは私にとって迷惑だ」
"Wouldn't you, ferryman, like to accept these clothes"
「渡し守さん、この服を受け取っていただけませんか」
"because you must know, I have no money to pay your fare"
「ご存知でしょうが、運賃を払うお金がありません」
"You're joking, sir," the ferryman laughed
「冗談でしょう」船頭は笑った。
"I'm not joking, friend"
「冗談じゃないよ、友よ」
"once before you have ferried me across this water in your boat"
「以前あなたは私をあなたのボートでこの海を渡らせてくれました」
"you did it for the immaterial reward of a good deed"
「あなたは善行という無形の報酬のためにそれをしたのです」
"ferry me across the river and accept my clothes for it"
「川を渡って私の服を受け取ってください」
"And do you, sir, intent to continue travelling without clothes?"
「それで、あなたは服を着ずに旅を続けるつもりですか？」
"Ah, most of all I wouldn't want to continue travelling at all"
「ああ、何よりも、私は旅行を続けるつもりはない」
"I would rather you gave me an old loincloth"
「古い腰布をくれたらよかったのに」
"I would like it if you kept me with you as your assistant"
「私をあなたのアシスタントとしてお連れいただければ幸いです」
"or rather, I would like if you accepted me as your trainee"
「というか、研修生として受け入れていただければ嬉しいです」
"because first I'll have to learn how to handle the boat"

「まずはボートの操縦方法を学ばなくてはならないから」

For a long time, the ferryman looked at the stranger
渡し守は長い間、見知らぬ人を見つめていた

he was searching in his memory for this strange man
彼は記憶の中でこの奇妙な男を探していた

"Now I recognise you," he finally said
「今、君だと分かったよ」彼はついに言った

"At one time, you've slept in my hut"
「かつて、あなたは私の小屋で寝たことがあった」

"this was a long time ago, possibly more than twenty years"
「これはかなり昔のこと、おそらく20年以上前のこと」

"and you've been ferried across the river by me"
「そしてあなたは私が川を渡って渡ったのです」

"that day we parted like good friends"
「その日、私たちは良い友達のように別れた」

"Haven't you been a Samana?"
「あなたはサマナではなかったのですか？」

"I can't think of your name anymore"
「もうあなたの名前が思い出せない」

"My name is Siddhartha, and I was a Samana"
「私の名前はシッダールタ、私はサマナでした」

"I had still been a Samana when you last saw me"
「あなたが最後に私を見たとき、私はまだサマナでした」

"So be welcome, Siddhartha. My name is Vasudeva"
「それでは、ようこそ、シッダールタ。私の名前はヴァスデーヴァです」

"You will, so I hope, be my guest today as well"
「今日も私のゲストになってくれるといいのですが」

"and you may sleep in my hut"
「私の小屋で寝てもいいよ」

"and you may tell me, where you're coming from"
「そして、あなたはどこから来たのか私に教えてくれるかもしれない」

"and you may tell me why these beautiful clothes are such a nuisance to you"
「そして、なぜこの美しい服があなたにとってそんなに厄介なのか教えてください」
They had reached the middle of the river
彼らは川の真ん中に到達した
Vasudeva pushed the oar with more strength
ヴァスデーヴァはもっと力を入れてオールを押した
in order to overcome the current
現状を克服するために
He worked calmly, with brawny arms
彼は力強い腕で落ち着いて働いた
his eyes were fixed in on the front of the boat
彼の目は船の前方に釘付けになっていた
Siddhartha sat and watched him
シッダールタは座って彼を見ていた
he remembered his time as a Samana
彼はサマナ時代を思い出した
he remembered how love for this man had stirred in his heart
彼はこの男への愛が自分の心の中でどのように湧き起こったかを思い出した
Gratefully, he accepted Vasudeva's invitation
彼は感謝の気持ちでヴァスデーヴァの招待を受け入れた
When they had reached the bank, he helped him to tie the boat to the stakes
岸に着くと、彼は船を杭に結びつけるのを手伝った。
after this, the ferryman asked him to enter the hut
その後、渡し守は彼に小屋に入るように頼んだ
he offered him bread and water, and Siddhartha ate with eager pleasure
彼はパンと水を与え、シッダールタは喜んで食べた。
and he also ate with eager pleasure of the mango fruits Vasudeva offered him
そして彼はヴァスデーヴァが差し出したマンゴーの実を喜んで食べた。

Afterwards, it was almost the time of the sunset
その後、日没の時間になりました
they sat on a log by the bank
彼らは川岸の丸太の上に座った
Siddhartha told the ferryman about where he originally came from
シッダールタは渡し守に自分が元々どこから来たのかを話した
he told him about his life as he had seen it today
彼は今日見た自分の人生について語った
the way he had seen it in that hour of despair
絶望の瞬間に彼が見たもの
the tale of his life lasted late into the night
彼の人生の物語は夜遅くまで続いた
Vasudeva listened with great attention
ヴァスデーヴァは熱心に耳を傾けた
Listening carefully, he let everything enter his mind
注意深く耳を傾け、彼はすべてを心に留めた
birthplace and childhood, all that learning
生まれ育った場所、学んだことすべて
all that searching, all joy, all distress
あらゆる探求、あらゆる喜び、あらゆる苦悩
This was one of the greatest virtues of the ferryman
これは渡し守の最大の美徳の一つであった。
like only a few, he knew how to listen
彼は、ごく少数の人のように、聞く方法を知っていた
he did not have to speak a word
彼は一言も話さなかった
but the speaker sensed how Vasudeva let his words enter his mind
しかし話し手はヴァスデーヴァが自分の言葉を自分の心に届けたことを察知した
his mind was quiet, open, and waiting
彼の心は静かで開かれていて、待っていた

he did not lose a single word
彼は一言も失わなかった
he did not await a single word with impatience
彼はいらだちながら一言も待たなかった
he did not add his praise or rebuke
彼は賞賛も非難も加えなかった
he was just listening, and nothing else
彼はただ聞いているだけで、他には何もなかった
Siddhartha felt what a happy fortune it is to confess to such a listener
シッダールタは、このような聞き手に告白できることはなんと幸せなことかと感じた。
he felt fortunate to bury in his heart his own life
彼は自分の命を心の中に埋めることができて幸運だと思った
he buried his own search and suffering
彼は自身の探求と苦しみを埋めた
he told the tale of Siddhartha's life
彼はシッダールタの生涯の物語を語った
when he spoke of the tree by the river
彼が川沿いの木について話したとき
when he spoke of his deep fall
彼が自身の深い堕落について語ったとき
when he spoke of the holy Om
彼が聖なるオームについて語ったとき
when he spoke of how he had felt such a love for the river
彼が川に対してどれほど愛を感じていたかを語ったとき
the ferryman listened to these things with twice as much attention
渡し守はこれらのことを二倍の注意を払って聞いた
he was entirely and completely absorbed by it
彼は完全にそれに夢中になった
he was listening with his eyes closed
彼は目を閉じて聞いていた
when Siddhartha fell silent a long silence occurred

シッダールタが沈黙すると、長い沈黙が続いた。
then Vasudeva spoke "It is as I thought"
するとヴァスデーヴァは「私が思った通りだ」と言った。
"The river has spoken to you"
「川があなたに語りかけています」
"the river is your friend as well"
「川もあなたの友達です」
"the river speaks to you as well"
「川もあなたに語りかけます」
"That is good, that is very good"
「それは良いことだ、とても良いことだ」
"Stay with me, Siddhartha, my friend"
「シッダールタ、友よ、私と一緒にいてください」
"I used to have a wife"
「私にはかつて妻がいました」
"her bed was next to mine"
「彼女のベッドは私のベッドの隣にあった」
"but she has died a long time ago"
「でも彼女はずっと前に亡くなってしまった」
"for a long time, I have lived alone"
「私は長い間、一人で暮らしてきました」
"Now, you shall live with me"
「さあ、私と一緒に暮らすんだ」
"there is enough space and food for both of us"
「二人で過ごすには十分なスペースと食べ物があります」
"I thank you," said Siddhartha
「ありがとう」とシッダールタは言った。
"I thank you and accept"
「感謝します、承ります」
"And I also thank you for this, Vasudeva"
「そして、ヴァスデーヴァ、これについても感謝します」
"I thank you for listening to me so well"

「私の話をよく聞いてくださってありがとうございます」
"people who know how to listen are rare"
「聞き方を知っている人は稀だ」
"I have not met a single person who knew it as well as you do"
「あなたほどそれをよく知っている人に会ったことはありません」
"I will also learn in this respect from you"
「この点についても、私はあなたから学びます」
"You will learn it," spoke Vasudeva
「あなたはそれを学ぶでしょう」とヴァスデーヴァは言った
"but you will not learn it from me"
「しかし、あなたは私からそれを学ぶことはできないでしょう」
"The river has taught me to listen"
「川は私に耳を傾けることを教えてくれた」
"you will learn to listen from the river as well"
「川からも聞くことを学ぶでしょう」
"It knows everything, the river"
「川はすべてを知っている」
"everything can be learned from the river"
「川からすべてを学ぶことができる」
"See, you've already learned this from the water too"
「ほら、あなたも水からこれをすでに学んだでしょう」
"you have learned that it is good to strive downwards"
「下に向かって努力することが良いことだと学んだ」
"you have learned to sink and to seek depth"
「あなたは沈み、深みを求めることを学んだ」
"The rich and elegant Siddhartha is becoming an oarsman's servant"
「裕福で優雅なシッダールタは漕ぎ手の召使になる」
"the learned Brahman Siddhartha becomes a ferryman"
「博学なバラモン、シッダールタが渡し守になる」

"this has also been told to you by the river"
「これは川からも伝えられている」

"You'll learn the other thing from it as well"
「他のことも学ぶでしょう」

Siddhartha spoke after a long pause
シッダールタは長い沈黙の後に話し始めた。

"What other things will I learn, Vasudeva?"
「ヴァスデーヴァ、他に何を学べるのでしょうか？」

Vasudeva rose. "It is late," he said
ヴァスデーヴァは立ち上がった。「もう遅い」と彼は言った。

and Vasudeva proposed going to sleep
そしてヴァスデーヴァは寝ることを提案した

"I can't tell you that other thing, oh friend"
「他のことは言えないよ、友よ」

"You'll learn the other thing, or perhaps you know it already"
「あなたは他のことを学ぶでしょう、あるいはすでに知っているかもしれません」

"See, I'm no learned man"
「ほら、私は学識のある人間じゃないんだ」

"I have no special skill in speaking"
「私は話すことに特別なスキルを持っていません」

"I also have no special skill in thinking"
「私も考えることに特別な才能はありません」

"All I'm able to do is to listen and to be godly"
「私にできるのは、ただ耳を傾け、敬虔になることだけです」

"I have learned nothing else"
「他には何も学んでいません」

"If I was able to say and teach it, I might be a wise man"
「もしそれを言い、教えることができたら、私は賢者になれるかもしれない」

"but like this I am only a ferryman"
「しかし、このままでは私はただの渡し守に過ぎない」

"and it is my task to ferry people across the river"
「そして人々を川の向こうへ運ぶのが私の仕事です」
"I have transported many thousands of people"
「私は何千人もの人々を輸送してきました」
"and to all of them, my river has been nothing but an obstacle"
「そして彼ら全員にとって、私の川は障害物でしかなかった」
"it was something that got in the way of their travels"
「それは彼らの旅行の邪魔になるものでした」
"they travelled to seek money and business"
「彼らはお金とビジネスを求めて旅をした」
"they travelled for weddings and pilgrimages"
「彼らは結婚式や巡礼のために旅をしました」
"and the river was obstructing their path"
「そして川が彼らの行く手を阻んでいた」
"the ferryman's job was to get them quickly across that obstacle"
「渡し守の仕事は、彼らをその障害物を素早く越えさせることだった」
"But for some among thousands, a few, the river has stopped being an obstacle"
「しかし、数千人のうちの少数の人々にとって、川はもはや障害物ではなくなった」
"they have heard its voice and they have listened to it"
「彼らはその声を聞き、それに耳を傾けた」
"and the river has become sacred to them"
「そして川は彼らにとって神聖なものとなった」
"it become sacred to them as it has become sacred to me"
「私にとって神聖なものとなったように、彼らにとっても神聖なものとなった」
"for now, let us rest, Siddhartha"
「今は休もう、シッダールタ」

Siddhartha stayed with the ferryman and learned to operate the boat
シッダールタは渡し守と一緒に船の操縦を学んだ
when there was nothing to do at the ferry, he worked with Vasudeva in the rice-field
渡し船で何もすることがなかったとき、彼はヴァスデーヴァと一緒に田んぼで働きました
he gathered wood and plucked the fruit off the banana-trees
彼は木を集め、バナナの木から実を摘んだ
He learned to build an oar and how to mend the boat
彼はオールの作り方とボートの修理の仕方を学んだ
he learned how to weave baskets and repaid the hut
彼はかごの編み方を学び、小屋の代金を返済した。
and he was joyful because of everything he learned
そして彼は学んだことすべてに喜びを感じた
the days and months passed quickly
日月日があっという間に過ぎた
But more than Vasudeva could teach him, he was taught by the river
しかし、ヴァスデーヴァが彼に教えたこと以上に、彼は川から教えを受けた。
Incessantly, he learned from the river
彼は絶えず川から学んだ
Most of all, he learned to listen
何よりも、彼は聞くことを学んだ
he learned to pay close attention with a quiet heart
彼は静かな心で細心の注意を払うことを学んだ
he learned to keep a waiting, open soul
彼は待つ心を持ち続けることを学んだ
he learned to listen without passion
彼は情熱を持たずに聞くことを学んだ
he learned to listen without a wish
彼は願わずに聞くことを学んだ
he learned to listen without judgement
彼は判断せずに聞くことを学んだ
he learned to listen without an opinion

彼は意見を言わずに聞くことを学んだ

In a friendly manner, he lived side by side with Vasudeva
彼は友好的にヴァスデーヴァと隣り合って暮らした
occasionally they exchanged some words
時折彼らは言葉を交わした
then, at length, they thought about the words
そして、ついに彼らは言葉について考えた
Vasudeva was no friend of words
ヴァスデーヴァは言葉の友ではなかった
Siddhartha rarely succeeded in persuading him to speak
シッダールタは彼に話すように説得することはほとんどできなかった
"did you too learn that secret from the river?"
「あなたも川からその秘密を知ったのですか？」
"the secret that there is no time?"
「時間がないという秘密？」
Vasudeva's face was filled with a bright smile
ヴァスデーヴァの顔は明るい笑顔で満ちていた
"Yes, Siddhartha," he spoke
「はい、シッダールタ」と彼は言った
"I learned that the river is everywhere at once"
「川はどこにでもあるということを知りました」
"it is at the source and at the mouth of the river"
「それは川の源流と河口にあります」
"it is at the waterfall and at the ferry"
「滝と渡し場にあります」
"it is at the rapids and in the sea"
「それは急流と海にあります」
"it is in the mountains and everywhere at once"
「それは山の中にあり、同時にどこにでもある」
"and I learned that there is only the present time for the river"
「そして私は川に今という時間しかないことを知った」
"it does not have the shadow of the past"

「過去の影はない」
"and it does not have the shadow of the future"
「そして未来の影はない」
"is this what you mean?" he asked
「これがあなたの言いたいことなのですか？」と彼は尋ねた
"This is what I meant," said Siddhartha
「これが私が言いたかったことだ」とシッダールタは言った。
"And when I had learned it, I looked at my life"
「そしてそれを学んだとき、私は自分の人生を見つめ直しました」
"and my life was also a river"
「そして私の人生もまた川だった」
"the boy Siddhartha was only separated from the man Siddhartha by a shadow"
「少年シッダールタと男のシッダールタを隔てていたのは影だけだった」
"and a shadow separated the man Siddhartha from the old man Siddhartha"
「そして影がシッダールタ男と老人シッダールタを隔てた」
"things are separated by a shadow, not by something real"
「物事は影によって隔てられているのであって、実体によって隔てられているのではない」
"Also, Siddhartha's previous births were not in the past"
「また、シッダールタの前世は過去のものではなかった」
"and his death and his return to Brahma is not in the future"
「彼の死とブラフマーへの帰還は未来のものではない」
"nothing was, nothing will be, but everything is"
「何もなかったし、何も起こらない、しかしすべては存在する」
"everything has existence and is present"
「すべてのものは存在し、存在している」

Siddhartha spoke with ecstasy
シッダールタは恍惚とした様子で語った
this enlightenment had delighted him deeply
この啓示は彼を大いに喜ばせた
"was not all suffering time?"
「すべては苦しみの時間ではなかったのか？」
"were not all forms of tormenting oneself a form of time?"
「自分自身を苦しめるあらゆる形態は時間の一種ではないのか？」
"was not everything hard and hostile because of time?"
「時間のせいですべてが困難で敵対的ではなかったのか？」
"is not everything evil overcome when one overcomes time?"
「時間を克服すれば、すべての悪も克服できるのではないか？」
"as soon as time leaves the mind, does suffering leave too?"
「時間が心から消え去れば、苦しみも消え去るのだろうか？」
Siddhartha had spoken in ecstatic delight
シッダールタは恍惚とした喜びの中で語った
but Vasudeva smiled at him brightly and nodded in confirmation
しかしヴァスデーヴァは彼に明るく微笑み、うなずいて確認した。
silently he nodded and brushed his hand over Siddhartha's shoulder
彼は黙ってうなずき、シッダールタの肩に手をかざした。
and then he turned back to his work
そして彼は仕事に戻った

And Siddhartha asked Vasudeva again another time
そしてシッダールタはヴァスデーヴァにもう一度尋ねた
the river had just increased its flow in the rainy season
川は雨期に水量が増えたばかりだった

and it made a powerful noise
そして大きな音がした
"Isn't it so, oh friend, the river has many voices?"
「そうではないか、友よ、川には多くの声があるのだ。」
"Hasn't it the voice of a king and of a warrior?"
「それは王と戦士の声ではないか？」
"Hasn't it the voice of of a bull and of a bird of the night?"
「それは雄牛の声と夜の鳥の声ではないか？」
"Hasn't it the voice of a woman giving birth and of a sighing man?"
「それは出産する女性とため息をつく男性の声ではないか？」
"and does it not also have a thousand other voices?"
「そして、他の千の声もあるのではないですか？」
"it is as you say it is," Vasudeva nodded
「おっしゃる通りです」ヴァスデーヴァはうなずいた
"all voices of the creatures are in its voice"
「生き物たちのすべての声はその声の中にある」
"And do you know..." Siddhartha continued
「そしてご存知ですか…」シッダールタは続けた
"what word does it speak when you succeed in hearing all of voices at once?"
「一度にすべての声を聞くことができたら、何という言葉を話すでしょうか？」
Happily, Vasudeva's face was smiling
幸いにもヴァスデーヴァの顔は笑っていた
he bent over to Siddhartha and spoke the holy Om into his ear
彼はシッダールタに身をかがめ、彼の耳元で聖なるオームを唱えた。
And this had been the very thing which Siddhartha had also been hearing
そしてこれはシッダールタも聞いていたことだった

time after time, his smile became more similar to the ferryman's
何度も、彼の笑顔は船頭の笑顔に似てきました
his smile became almost just as bright as the ferryman's
彼の笑顔は渡し守の笑顔と同じくらい明るくなった
it was almost just as thoroughly glowing with bliss
それは至福で輝いていた
shining out of thousand small wrinkles
何千もの小さなしわから輝く
just like the smile of a child
まるで子供の笑顔のように
just like the smile of an old man
老人の笑顔のように
Many travellers, seeing the two ferrymen, thought they were brothers
多くの旅行者は、二人の渡し守を見て、彼らが兄弟だと思った。
Often, they sat in the evening together by the bank
夕方になると、彼らはよく一緒に銀行のそばに座っていた。
they said nothing and both listened to the water
彼らは何も言わず、水の音を聞いていた
the water, which was not water to them
彼らにとって水ではなかった水
it wasn't water, but the voice of life
それは水ではなく、生命の声だった
the voice of what exists and what is eternally taking shape
存在するものの声、そして永遠に形作られるものの声
it happened from time to time that both thought of the same thing
時々二人は同じことを考えていた
they thought of a conversation from the day before
彼らは前日の会話を思い出した
they thought of one of their travellers
彼らは旅人の一人のことを思い浮かべた
they thought of death and their childhood

彼らは死と子供時代について考えた
they heard the river tell them the same thing
彼らは川が同じことを言っているのを聞いた
both delighted about the same answer to the same question
二人とも、同じ質問に対する同じ答えに大喜びした
There was something about the two ferrymen which was transmitted to others
二人の渡し守には他の人に伝わる何かがあった
it was something which many of the travellers felt
それは多くの旅行者が感じたことだった
travellers would occasionally look at the faces of the ferrymen
旅行者は時々渡し守の顔を見る
and then they told the story of their life
そして彼らは自分たちの人生の物語を語った
they confessed all sorts of evil things
彼らはあらゆる悪事を告白した
and they asked for comfort and advice
そして彼らは慰めと助言を求めた
occasionally someone asked for permission to stay for a night
時々誰かが一晩泊まる許可を求めてきた
they also wanted to listen to the river
彼らは川の音も聞きたかった
It also happened that curious people came
好奇心旺盛な人たちもやって来て
they had been told that there were two wise men
彼らは二人の賢者がいると聞いていた
or they had been told there were two sorcerers
あるいは二人の魔術師がいると聞かされていた
The curious people asked many questions
好奇心旺盛な人々は多くの質問をした
but they got no answers to their questions
しかし、彼らの質問に対する答えは得られなかった
they found neither sorcerers nor wise men
彼らは魔術師も賢者も見つけられなかった

they only found two friendly little old men, who seemed to be mute
彼らが見つけたのは、口がきけないように見える、友好的な老人二人だけだった。
they seemed to have become a bit strange in the forest by themselves
彼らは森の中で少し奇妙になったようだった
And the curious people laughed about what they had heard
そして好奇心旺盛な人々は聞いた話を聞いて笑った
they said common people were foolishly spreading empty rumours
彼らは一般の人々が愚かにも根拠のない噂を広めていると言った

The years passed by, and nobody counted them
年月が過ぎていったが、誰もそれを数えなかった
Then, at one time, monks came by on a pilgrimage
そして、ある時、修道士たちが巡礼にやって来た
they were followers of Gotama, the Buddha
彼らはゴータマ、仏陀の信奉者であった
they asked to be ferried across the river
彼らは川を渡ってもらうよう頼んだ
they told them they were in a hurry to get back to their wise teacher
彼らは賢明な先生のところへ急いで戻らなければならないと言った
news had spread the exalted one was deadly sick
尊者が重病であるという知らせが広まった
he would soon die his last human death
彼は間もなく最後の人間としての死を迎えるだろう
in order to become one with the salvation
救いと一体になるために
It was not long until a new flock of monks came
間もなく新しい僧侶の群れがやって来た
they were also on their pilgrimage

彼らも巡礼の旅に出ていた
most of the travellers spoke of nothing other than Gotama
旅行者のほとんどはゴータマについてしか話さなかった
his impending death was all they thought about
彼らが考えていたのは彼の差し迫った死だけだった
if there had been war, just as many would travel
もし戦争があったら、同じように多くの人が旅行するだろう
just as many would come to the coronation of a king
王の戴冠式に多くの人が集まるのと同じように
they gathered like ants in droves
彼らは蟻のように群れをなして集まった
they flocked, like being drawn onwards by a magic spell
彼らはまるで魔法に引き寄せられたかのように群がった
they went to where the great Buddha was awaiting his death
彼らは大仏が死を待つ場所へ行った
the perfected one of an era was to become one with the glory
時代の完成者は栄光と一体になることだった
Often, Siddhartha thought in those days of the dying wise man
シッダールタは当時、死にゆく賢者のことをよく考えていた
the great teacher whose voice had admonished nations
声によって諸国を戒めた偉大な教師
the one who had awoken hundreds of thousands
何十万人もの人々を目覚めさせた
a man whose voice he had also once heard
彼もかつてその声を聞いたことがある男
a teacher whose holy face he had also once seen with respect
彼もまたかつてその聖なる顔を尊敬の念をもって見ていた教師
Kindly, he thought of him
親切に、彼は彼のことを考えた
he saw his path to perfection before his eyes
彼は完璧への道を目の前に見た

and he remembered with a smile those words he had said to him
そして彼は微笑みながら、彼に言った言葉を思い出しました
when he was a young man and spoke to the exalted one
彼が若いころ、高貴な方に話しかけたとき
They had been, so it seemed to him, proud and precious words
それは、彼には誇らしくて貴重な言葉のように思えた。
with a smile, he remembered the the words
彼は微笑みながら、その言葉を思い出しました
he knew that there was nothing standing between Gotama and him any more
彼はゴータマと自分との間にはもう何も立ちはだかっていないことを知っていた
he had known this for a long time already
彼はすでにずっと前からこのことを知っていた
though he was still unable to accept his teachings
彼はまだ彼の教えを受け入れることができなかったが
there was no teaching a truly searching person
真に探求する人に教えることはなかった
someone who truly wanted to find, could accept
本当に見つけたい人は受け入れることができる
But he who had found the answer could approve of any teaching
しかし、答えを見つけた者は、どんな教えも認めることができる
every path, every goal, they were all the same
全ての道、全ての目標、それらはすべて同じだった
there was nothing standing between him and all the other thousands any more
彼と他の何千人もの人々の間にはもはや何も立ちはだかっていなかった
the thousands who lived in that what is eternal
永遠の中に生きた何千人もの
the thousands who breathed what is divine

神聖なものを呼吸した何千人もの

On one of these days, Kamala also went to him
ある日、カマラも彼のところへ行きました
she used to be the most beautiful of the courtesans
彼女はかつて遊女の中で最も美しかった
A long time ago, she had retired from her previous life
彼女はずっと前に前世から引退していた
she had given her garden to the monks of Gotama as a gift
彼女は自分の庭をゴータマの僧侶たちに贈り物として与えた。
she had taken her refuge in the teachings
彼女は教えに頼っていた
she was among the friends and benefactors of the pilgrims
彼女は巡礼者たちの友人であり恩人であった
she was together with Siddhartha, the boy
彼女は少年シッダールタと一緒にいた
Siddhartha the boy was her son
シッダールタ少年は彼女の息子だった
she had gone on her way due to the news of the near death of Gotama
彼女はゴータマが死に瀕しているという知らせを受けて旅立った。
she was in simple clothes and on foot
彼女はシンプルな服を着て歩いていた
and she was With her little son
彼女は幼い息子と一緒に
she was travelling by the river
彼女は川沿いを旅していた
but the boy had soon grown tired
しかし少年はすぐに飽きてしまった
he desired to go back home
彼は家に帰りたいと思った
he desired to rest and eat
彼は休んで食事をしたかった

he became disobedient and started whining
彼は言うことを聞かなくなり、泣き言を言い始めた
Kamala often had to take a rest with him
カマラはよく彼と一緒に休憩しなければならなかった
he was accustomed to getting what he wanted
彼は欲しいものを手に入れることに慣れていた
she had to feed him and comfort him
彼女は彼に食事を与え、慰めなければならなかった
she had to scold him for his behaviour
彼女は彼の行動を叱らなければならなかった
He did not comprehend why he had to go on this exhausting pilgrimage
彼はなぜこの疲れる巡礼に出なければならないのか理解できなかった
he did not know why he had to go to an unknown place
彼はなぜ知らない場所に行かなければならないのか分からなかった
he did know why he had to see a holy dying stranger
彼はなぜ死にゆく聖なる見知らぬ人に会わなければならなかったのか知っていた
"So what if he died?" he complained
「死んだらどうするんだ?」と彼は不満を漏らした。
why should this concern him?
なぜ彼はこれに関心を持つべきなのでしょうか?
The pilgrims were getting close to Vasudeva's ferry
巡礼者たちはヴァスデーヴァの渡し船に近づいていた
little Siddhartha once again forced his mother to rest
幼いシッダールタは再び母親に休むよう強制した
Kamala had also become tired
カマラも疲れていた
while the boy was chewing a banana, she crouched down on the ground
少年がバナナを噛んでいる間、彼女は地面にしゃがみ込んだ
she closed her eyes a bit and rested

彼女は少し目を閉じて休んだ
But suddenly, she uttered a wailing scream
しかし突然、彼女は泣き叫んだ
the boy looked at her in fear
少年は恐怖しながら彼女を見た
he saw her face had grown pale from horror
彼は彼女の顔が恐怖で青ざめているのに気づいた
and from under her dress, a small, black snake fled
そして彼女のドレスの下から小さな黒い蛇が逃げ出した
a snake by which Kamala had been bitten
カマラが噛まれた蛇
Hurriedly, they both ran along the path, to reach people
二人は急いで道に沿って走り、人々に近づいた。
they got near to the ferry and Kamala collapsed
彼らはフェリーに近づき、カマラは倒れた
she was not able to go any further
彼女はそれ以上進むことができなかった
the boy started crying miserably
少年は悲しそうに泣き始めた
his cries were only interrupted when he kissed his mother
彼の泣き声は母親にキスをしたときだけ止まった
she also joined his loud screams for help
彼女も助けを求めて大声で叫んだ
she screamed until the sound reached Vasudeva's ears
彼女はヴァスデーヴァの耳に届くまで叫び続けた
Vasudeva quickly came and took the woman on his arms
ヴァスデーヴァはすぐにやって来て女性を抱きかかえました
he carried her into the boat and the boy ran along
彼は彼女をボートに運び、少年は一緒に走っていった
soon they reached the hut, where Siddhartha stood by the stove
やがて彼らは小屋に到着し、シッダールタはストーブのそばに立っていた。
he was just lighting the fire

彼はただ火をつけていた
He looked up and first saw the boy's face
彼は顔を上げて最初に少年の顔を見た
it wondrously reminded him of something
それは不思議なことに彼に何かを思い出させた
like a warning to remember something he had forgotten
忘れていたことを思い出すようにという警告のように
Then he saw Kamala, whom he instantly recognised
すると彼はカマラを見た。彼はすぐにカマラだと分かった。
she lay unconscious in the ferryman's arms
彼女は船頭の腕の中で意識を失っていた
now he knew that it was his own son
彼はそれが自分の息子だと知った
his son whose face had been such a warning reminder to him
彼にとってその顔は警告の念を抱かせた息子
and the heart stirred in his chest
そして彼の胸の中で心が動いた
Kamala's wound was washed, but had already turned black
カマラの傷は洗われたが、すでに黒くなっていた
and her body was swollen
彼女の体は腫れていた
she was made to drink a healing potion
彼女は治癒薬を飲まされた
Her consciousness returned and she lay on Siddhartha's bed
彼女は意識を取り戻し、シッダールタのベッドに横たわった。
Siddhartha stood over Kamala, who he used to love so much
シッダールタはかつて愛していたカマラのそばに立っていた
It seemed like a dream to her
彼女にとっては夢のようだった
with a smile, she looked at her friend's face
彼女は微笑みながら友人の顔を見た

slowly she realized her situation
彼女はゆっくりと自分の状況に気づきました
she remembered she had been bitten
彼女は噛まれたことを思い出した
and she timidly called for her son
そして彼女は恐る恐る息子を呼びました
"He's with you, don't worry," said Siddhartha
「彼はあなたと一緒にいます、心配しないでください」
とシッダールタは言った
Kamala looked into his eyes
カマラは彼の目を見つめた
She spoke with a heavy tongue, paralysed by the poison
彼女は毒に麻痺したように重い舌で話した
"You've become old, my dear," she said
「あなたは年老いたのよ、愛しい人よ」と彼女は言った
"you've become gray," she added
「白髪になったわね」と彼女は付け加えた。
"But you are like the young Samana, who came without clothes"
「しかし、あなたは裸でやって来た若いサマナのようだ」
"you're like the Samana who came into my garden with dusty feet"
「あなたは埃まみれの足で私の庭に入ってきたサマナのようだ」
"You are much more like him than you were when you left me"
「あなたは私と別れた時よりもずっと彼に似ている」
"In the eyes, you're like him, Siddhartha"
「あなたの目は彼に似ているわ、シッダールタ」
"Alas, I have also grown old"
「ああ、私も年をとってしまった」
"could you still recognise me?"
「まだ私を認識できますか？」
Siddhartha smiled, "Instantly, I recognised you, Kamala, my dear"

シッダールタは微笑んで言った。「すぐにあなたがカマラだと分かりました、私の愛しい人よ」
Kamala pointed to her boy
カマラは息子を指差した
"Did you recognise him as well?"
「あなたも彼を認識しましたか？」
"He is your son," she confirmed
「彼はあなたの息子です」と彼女は確認した。
Her eyes became confused and fell shut
彼女の目は混乱して閉じてしまった
The boy wept and Siddhartha took him on his knees
少年は泣き、シッダールタは彼をひざまずかせた
he let him weep and petted his hair
彼は彼を泣かせ、彼の髪を撫でた
at the sight of the child's face, a Brahman prayer came to his mind
その子の顔を見て、ブラフマンの祈りが心に浮かんだ。
a prayer which he had learned a long time ago
彼が昔学んだ祈り
a time when he had been a little boy himself
彼自身がまだ少年だった頃
Slowly, with a singing voice, he started to speak
彼はゆっくりと歌うような声で話し始めた
from his past and childhood, the words came flowing to him
彼の過去と幼少時代から、言葉が流れ出てきた
And with that song, the boy became calm
そしてその歌で少年は落ち着いた
he was only now and then uttering a sob
彼は時々すすり泣くだけだった
and finally he fell asleep
そしてついに彼は眠りについた
Siddhartha placed him on Vasudeva's bed
シッダールタは彼をヴァスデーヴァのベッドに寝かせた
Vasudeva stood by the stove and cooked rice
ヴァスデーヴァはストーブのそばに立ってご飯を炊いた

Siddhartha gave him a look, which he returned with a smile
シッダールタは彼に視線を向け、彼は微笑み返した。
"She'll die," Siddhartha said quietly
「彼女は死ぬだろう」シッダールタは静かに言った
Vasudeva knew it was true, and nodded
ヴァスデーヴァはそれが真実だと知り、うなずいた。
over his friendly face ran the light of the stove's fire
彼の優しい顔の上にストーブの火の光が走った
once again, Kamala returned to consciousness
再びカマラは意識を取り戻した
the pain of the poison distorted her face
毒の痛みが彼女の顔を歪めた
Siddhartha's eyes read the suffering on her mouth
シッダールタの目は彼女の口元に苦しみを読んだ
from her pale cheeks he could see that she was suffering
彼女の青白い頬から、彼は彼女が苦しんでいるのを見ました
Quietly, he read the pain in her eyes
彼は静かに彼女の目に痛みを感じた
attentively, waiting, his mind become one with her suffering
注意深く、待ちながら、彼の心は彼女の苦しみと一体となった
Kamala felt it and her gaze sought his eyes
カマラはそれを感じ、彼の目を見つめた
Looking at him, she spoke
彼女は彼を見て言った
"Now I see that your eyes have changed as well"
「あなたの目も変わったのがわかりました」
"They've become completely different"
「彼らは完全に別人になった」
"what do I still recognise in you that is Siddhartha?
「あなたの中にシッダールタであるものがまだ何だと私は認めますか？
"It's you, and it's not you"
「それはあなたであり、あなたではない」

Siddhartha said nothing, quietly his eyes looked at hers
シッダールタは何も言わず、静かに彼女の目を見つめた。
"You have achieved it?" she asked
「あなたはそれを達成したのですか?」彼女は尋ねた
"You have found peace?"
「あなたは平和を見つけましたか?」
He smiled and placed his hand on hers
彼は微笑んで彼女の手に手を置いた
"I'm seeing it" she said
「見えてるわ」と彼女は言った
"I too will find peace"
「私も平和を見つけるだろう」
"You have found it," Siddhartha spoke in a whisper
「あなたはそれを見つけた」シッダールタはささやき声で言った
Kamala never stopped looking into his eyes
カマラは彼の目を見つめ続けた
She thought about her pilgrimage to Gotama
彼女はゴータマへの巡礼について考えた
the pilgrimage which she wanted to take
彼女が行きたかった巡礼
in order to see the face of the perfected one
完成された者の顔を見るために
in order to breathe his peace
平穏を呼吸するために
but she had now found it in another place
しかし彼女は今、別の場所でそれを見つけた
and this she thought that was good too
そして彼女はそれが良いと思った
it was just as good as if she had seen the other one
それはまるで彼女が他のものを見たのと同じくらい良かった
She wanted to tell this to him
彼女は彼にこれを伝えたかった

but her tongue no longer obeyed her will
しかし彼女の舌はもはや彼女の意志に従わなかった
Without speaking, she looked at him
彼女は何も言わずに彼を見つめた
he saw the life fading from her eyes
彼は彼女の目から命が消えていくのを見た
the final pain filled her eyes and made them grow dim
最後の痛みが彼女の目を満たし、彼女の目は暗くなった
the final shiver ran through her limbs
彼女の手足に最後の震えが走った
his finger closed her eyelids
彼の指が彼女のまぶたを閉じた

For a long time, he sat and looked at her peacefully dead face
彼は長い間、彼女の安らかに死んだ顔を見つめていた
For a long time, he observed her mouth
彼は長い間彼女の口を観察していた
her old, tired mouth, with those lips, which had become thin
彼女の年老いて疲れた口と薄くなった唇
he remembered he used to compare this mouth with a freshly cracked fig
彼はこの口を割ったばかりのイチジクに例えていたことを思い出した
this was in the spring of his years
それは彼の年の春のことでした
For a long time, he sat and read the pale face
彼は長い間座って青白い顔を読んだ
he read the tired wrinkles
彼は疲れたしわを読んだ
he filled himself with this sight
彼はこの光景に満足した
he saw his own face in the same manner
彼は自分の顔も同じように見た
he saw his face was just as white

彼は自分の顔が同じように青ざめているのに気づいた
he saw his face was just as quenched out
彼は自分の顔が同じように潤っているのに気づいた
at the same time he saw his face and hers being young
同時に彼は自分の顔と彼女の顔が若かったことに気づいた
their faces with red lips and fiery eyes
赤い唇と燃えるような目をした彼らの顔
the feeling of both being real at the same time
両方が同時に現実であるという感覚
the feeling of eternity completely filled every aspect of his being
永遠の感覚が彼の存在のあらゆる側面を完全に満たした。
in this hour he felt more deeply than than he had ever felt before
この時、彼は今まで感じたことのないほど深い感情を抱いた。
he felt the indestructibility of every life
彼はすべての生命の不滅性を感じた
he felt the eternity of every moment
彼は一瞬一瞬の永遠を感じた
When he rose, Vasudeva had prepared rice for him
彼が起き上がると、ヴァスデーヴァは彼のためにご飯を用意していた
But Siddhartha did not eat that night
しかしシッダールタはその夜何も食べなかった
In the stable their goat stood
馬小屋にヤギが立っていた
the two old men prepared beds of straw for themselves
二人の老人はわらのベッドを用意した
Vasudeva laid himself down to sleep
ヴァスデーヴァは眠りについた
But Siddhartha went outside and sat before the hut
しかしシッダールタは外に出て小屋の前に座った

he listened to the river, surrounded by the past
彼は過去に囲まれながら川の音を聞いた
he was touched and encircled by all times of his life at the same time
彼は人生のあらゆる瞬間に感動し、包まれていた
occasionally he rose and he stepped to the door of the hut
時折彼は立ち上がり、小屋のドアまで歩いた
he listened whether the boy was sleeping
彼は少年が眠っているかどうか聞いた

before the sun could be seen, Vasudeva came out of the stable
太陽が見える前にヴァスデーヴァは馬小屋から出てきた
he walked over to his friend
彼は友人のところへ歩いて行った
"You haven't slept," he said
「寝てないね」と彼は言った
"No, Vasudeva. I sat here"
「いいえ、ヴァスデーヴァ。私はここに座っていました」
"I was listening to the river"
「川の音を聞いていた」
"the river has told me a lot"
「川は私に多くのことを教えてくれた」
"it has deeply filled me with the healing thought of oneness"
「それは私を一体感の癒しの思いで深く満たしてくれました」
"You've experienced suffering, Siddhartha"
「あなたは苦しみを経験した、シッダールタ」
"but I see no sadness has entered your heart"
「しかし、あなたの心には悲しみは入っていませんね」
"No, my dear, how should I be sad?"
「いいえ、愛しい人よ、どうして悲しむべきなのでしょう?」
"I, who have been rich and happy"

「裕福で幸せだった私」
"I have become even richer and happier now"
「私は今、さらに豊かになり、幸せになりました」
"My son has been given to me"
「息子は私に与えられた」
"Your son shall be welcome to me as well"
「あなたの息子も歓迎します」
"But now, Siddhartha, let's get to work"
「しかし、シッダールタ、仕事に取り掛かりましょう」
"there is much to be done"
「やるべきことはたくさんある」
"Kamala has died on the same bed on which my wife had died"
「カマラは私の妻が亡くなったのと同じベッドで亡くなった」
"Let us build Kamala's funeral pile on the hill"
「丘の上にカマラの墓を建てよう」
"the hill on which I my wife's funeral pile is"
「私の妻の葬儀の墓がある丘」
While the boy was still asleep, they built the funeral pile
少年がまだ眠っている間に、彼らは葬式の火葬場を建てた。

The Son
息子

Timid and weeping, the boy had attended his mother's funeral
少年は臆病で泣きながら母親の葬儀に出席した。
gloomy and shy, he had listened to Siddhartha
彼は陰気で内気な性格で、シッダールタの教えを聞いていた。
Siddhartha greeted him as his son
シッダールタは彼を息子として迎えた
he welcomed him at his place in Vasudeva's hut
彼はヴァスデーヴァの小屋で彼を歓迎した
Pale, he sat for many days by the hill of the dead
彼は青ざめ、死者の丘のそばに何日も座っていた
he did not want to eat
彼は食べたくなかった
he did not look at anyone
彼は誰にも目を向けなかった
he did not open his heart
彼は心を開かなかった
he met his fate with resistance and denial
彼は抵抗と否定で運命を迎えた
Siddhartha spared giving him lessons
シッダールタは彼に教訓を与えることを惜しまなかった
and he let him do as he pleased
そして彼は彼の好きなようにさせた
Siddhartha honoured his son's mourning
シッダールタは息子の喪を尊重した
he understood that his son did not know him
彼は息子が自分を知らないことを理解した
he understood that he could not love him like a father
彼は父親のように彼を愛することはできないと理解した
Slowly, he also understood that the eleven-year-old was a pampered boy

ゆっくりと、彼は11歳の少年が甘やかされた少年であることを理解した。
he saw that he was a mother's boy
彼は自分が母親の息子であることを知った
he saw that he had grown up in the habits of rich people
彼は自分が金持ちの習慣の中で育ったことに気づいた
he was accustomed to finer food and a soft bed
彼は上質な食事と柔らかいベッドに慣れていた
he was accustomed to giving orders to servants
彼は召使に命令することに慣れていた
the mourning child could not suddenly be content with a life among strangers
悲しみに暮れる子供は、突然見知らぬ人々の中での生活に満足することはできなかった
Siddhartha understood the pampered child would not willingly be in poverty
シッダールタは甘やかされた子供が自ら貧困に陥ることはないだろうと理解していた
He did not force him to do these these things
彼はこれらのことを強制しなかった
Siddhartha did many chores for the boy
シッダールタは少年のために多くの雑用をした
he always saved the best piece of the meal for him
彼はいつも食事の一番おいしい部分を自分のために取っておいた
Slowly, he hoped to win him over, by friendly patience
彼はゆっくりと、友好的な忍耐によって彼を味方につけようとした。
Rich and happy, he had called himself, when the boy had come to him
少年が彼のところに来た時、彼は自分を裕福で幸せだと称していた
Since then some time had passed
それからしばらく経った
but the boy remained a stranger and in a gloomy disposition

しかし少年は見知らぬ人のままで、暗い性格のままだった

he displayed a proud and stubbornly disobedient heart
彼は傲慢で頑固に不従順な心を示した

he did not want to do any work
彼は仕事をしたくなかった

he did not pay his respect to the old men
彼は老人たちに敬意を払わなかった

he stole from Vasudeva's fruit-trees
彼はヴァスデーヴァの果樹から盗んだ

his son had not brought him happiness and peace
息子は彼に幸福と平和をもたらさなかった

the boy had brought him suffering and worry
その少年は彼に苦しみと心配をもたらした

slowly Siddhartha began to understand this
シッダールタはゆっくりとこれを理解し始めた

But he loved him regardless of the suffering he brought him
しかし、彼がどんな苦しみをもたらしたとしても、彼は彼を愛していた

he preferred the suffering and worries of love over happiness and joy without the boy
彼は息子のいない幸せや喜びよりも、愛の苦しみや心配を好んだ

from when young Siddhartha was in the hut the old men had split the work
若いシッダールタが小屋にいた頃から老人たちは仕事を分担していた

Vasudeva had again taken on the job of the ferryman
ヴァスデーヴァは再び渡し守の仕事を引き受けた

and Siddhartha, in order to be with his son, did the work in the hut and the field
シッダールタは息子と一緒にいるために小屋や畑で仕事をした

for long months Siddhartha waited for his son to understand him
シッダールタは息子が自分を理解するのを何ヶ月も待った
he waited for him to accept his love
彼は彼が自分の愛を受け入れるのを待った
and he waited for his son to perhaps reciprocate his love
そして彼は息子が彼の愛に応えてくれるのを待った
For long months Vasudeva waited, watching
ヴァスデーヴァは長い月日を待ち続け、
he waited and said nothing
彼は何も言わずに待っていた
One day, young Siddhartha tormented his father very much
ある日、若いシッダールタは父親をひどく苦しめた。
he had broken both of his rice-bowls
彼は両方の飯碗を割ってしまった
Vasudeva took his friend aside and talked to him
ヴァスデーヴァは友人を脇に連れて行き、話しかけた。
"Pardon me," he said to Siddhartha
「失礼」と彼はシッダールタに言った
"from a friendly heart, I'm talking to you"
「友好的な心から、私はあなたに話しています」
"I'm seeing that you are tormenting yourself"
「あなたが自分自身を苦しめているのがわかります」
"I'm seeing that you're in grief"
「あなたが悲しんでいるのがわかります」
"Your son, my dear, is worrying you"
「あなたの息子が心配しているのよ」
"and he is also worrying me"
「そして彼は私を心配させている」
"That young bird is accustomed to a different life"
「あの若い鳥は違う生活に慣れている」
"he is used to living in a different nest"
「彼は別の巣に住むことに慣れている」
"he has not, like you, run away from riches and the city"

「彼はあなたのように富と都市から逃げたのではない」
"he was not disgusted and fed up with the life in Sansara"
「彼はサンサーラでの生活に嫌悪感や飽きを感じていなかった」
"he had to do all these things against his will"
「彼は自分の意志に反してこれらすべてのことをしなければならなかった」
"he had to leave all this behind"
「彼はこれらすべてを捨て去らなければならなかった」
"I asked the river, oh friend"
「私は川に尋ねた、ああ友よ」
"many times I have asked the river"
「何度も川に尋ねました」
"But the river laughs at all of this"
「しかし川はこれらすべてを笑っている」
"it laughs at me and it laughs at you"
「それは私を笑い、あなたを笑う」
"the river is shaking with laughter at our foolishness"
「川は我々の愚かさを笑いながら震えている」
"Water wants to join water as youth wants to join youth"
「若者が若者に加わることを望むように、水は水に加わることを望む」
"your son is not in the place where he can prosper"
「あなたの息子は繁栄できる場所にいません」
"you too should ask the river"
「あなたも川に聞いてみなさい」
"you too should listen to it!"
「あなたも聞いてみて！」
Troubled, Siddhartha looked into his friendly face
困惑したシッダールタは彼の優しい顔を見つめた
he looked at the many wrinkles in which there was incessant cheerfulness
彼は、絶え間ない明るさが感じられる多くのしわを眺めた。
"How could I part with him?" he said quietly, ashamed

「どうして彼と別れられるんだ?」彼は恥ずかしそうに静かに言った。
"Give me some more time, my dear"
「もう少し時間をください、愛しい人よ」
"See, I'm fighting for him"
「ほら、私は彼のために戦っている」
"I'm seeking to win his heart"
「私は彼の心を勝ち取りたいのです」
"with love and with friendly patience I intend to capture it"
「愛と友好的な忍耐をもって、私はそれを捕らえるつもりです」
"One day, the river shall also talk to him"
「いつか川も彼に話しかけるだろう」
"he also is called upon"
「彼もまた呼ばれている」
Vasudeva's smile flourished more warmly
ヴァスデーヴァの笑顔はより温かく輝いた
"Oh yes, he too is called upon"
「ああ、そうだ、彼も呼ばれているんだ」
"he too is of the eternal life"
「彼もまた永遠の命の者です」
"But do we, you and me, know what he is called upon to do?"
「しかし、私たち、つまりあなたと私は、彼が何をするように求められているか知っていますか?」
"we know what path to take and what actions to perform"
「私たちはどの道を進むべきか、どのような行動を取るべきかを知っています」
"we know what pain we have to endure"
「私たちはどんな痛みに耐えなければならないか知っています」
"but does he know these things?"
「しかし、彼はこれらのことを知っているのでしょうか?」
"Not a small one, his pain will be"

「小さな痛みではない、彼の痛みは」
"after all, his heart is proud and hard"
「結局、彼の心は傲慢で厳しいのです」
"people like this have to suffer and err a lot"
「このような人は苦しみ、多くの過ちを犯さなければならない」
"they have to do much injustice"
「彼らは多くの不正をしなければならない」
"and they have burden themselves with much sin"
「彼らは多くの罪を背負っている」
"Tell me, my dear," he asked of Siddhartha
「教えてください、愛しい人よ」彼はシッダールタに尋ねた。
"you're not taking control of your son's upbringing?"
「息子さんの子育てを自分でコントロールしていないんですか？」
"You don't force him, beat him, or punish him?"
「彼に強制したり、殴ったり、罰を与えたりしないのですか？」
"No, Vasudeva, I don't do any of these things"
「いいえ、ヴァスデーヴァ、私はそんなことはしません」
"I knew it. You don't force him"
「やっぱり。無理強いはダメだよ」
"you don't beat him and you don't give him orders"
「彼を殴ったり命令したりしてはいけない」
"because you know softness is stronger than hard"
「柔らかさは硬さよりも強いことを知っているから」
"you know water is stronger than rocks"
「水は岩よりも強いのはご存じでしょう」
"and you know love is stronger than force"
「そしてあなたは愛が力よりも強いことを知っています」
"Very good, I praise you for this"
「とてもよかった、褒めてあげるよ」

"But aren't you mistaken in some way?"
「でも、何か間違ってるんじゃないの？」
"don't you think that you are forcing him?"
「あなたは彼を強制しているとは思わないのですか？」
"don't you perhaps punish him a different way?"
「もっと違う方法で彼を罰することはできないでしょうか？」
"Don't you shackle him with your love?"
「あなたの愛で彼を縛り付けているんじゃないの？」
"Don't you make him feel inferior every day?"
「あなたは彼に毎日劣等感を感じさせていませんか？」
"doesn't your kindness and patience make it even harder for him?"
「あなたの優しさと忍耐が、彼にとってさらに辛いことにならないでしょうか？」
"aren't you forcing him to live in a hut with two old banana-eaters?"
「バナナを食べる老人二人と一緒に小屋に住むことを彼に強制しているんじゃないの？」
"old men to whom even rice is a delicacy"
「米さえもご馳走である老人」
"old men whose thoughts can't be his"
「自分の考えとは違う老人」
"old men whose hearts are old and quiet"
「心が老いて静かな老人」
"old men whose hearts beat in a different pace than his"
「彼とは心臓の鼓動の速さが違う老人」
"Isn't he forced and punished by all this?""
「彼はこれらすべてによって強制され、罰せられているのではないですか？」
Troubled, Siddhartha looked to the ground
困惑したシッダールタは地面を見下ろした
Quietly, he asked, "What do you think should I do?"
彼は静かに尋ねました。「どうしたらいいと思いますか？」

Vasudeva spoke, "Bring him into the city"
ヴァスデーヴァは言った。「彼を街に連れて行きなさい」

"bring him into his mother's house"
「彼を母親の家に連れて行きなさい」

"there'll still be servants around, give him to them"
「まだ召使が残っているから、彼を彼らに渡して」

"And if there aren't any servants, bring him to a teacher"
「召使がいないなら、先生のところに連れて行ってください」

"but don't bring him to a teacher for teachings' sake"
「しかし、教えのために先生のところに連れて行かないでください」

"bring him to a teacher so that he is among other children"
「彼を先生のところに連れて行き、他の子供たちと一緒にいられるようにしてください」

"and bring him to the world which is his own"
「そして彼を彼自身の世界に連れて行く」

"have you never thought of this?"
「これについて考えたことはなかったのですか？」

"you're seeing into my heart," Siddhartha spoke sadly
「あなたは私の心を見ている」シッダールタは悲しそうに言った

"Often, I have thought of this"
「私はよくこのことを考えていました」

"but how can I put him into this world?"
「でも、どうやって彼をこの世に送り出せばいいの？」

"Won't he become exuberant?"
「彼は元気になりませんか？」

"won't he lose himself to pleasure and power?"
「彼は快楽と権力に溺れてしまうのではないか？」

"won't he repeat all of his father's mistakes?"
「彼は父親の過ちを繰り返すのではないだろうか？」

"won't he perhaps get entirely lost in Sansara?"

「彼はサンサーラで完全に迷子になってしまうのではないか？」
Brightly, the ferryman's smile lit up
船頭の笑顔が明るくなった
softly, he touched Siddhartha's arm
彼はそっとシッダールタの腕に触れた
"Ask the river about it, my friend!"
「川に聞いてみろよ、友よ！」
"Hear the river laugh about it!"
「川の笑い声が聞こえますよ！」
"Would you actually believe that you had committed your foolish acts?
「あなたは本当に自分が愚かな行為を犯したと信じますか？
"in order to spare your son from committing them too"
「あなたの息子が同じようなことを犯さないようにするため」
"And could you in any way protect your son from Sansara?"
「それで、あなたは息子をサンサーラから何らかの方法で守ることができるでしょうか？」
"How could you protect him from Sansara?"
「どうやって彼をサンサーラから守ったのですか？」
"By means of teachings, prayer, admonition?"
「教え、祈り、訓戒によって？」
"My dear, have you entirely forgotten that story?"
「おやおや、その話はすっかり忘れてしまったのかい？」
"the story containing so many lessons"
「多くの教訓を含んだ物語」
"the story about Siddhartha, a Brahman's son"
「バラモンの息子シッダールタの物語」
"the story which you once told me here on this very spot?"
「かつてこの場所で私に話してくれた話ですか？」
"Who has kept the Samana Siddhartha safe from Sansara?"

「誰がサマナ・シッダールタをサンサーラから守ったのか？」
"who has kept him from sin, greed, and foolishness?"
「だれが彼を罪と貪欲と愚かさから守ったのか？」
"Were his father's religious devotion able to keep him safe?
「父親の信仰心が彼を安全に守ることができたのだろうか？
"were his teacher's warnings able to keep him safe?"
「先生の警告は彼を安全に保つことができたでしょうか？」
"could his own knowledge keep him safe?"
「彼自身の知識が彼を安全に保ってくれるだろうか？」
"was his own search able to keep him safe?"
「彼自身の捜索は彼を安全に保つことができたのか？」
"What father has been able to protect his son?"
「どんな父親が息子を守ることができただろうか？」
"what father could keep his son from living his life for himself?"
「息子が自分のために生きることを止められる父親がいるだろうか？」
"what teacher has been able to protect his student?"
「どの教師が生徒を守ることができただろうか？」
"what teacher can stop his student from soiling himself with life?"
「生徒が人生で自分自身を汚すのを止められる教師がいるだろうか？」
"who could stop him from burdening himself with guilt?"
「彼が罪悪感を背負うのを誰が止められるだろうか？」
"who could stop him from drinking the bitter drink for himself?"
「彼が自分で苦い飲み物を飲むのを誰が止めることができようか？」
"who could stop him from finding his path for himself?"
「彼が自分自身の道を見つけることを誰が止められるだろうか？」

"did you think anybody could be spared from taking this path?"
「この道を通らずに済む人がいるとお考えですか?」
"did you think that perhaps your little son would be spared?"
「あなたの幼い息子は助かるかもしれないと考えたのですか?」
"did you think your love could do all that?"
「あなたの愛がそんなことができると思ったの?」
"did you think your love could keep him from suffering"
「あなたの愛が彼を苦しませないようにできると思ったの?」
"did you think your love could protect him from pain and disappointment?
「あなたの愛が彼を痛みや失望から守れると思ったの?
"you could die ten times for him"
「彼のためなら10回死んでもいい」
"but you could take no part of his destiny upon yourself"
「しかし、あなたは彼の運命の一部を自分で引き受けることはできない」
Never before, Vasudeva had spoken so many words
ヴァスデーヴァはこれまでこれほど多くの言葉を語ったことはなかった
Kindly, Siddhartha thanked him
シッダールタは彼に感謝した。
he went troubled into the hut
彼は困惑しながら小屋に入った

he could not sleep for a long time
彼は長い間眠れなかった
Vasudeva had told him nothing he had not already thought and known
ヴァスデーヴァは彼がすでに考え、知っていたこと以外のことは何も語らなかった。
But this was a knowledge he could not act upon

しかし、彼はこの知識に基づいて行動することはできなかった。
stronger than knowledge was his love for the boy
知識よりも強かったのは少年に対する彼の愛だった
stronger than knowledge was his tenderness
知識よりも彼の優しさが強かった
stronger than knowledge was his fear to lose him
知識よりも強かったのは彼を失うことへの恐怖だった
had he ever lost his heart so much to something?
彼は何かに対してこれほどまでに心を奪われたことがあっただろうか？
had he ever loved any person so blindly?
彼はかつてこれほど盲目的に誰かを愛したことがあるだろうか？
had he ever suffered for someone so unsuccessfully?
彼はこれまで誰かのためにこれほど失敗した苦しみを味わったことがあるだろうか？
had he ever made such sacrifices for anyone and yet been so unhappy?
彼はこれまで誰かのためにこれほど犠牲を払って、それでもこれほど不幸だったことがあるだろうか？
Siddhartha could not heed his friend's advice
シッダールタは友人の忠告に従わなかった
he could not give up the boy
彼はその少年を諦めることができなかった
He let the boy give him orders
彼は少年に命令をさせた
he let him disregard him
彼は彼を無視させた
He said nothing and waited
彼は何も言わずに待った
daily, he attempted the struggle of friendliness
彼は毎日、友情の闘いに挑戦した
he initiated the silent war of patience
彼は沈黙の忍耐の戦いを始めた

Vasudeva also said nothing and waited
ヴァスデーヴァも何も言わずに待った
They were both masters of patience
彼らは二人とも忍耐の達人だった

one time the boy's face reminded him very much of Kamala
ある時、その少年の顔はカマラにとてもよく似ていた。
Siddhartha suddenly had to think of something Kamala had once said
シッダールタは突然、カマラがかつて言ったことを思い出さなければならなかった
"You cannot love" she had said to him
「あなたは愛することはできない」と彼女は彼に言った
and he had agreed with her
そして彼は彼女に同意した
and he had compared himself with a star
そして彼は自分を星に例えた
and he had compared the childlike people with falling leaves
そして彼は子供のような人々を落ち葉に例えた
but nevertheless, he had also sensed an accusation in that line
しかし、彼はその言葉に非難の念も感じていた。
Indeed, he had never been able to love
確かに彼は愛することができなかった
he had never been able to devote himself completely to another person
彼は他人に完全に身を捧げることができなかった
he had never been able to to forget himself
彼は自分自身を忘れることができなかった
he had never been able to commit foolish acts for the love of another person
彼は他人への愛のために愚かな行為をすることは決してできなかった
at that time it seemed to set him apart from the childlike people

当時、彼は子供っぽい人々とは一線を画していたようだった
But ever since his son was here, Siddhartha also become a childlike person
しかし息子がここに来てから、シッダールタも子供のような人間になった
he was suffering for the sake of another person
彼は他の人のために苦しんでいた
he was loving another person
彼は他の人を愛していた
he was lost to a love for someone else
彼は他の誰かへの愛に溺れてしまった
he had become a fool on account of love
彼は愛のせいで愚か者になった
Now he too felt the strongest and strangest of all passions
今、彼もまた、最も強く、最も奇妙な情熱を感じていた
he suffered from this passion miserably
彼はこの情熱にひどく苦しんだ
and he was nevertheless in bliss
それでも彼は至福の時を過ごしていた
he was nevertheless renewed in one respect
彼はそれにもかかわらず、ある点において新しくなった。
he was enriched by this one thing
彼はこの一つのことで豊かになった
He sensed very well that this blind love for his son was a passion
彼は息子に対するこの盲目的な愛情が情熱であることをよく感じていた
he knew that it was something very human
彼はそれがとても人間的なものだということを知っていました
he knew that it was Sansara
彼はそれがサンサーラだと知っていた
he knew that it was a murky source, dark waters

彼はそれが濁った源、暗い水であることを知っていた
but he felt it was not worthless, but necessary
しかし彼はそれが無価値ではなく必要だと感じた
it came from the essence of his own being
それは彼自身の本質から生まれたものだった
This pleasure also had to be atoned for
この喜びもまた償わなければならなかった
this pain also had to be endured
この痛みも耐えなければならなかった
these foolish acts also had to be committed
これらの愚かな行為も犯されなければならなかった
Through all this, the son let him commit his foolish acts
これらすべてを通して、息子は彼の愚かな行為を許した
he let him court for his affection
彼は愛情を得るために彼に求愛した
he let him humiliate himself every day
彼は毎日自分を辱めた
he gave in to the moods of his son
彼は息子の気分に屈した
his father had nothing which could have delighted him
彼の父親には彼を喜ばせるようなものは何もなかった
and he nothing that the boy feared
そして少年は何も恐れていなかった
He was a good man, this father
この父親は良い人だった
he was a good, kind, soft man
彼は善良で、優しく、温厚な人だった
perhaps he was a very devout man
おそらく彼は非常に信心深い人だったのだろう
perhaps he was a saint, the boy thought
おそらく彼は聖人なのだろう、と少年は思った
but all these attributes could not win the boy over
しかし、これらの特徴の全てが少年を魅了することはできなかった
He was bored by this father, who kept him imprisoned

彼は監禁されたままの父親に飽き飽きしていた
a prisoner in this miserable hut of his
このみじめな小屋に囚われている
he was bored of him answering every naughtiness with a smile
彼は、どんないたずらにも笑顔で答える彼にうんざりしていた。
he didn't appreciate insults being responded to by friendliness
彼は侮辱に対して友好的な態度で応じられることを好まなかった
he didn't like viciousness returned in kindness
彼は悪意が優しさで返されることを好まなかった
this very thing was the hated trick of this old sneak
まさにこれがこの老いた卑劣漢の嫌われ者の策略だった
Much more the boy would have liked it if he had been threatened by him
少年は彼に脅されていたらもっと喜んだだろう
he wanted to be abused by him
彼は彼に虐待されたかった

A day came when young Siddhartha had had enough
ある日、若きシッダールタはもう我慢できなくなった。
what was on his mind came bursting forth
彼の心にあったものが一気に溢れ出た
and he openly turned against his father
そして彼は公然と父親に反抗した
Siddhartha had given him a task
シッダールタは彼に課題を与えた
he had told him to gather brushwood
彼は彼に柴を集めるように言った
But the boy did not leave the hut
しかし少年は小屋から出なかった
in stubborn disobedience and rage, he stayed where he was
彼は頑固な不服従と怒りでその場に留まった

he thumped on the ground with his feet
彼は足で地面を踏み鳴らした
he clenched his fists and screamed in a powerful outburst
彼は拳を握りしめて力強く叫んだ
he screamed his hatred and contempt into his father's face
彼は父親の顔に向かって憎しみと軽蔑を叫んだ
"Get the brushwood for yourself!" he shouted, foaming at the mouth
「自分で薪を取ってこい！」彼は口から泡を吹きながら叫んだ。
"I'm not your servant"
「私はあなたの召使いではありません」
"I know that you won't hit me, you wouldn't dare"
「あなたは私を殴らないだろう、殴る勇気はないだろう」
"I know that you constantly want to punish me"
「あなたがいつも私を罰したいと思っているのはわかっています」
"you want to put me down with your religious devotion and your indulgence"
「あなたはあなたの宗教的信仰と耽溺で私を貶めたいのです」
"You want me to become like you"
「あなたは私をあなたのようになってほしいのね」
"you want me to be just as devout, soft, and wise as you"
「あなたは私にあなたと同じように敬虔で、優しく、そして賢くなってほしいと願っている」
"but I won't do it, just to make you suffer"
「でも、あなたを苦しめるためにそんなことはしません」
"I would rather become a highway-robber than be as soft as you"
「私はあなたのように甘やかされるよりはむしろ強盗になりたい」
"I would rather be a murderer than be as wise as you"

「私はあなたのように賢くなるよりは殺人者になりたい」

"I would rather go to hell, than to become like you!"
「あなたのようになるくらいなら、地獄に落ちたほうがましだ！」

"I hate you, you're not my father
「あなたが嫌いよ、あなたは私の父親じゃない

"even if you've slept with my mother ten times, you are not my father!"
「たとえ私の母と10回寝たとしても、あなたは私の父ではない！」

Rage and grief boiled over in him
怒りと悲しみが彼の中に沸き起こった

he foamed at his father in a hundred savage and evil words
彼は父親に向かって、百もの残酷で邪悪な言葉を吐き出した。

Then the boy ran away into the forest
それから少年は森へ逃げていった

it was late at night when the boy returned
少年が帰ってきたのは夜遅くだった

But the next morning, he had disappeared
しかし翌朝、彼は姿を消した

What had also disappeared was a small basket
小さなバスケットも消えていた

the basket in which the ferrymen kept those copper and silver coins
渡し守が銅貨や銀貨を入れていた籠

the coins which they received as a fare
運賃として受け取ったコイン

The boat had also disappeared
ボートも消えていた

Siddhartha saw the boat lying by the opposite bank
シッダールタは対岸に停泊している船を見た

Siddhartha had been shivering with grief
シッダールタは悲しみに震えていた

the ranting speeches the boy had made touched him
少年が暴言を吐いたことが彼の心を打った
"I must follow him," said Siddhartha
「私は彼に従わなければならない」とシッダールタは言った
"A child can't go through the forest all alone, he'll perish"
「子供は一人で森を抜けることはできない、死んでしまうだろう」
"We must build a raft, Vasudeva, to get over the water"
「ヴァスデーヴァよ、水を渡るためにはいかだを作らなければなりません」
"We will build a raft" said Vasudeva
「私たちはいかだを作ります」とヴァスデーヴァは言った
"we will build it to get our boat back"
「私たちは船を取り戻すためにそれを作ります」
"But you shall not run after your child, my friend"
「しかし、子供を追いかけてはいけませんよ、友よ」
"he is no child anymore"
「彼はもう子供ではない」
"he knows how to get around"
「彼はどうやって移動するかを知っている」
"He's looking for the path to the city"
「彼は街への道を探している」
"and he is right, don't forget that"
「彼は正しい、それを忘れないで」
"he's doing what you've failed to do yourself"
「彼はあなたが自分でできなかったことをやっている」
"he's taking care of himself"
「彼は自分の面倒を見ている」
"he's taking his course for himself"
「彼は自分の道を自分で進んでいる」
"Alas, Siddhartha, I see you suffering"
「ああ、シッダールタよ、あなたが苦しんでいるのが見えます」

"but you're suffering a pain at which one would like to laugh"
「しかし、あなたは笑いたくなるような痛みに苦しんでいるのです」
"you're suffering a pain at which you'll soon laugh yourself"
「あなたは、すぐに自分自身が笑ってしまうほどの痛みに苦しんでいます」
Siddhartha did not answer his friend
シッダールタは友人に答えなかった
He already held the axe in his hands
彼はすでに斧を手にしていた
and he began to make a raft of bamboo
そして彼は竹でいかだを作り始めた
Vasudeva helped him to tie the canes together with ropes of grass
ヴァスデーヴァは彼が草のロープで杖を結ぶのを手伝った。
When they crossed the river they drifted far off their course
彼らは川を渡ったとき、進路から大きく外れてしまった
they pulled the raft upriver on the opposite bank
彼らは対岸の上流にいかだを引っ張った
"Why did you take the axe along?" asked Siddhartha
「なぜ斧を持ってきたのか？」シッダールタは尋ねた。
"It might have been possible that the oar of our boat got lost"
「私たちのボートのオールが紛失した可能性もあったかもしれません」
But Siddhartha knew what his friend was thinking
しかしシッダールタは友人が何を考えているか知っていた
He thought, the boy would have thrown away the oar
彼は、少年はオールを投げ捨てるだろうと思った
in order to get some kind of revenge
何らかの復讐をするために
and in order to keep them from following him
そして彼らが彼に従うのを防ぐために

And in fact, there was no oar left in the boat
そして実際、ボートにはオールが残っていなかった
Vasudeva pointed to the bottom of the boat
ヴァスデーヴァは船底を指差した
and he looked at his friend with a smile
そして彼は笑顔で友人を見た
he smiled as if he wanted to say something
彼は何か言いたげに微笑んだ
"Don't you see what your son is trying to tell you?"
「息子さんがあなたに何を伝えようとしているのか分からないのですか？」
"Don't you see that he doesn't want to be followed?"
「彼は尾行されたくないのが分からないの？」
But he did not say this in words
しかし彼は言葉では言わなかった
He started making a new oar
彼は新しいオールを作り始めた
But Siddhartha bid his farewell, to look for the run-away
しかしシッダールタは逃亡者を探すために別れを告げた
Vasudeva did not stop him from looking for his child
ヴァスデーヴァは彼が子供を探すのを止めなかった

Siddhartha had been walking through the forest for a long time
シッダールタは長い間森の中を歩いていた
the thought occurred to him that his search was useless
彼の捜索は無駄だという思いが浮かんだ
Either the boy was far ahead and had already reached the city
少年は遥か先にいて、すでに街に到着していたのかもしれない
or he would conceal himself from him
あるいは彼から身を隠すだろう
he continued thinking about his son
彼は息子のことを考え続けた

he found that he was not worried for his son
彼は息子のことを心配していないことに気づいた
he knew deep inside that he had not perished
彼は心の底では自分が死んでいないことを知っていた
nor was he in any danger in the forest
彼は森の中で危険にさらされることもなかった
Nevertheless, he ran without stopping
それでも彼は止まることなく走り続けた
he was not running to save him
彼は彼を救うために走っていたのではない
he was running to satisfy his desire
彼は欲望を満たすために走っていた
he wanted to perhaps see him one more time
彼はもう一度彼に会いたかった
And he ran up to just outside of the city
そして彼は街のすぐ外まで走って行った
When, near the city, he reached a wide road
街の近くで広い道に着いたとき
he stopped, by the entrance of the beautiful pleasure-garden
彼は美しい遊園地の入り口で立ち止まった
the garden which used to belong to Kamala
かつてカマラが所有していた庭園
the garden where he had seen her for the first time
彼が彼女を初めて見た庭
when she was sitting in her sedan-chair
彼女がセダンチェアに座っていたとき
The past rose up in his soul
過去が彼の魂に蘇った
again, he saw himself standing there
再び、彼は自分がそこに立っているのを見た
a young, bearded, naked Samana
若くて髭を生やした裸のサマナ
his hair hair was full of dust
彼の髪はほこりでいっぱいだった
For a long time, Siddhartha stood there

シッダールタは長い間そこに立っていた
he looked through the open gate into the garden
彼は開いた門から庭を眺めた
he saw monks in yellow robes walking among the beautiful trees
彼は黄色い僧衣を着た僧侶たちが美しい木々の間を歩いているのを見た
For a long time, he stood there, pondering
彼は長い間そこに立って考えていた
he saw images and listened to the story of his life
彼は映像を見て、彼の人生の物語を聞いた
For a long time, he stood there looking at the monks
彼は長い間そこに立って僧侶たちを眺めていた
he saw young Siddhartha in their place
彼は彼らの代わりに若きシッダールタを見た
he saw young Kamala walking among the high trees
彼は若いカマラが高い木々の間を歩いているのを見た
Clearly, he saw himself being served food and drink by Kamala
明らかに彼はカマラから食べ物や飲み物を出されるのを見ていた。
he saw himself receiving his first kiss from her
彼は彼女から初めてのキスを受けるのを想像した
he saw himself looking proudly and disdainfully back on his life as a Brahman
彼はブラフマンとしての人生を誇らしげに、そして軽蔑的に振り返っている自分自身を見た。
he saw himself beginning his worldly life, proudly and full of desire
彼は誇りと欲望に満ちたこの世での人生を始める自分自身を見た
He saw Kamaswami, the servants, the orgies
彼はカマスワミ、召使い、乱交パーティーを見た
he saw the gamblers with the dice
彼はサイコロを振るギャンブラーたちを見た

he saw Kamala's song-bird in the cage
彼はカマラの鳴き鳥が檻の中にいるのを見た
he lived through all this again
彼はまたこのすべてを生き抜いた
he breathed Sansara and was once again old and tired
彼はサンサーラを呼吸し、再び老いて疲れ果てた
he felt the disgust and the wish to annihilate himself again
彼は嫌悪感と再び自分自身を滅ぼしたいという願望を感じた
and he was healed again by the holy Om
そして彼は聖なるオームによって再び癒された
for a long time Siddhartha had stood by the gate
シッダールタは長い間門のそばに立っていた
he realised his desire was foolish
彼は自分の欲望が愚かであることに気づいた
he realized it was foolishness which had made him go up to this place
彼は自分がこの場所へ来たのは愚かなことだったと悟った
he realized he could not help his son
彼は息子を助けることができないことに気づいた
and he realized that he was not allowed to cling to him
そして彼は、彼に執着することは許されないことに気づいた
he felt the love for the run-away deeply in his heart
彼は家出人への愛情を心の底から感じた
the love for his son felt like a wound
息子への愛は傷のように感じられた
but this wound had not been given to him in order to turn the knife in it
しかし、この傷はナイフを突き刺すために与えられたものではない。
the wound had to become a blossom
傷は花にならなければならなかった
and his wound had to shine

そして彼の傷は光り輝かなければならなかった
That this wound did not blossom or shine yet made him sad
この傷がまだ花を咲かせたり輝いたりしていないことが彼を悲しませた
Instead of the desired goal, there was emptiness
望んだ目標の代わりに空虚があった
emptiness had drawn him here, and sadly he sat down
空虚が彼をここに引き寄せ、悲しく彼は座った
he felt something dying in his heart
彼は心の中で何かが死ぬのを感じた
he experienced emptiness and saw no joy any more
彼は空虚さを感じ、もはや喜びを感じなくなった
there was no goal for which to aim for
目指すべき目標がなかった
He sat lost in thought and waited
彼は考えながら座って待っていた
This he had learned by the river
彼は川でこれを学んだ
waiting, having patience, listening attentively
待つこと、忍耐すること、注意深く聞くこと
And he sat and listened, in the dust of the road
そして彼は道の埃の中に座って聞いていた
he listened to his heart, beating tiredly and sadly
彼は疲れて悲しく鼓動する自分の心臓の音を聞いた
and he waited for a voice
そして彼は声を待った
Many an hour he crouched, listening
彼は何時間もしゃがみ込んで耳をすませた
he saw no images any more
彼はもう何も見なかった
he fell into emptiness and let himself fall
彼は虚無に陥り、自ら落ちていった
he could see no path in front of him
彼は目の前に道が見えなかった

And when he felt the wound burning, he silently spoke the Om
そして傷が焼けるのを感じた時、彼は静かにオームを唱えた。
he filled himself with Om
彼はオームで満たされた
The monks in the garden saw him
庭の修道士たちは彼を見た
dust was gathering on his gray hair
彼の白髪には埃が積もっていた
since he crouched for many hours, one of monks placed two bananas in front of him
彼が何時間もしゃがんでいたので、僧侶の一人が彼の前にバナナを2本置いた。
The old man did not see him
老人は彼に気づかなかった

From this petrified state, he was awoken by a hand touching his shoulder
この凍り付いた状態から、彼は肩に触れる手によって目覚めた。
Instantly, he recognised this tender bashful touch
彼はすぐにこの優しくて恥ずかしそうなタッチに気づいた
Vasudeva had followed him and waited
ヴァスデーヴァは彼を追いかけて待っていた
he regained his senses and rose to greet Vasudeva
彼は正気を取り戻し、ヴァスデーヴァに挨拶するために立ち上がった。
he looked into Vasudeva's friendly face
彼はヴァスデーヴァの優しい顔を見つめた
he looked into the small wrinkles
彼は小さなしわを覗き込んだ
his wrinkles were as if they were filled with nothing but his smile

彼のしわはまるで笑顔だけで満たされているかのようだった
he looked into the happy eyes, and then he smiled too
彼は幸せそうな目を見つめ、そして微笑んだ
Now he saw the bananas lying in front of him
今、彼は目の前にバナナが横たわっているのを見た
he picked the bananas up and gave one to the ferryman
彼はバナナを拾い、渡し守に一つ渡した。
After eating the bananas, they silently went back into the forest
バナナを食べた後、彼らは黙って森に戻っていった
they returned home to the ferry
彼らはフェリーで家に戻った
Neither one talked about what had happened that day
二人ともその日に何が起こったのか話さなかった
neither one mentioned the boy's name
どちらも少年の名前を言わなかった
neither one spoke about him running away
誰も彼が逃げたことについては話さなかった
neither one spoke about the wound
誰も傷については話さなかった
In the hut, Siddhartha lay down on his bed
小屋の中で、シッダールタはベッドに横たわった
after a while Vasudeva came to him
しばらくしてヴァスデーヴァが彼のところにやって来た
he offered him a bowl of coconut-milk
彼はココナッツミルクの入ったボウルを彼に差し出した
but he was already asleep
しかし彼はすでに眠っていた

Om
オム

For a long time the wound continued to burn
長い間、傷は焼けるように痛み続けた
Siddhartha had to ferry many travellers across the river
シッダールタは多くの旅人を川を渡らなければならなかった
many of the travellers were accompanied by a son or a daughter
旅行者の多くは息子か娘を連れていた
and he saw none of them without envying them
そして彼は彼らを羨ましがらずにはいられなかった
he couldn't see them without thinking about his lost son
彼は亡くなった息子のことを考えずには彼らを見ることはできなかった
"So many thousands possess the sweetest of good fortunes"
「何千人もの人々が最も素晴らしい幸運を手にしている」
"why don't I also possess this good fortune?"
「なぜ私もこの幸運を持たないのか？」
"even thieves and robbers have children and love them"
「泥棒や強盗でさえ子供を産み、愛する」
"and they are being loved by their children"
「そして彼らは子供たちに愛されている」
"all are loved by their children except for me"
「私以外はみんな子供に愛されている」
he now thought like the childlike people, without reason
彼は今、理由もなく子供のように考えていた
he had become one of the childlike people
彼は子供のような人々の一人になった
he looked upon people differently than before
彼は以前とは違った目で人々を見た
he was less smart and less proud of himself
彼は賢くなく、自分に誇りもなかった

but instead, he was warmer and more curious
しかし、彼はより温かく、より好奇心旺盛だった
when he ferried travellers, he was more involved than before
旅人を運ぶとき、彼は以前よりももっと関わるようになった
childlike people, businessmen, warriors, women
子供のような人々、ビジネスマン、戦士、女性
these people did not seem alien to him, as they used to
これらの人々は彼にとって、以前のように異質なものには見えなかった。
he understood them and shared their life
彼は彼らを理解し、彼らの人生を共有した
a life which was not guided by thoughts and insight
思考と洞察力に導かれなかった人生
but a life guided solely by urges and wishes
衝動と願望のみに導かれた人生
he felt like the the childlike people
彼は子供のような人々のように感じた
he was bearing his final wound
彼は最後の傷を負っていた
he was nearing perfection
彼は完璧に近づきつつあった
but the childlike people still seemed like his brothers
しかし、子供のような人々はまだ彼の兄弟のように見えました
their vanities, desires for possession were no longer ridiculous to him
彼らの虚栄心や所有欲はもはや彼にとって馬鹿げたことではなかった
they became understandable and lovable
彼らは理解しやすく愛らしくなった
they even became worthy of veneration to him
彼らは彼にとって崇拝に値する存在となった
The blind love of a mother for her child

母親の子供に対する盲目的な愛

the stupid, blind pride of a conceited father for his only son
うぬぼれた父親の、一人息子に対する愚かで盲目的な自尊心

the blind, wild desire of a young, vain woman for jewellery
若くてうぬぼれの強い女性の宝石に対する盲目的で激しい欲望

her wish for admiring glances from men
男性からの賞賛の視線を求める彼女の願い

all of these simple urges were not childish notions
これらの単純な衝動は子供じみた考えではなかった

but they were immensely strong, living, and prevailing urges
しかし、それらは非常に強く、生き生きとした、そして支配的な衝動であった

he saw people living for the sake of their urges
彼は人々が自分の衝動のために生きているのを見た

he saw people achieving rare things for their urges
彼は人々が衝動のために稀なことを成し遂げるのを見た

travelling, conducting wars, suffering
旅をし、戦争をし、苦しみ

they bore an infinite amount of suffering
彼らは限りない苦しみに耐えた

and he could love them for it, because he saw life
そして彼は彼らを愛することができた。なぜなら彼は人生を

that what is alive was in each of their passions
生きているものはそれぞれの情熱の中にあった

that what is is indestructible was in their urges, the Brahman
破壊できないものは彼らの衝動の中にあった、ブラフマン

these people were worthy of love and admiration
これらの人々は愛と賞賛に値する

they deserved it for their blind loyalty and blind strength
彼らは盲目的な忠誠心と盲目的な強さでそれに値する

there was nothing that they lacked
彼らには何も欠けていなかった
Siddhartha had nothing which would put him above the rest, except one thing
シッダールタには他の人より優れているところは何もなかったが、一つだけ例外があった。
there still was a small thing he had which they didn't
彼らが持っていなかった小さなものがまだ残っていた
he had the conscious thought of the oneness of all life
彼はすべての生命は一つであるという意識的な考えを持っていた
but Siddhartha even doubted whether this knowledge should be valued so highly
しかしシッダールタは、この知識がそれほど高く評価されるべきかどうかさえ疑問視した。
it might also be a childish idea of the thinking people
それは思慮深い人々の幼稚な考えかもしれない
the worldly people were of equal rank to the wise men
世俗の人々は賢者と同等の地位にあった
animals too can in some moments seem to be superior to humans
動物も時には人間より優れているように見えることがある
they are superior in their tough, unrelenting performance of what is necessary
彼らは必要なことを厳しく、容赦なく遂行することに優れている
an idea slowly blossomed in Siddhartha
シッダールタの中でゆっくりとアイデアが開花した
and the idea slowly ripened in him
そしてその考えはゆっくりと彼の中で熟成していった
he began to see what wisdom actually was
彼は知恵が実際に何であるかを理解し始めた
he saw what the goal of his long search was
彼は長い探求の目的が何であったかを知った

his search was nothing but a readiness of the soul
彼の探求は魂の準備以外の何ものでもなかった
a secret art to think every moment, while living his life
人生を生きながら、一瞬一瞬考えるという秘密の芸術
it was the thought of oneness
それは一体感の考えだった
to be able to feel and inhale the oneness
一体感を感じ、吸い込むことができる
Slowly this awareness blossomed in him
ゆっくりとこの認識が彼の中で開花した
it was shining back at him from Vasudeva's old, childlike face
それはヴァスデーヴァの年老いた子供のような顔から彼に輝き返していた
harmony and knowledge of the eternal perfection of the world
世界の永遠の完全性についての調和と知識
smiling and to be part of the oneness
笑顔で一体感を味わう
But the wound still burned
しかし傷はまだ焼けていた
longingly and bitterly Siddhartha thought of his son
シッダールタは息子のことを切実に思い、
he nurtured his love and tenderness in his heart
彼は心の中に愛と優しさを育んだ
he allowed the pain to gnaw at him
彼は痛みに苦しんだ
he committed all foolish acts of love
彼は愚かな愛の行為を犯した
this flame would not go out by itself
この炎は自然に消えることはない

one day the wound burned violently
ある日、傷口が激しく焼けた
driven by a yearning, Siddhartha crossed the river

憧れに駆られてシッダールタは川を渡った
he got off the boat and was willing to go to the city
彼は船を降りて街に行くつもりだった
he wanted to look for his son again
彼は息子をもう一度探したかった
The river flowed softly and quietly
川は静かに流れていた
it was the dry season, but its voice sounded strange
乾季だったが、その声は奇妙に聞こえた
it was clear to hear that the river laughed
川が笑っているのがはっきりと聞こえた
it laughed brightly and clearly at the old ferryman
それは年老いた渡し守に向かって明るくはっきりと笑った
he bent over the water, in order to hear even better
彼はもっとよく聞こえるように水の上に身をかがめた
and he saw his face reflected in the quietly moving waters
そして静かに流れる水面に自分の顔が映った。
in this reflected face there was something
この映った顔には何かがあった
something which reminded him, but he had forgotten
彼に思い出させたが、彼は忘れていた
as he thought about it, he found it
考えてみると、彼はそれを見つけた
this face resembled another face which he used to know and love
この顔は彼がかつて知っていて愛していた別の顔に似ていた
but he also used to fear this face
しかし彼はこの顔を恐れていた
It resembled his father's face, the Brahman
それは彼の父、ブラフマンの顔に似ていた。
he remembered how he had forced his father to let him go
彼は父親に強制的に行かせたことを思い出した
he remembered how he had bid his farewell to him

彼は彼に別れを告げた時のことを思い出した
he remembered how he had gone and had never come back
彼は自分がどうやって去って、二度と戻ってこなかったかを思い出した

Had his father not also suffered the same pain for him?
彼の父親もまた、彼のために同じ苦しみを味わったのではないだろうか？

was his father's pain not the pain Siddhartha is suffering now?
彼の父親の痛みは、シッダールタが今苦しんでいる痛みではなかったのでしょうか？

Had his father not long since died?
彼の父親はつい最近亡くなったのだろうか？

had he died without having seen his son again?
彼は息子に再び会うことなく亡くなったのだろうか？

Did he not have to expect the same fate for himself?
彼自身にも同じ運命が訪れることを覚悟しなければならなかったのではないだろうか？

Was it not a comedy in a fateful circle?
それは運命の輪の中の喜劇ではなかったのか？

The river laughed about all of this
川はこれらすべてを笑った

everything came back which had not been suffered
受けなかったものはすべて戻ってきた

everything came back which had not been solved
解決できなかったことはすべて戻ってきた

the same pain was suffered over and over again
同じ痛みが何度も繰り返された

Siddhartha went back into the boat
シッダールタは船に戻った

and he returned back to the hut
そして彼は小屋に戻った

he was thinking of his father and of his son
彼は父親と息子のことを考えていた

he thought of having been laughed at by the river

彼は川に笑われたと思った
he was at odds with himself and tending towards despair
彼は自分自身と対立し、絶望に陥りがちだった
but he was also tempted to laugh
しかし彼は笑いたくなった
he could laugh at himself and the entire world
彼は自分自身と世界全体を笑うことができた
Alas, the wound was not blossoming yet
悲しいかな、傷はまだ癒えていなかった
his heart was still fighting his fate
彼の心はまだ運命と戦っていた
cheerfulness and victory were not yet shining from his suffering
彼の苦しみからはまだ明るさと勝利は生まれていなかった
Nevertheless, he felt hope along with the despair
それでも彼は絶望とともに希望も感じていた
once he returned to the hut he felt an undefeatable desire to open up to Vasudeva
小屋に戻ると、彼はヴァスデーヴァに心を開きたいという抑えきれない欲求を感じた。
he wanted to show him everything
彼は彼にすべてを見せたかった
he wanted to say everything to the master of listening
彼は聞くことの達人にすべてを話したかった

Vasudeva was sitting in the hut, weaving a basket
ヴァスデーヴァは小屋に座って籠を編んでいた
He no longer used the ferry-boat
彼はもう渡し船を使わなくなった
his eyes were starting to get weak
彼の目は弱くなり始めていた
his arms and hands were getting weak as well
彼の腕と手も弱くなっていた

only the joy and cheerful benevolence of his face was unchanging
彼の顔の喜びと明るい慈悲だけが変わらなかった
Siddhartha sat down next to the old man
シッダールタは老人の隣に座った
slowly, he started talking about what they had never spoke about
彼はゆっくりと、これまで話したことのなかったことを話し始めた
he told him of his walk to the city
彼は街まで歩いたことを話した
he told at him of the burning wound
彼は焼けるような傷について彼に話した
he told him about the envy of seeing happy fathers
彼は幸せな父親を見てうらやましがったと話した
his knowledge of the foolishness of such wishes
そのような願いの愚かさを知っている
his futile fight against his wishes
彼の願いに反する無駄な戦い
he was able to say everything, even the most embarrassing parts
彼は、最も恥ずかしい部分さえもすべて話すことができた。
he told him everything he could tell him
彼は彼に話せることはすべて話した
he showed him everything he could show him
彼は彼に見せられるものはすべて見せた
He presented his wound to him
彼は傷を彼に見せた
he also told him how he had fled today
彼はまた、今日どのように逃げたかを話した。
he told him how he ferried across the water
彼はどうやって水を渡ったかを話した
a childish run-away, willing to walk to the city
街まで歩いて行こうとする子供じみた家出
and he told him how the river had laughed

そして彼は川が笑ったことを話した
he spoke for a long time
彼は長い間話した
Vasudeva was listening with a quiet face
ヴァスデーヴァは静かな顔で聞いていた
Vasudeva's listening gave Siddhartha a stronger sensation than ever before
ヴァスデーヴァの聴取はシッダールタにかつてないほど強い感覚を与えた。
he sensed how his pain and fears flowed over to him
彼は自分の痛みと恐怖が自分に流れ込んでくるのを感じた
he sensed how his secret hope flowed over him
彼は自分の秘めた希望が自分の中で溢れていることを感じた
To show his wound to this listener was the same as bathing it in the river
この聴衆に傷を見せることは、川で傷を洗うのと同じことだ
the river would have cooled Siddhartha's wound
川はシッダールタの傷を冷やしたであろう
the quiet listening cooled Siddhartha's wound
静かに聞くことでシッダールタの傷は癒された
it cooled him until he become one with the river
それは彼を冷やし、川と一体化するまで続いた
While he was still speaking, still admitting and confessing
彼がまだ話し続け、認め、告白している間
Siddhartha felt more and more that this was no longer Vasudeva
シッダールタは、これがもはやヴァスデーヴァではないとますます感じていた。
it was no longer a human being who was listening to him
彼の話を聞いていたのはもはや人間ではなかった
this motionless listener was absorbing his confession into himself

この動かない聞き手は彼の告白を自分の中に吸収していた
this motionless listener was like a tree the rain
この動かない聞き手は雨の木のようだった
this motionless man was the river itself
この動かない男は川そのものでした
this motionless man was God himself
この動かない男は神そのものでした
the motionless man was the eternal itself
動かない人間は永遠そのものである
Siddhartha stopped thinking of himself and his wound
シッダールタは自分自身と傷について考えるのをやめた
this realisation of Vasudeva's changed character took possession of him
ヴァスデーヴァの性格の変化に気づいた彼は
and the more he entered into it, the less wondrous it became
そして彼がそれに入るほど、それは不思議ではなくなった。
the more he realised that everything was in order and natural
すべてが秩序正しく自然であることを彼はより実感した
he realised that Vasudeva had already been like this for a long time
彼はヴァスデーヴァが長い間このような状態だったことに気づいた
he had just not quite recognised it yet
彼はまだそれを認識していなかった
yes, he himself had almost reached the same state
そう、彼自身もほぼ同じ状態に達していた
He felt, that he was now seeing old Vasudeva as the people see the gods
彼は、人々が神々を見るのと同じように、老いたヴァスデーヴァを見ていると感じた。
and he felt that this could not last
そして彼はこれが長く続くはずがないと感じた

in his heart, he started bidding his farewell to Vasudeva
彼は心の中でヴァスデーヴァに別れを告げ始めた
Throughout all this, he talked incessantly
その間ずっと彼は絶え間なく話していた
When he had finished talking, Vasudeva turned his friendly eyes at him
彼が話を終えると、ヴァスデーヴァは彼に友好的な目を向けた。
the eyes which had grown slightly weak
少し弱くなった目
he said nothing, but let his silent love and cheerfulness shine
彼は何も言わなかったが、静かな愛と明るさを輝かせた
his understanding and knowledge shone from him
彼の理解力と知識は輝いていた
He took Siddhartha's hand and led him to the seat by the bank
彼はシッダールタの手を取って、岸辺の席まで連れて行った。
he sat down with him and smiled at the river
彼は彼と一緒に座り、川に向かって微笑んだ
"You've heard it laugh," he said
「笑う声を聞いたことがあるだろう」と彼は言った
"But you haven't heard everything"
「でも、まだ全部聞いてないよ」
"Let's listen, you'll hear more"
「聞いてみろよ、もっと聞けるぞ」
Softly sounded the river, singing in many voices
川の音が静かに響き、様々な声が歌っていた
Siddhartha looked into the water
シッダールタは水の中を見つめた
images appeared to him in the moving water
流れる水の中に彼の目に映った映像
his father appeared, lonely and mourning for his son
父親は息子を亡くして寂しく嘆きながら現れた。
he himself appeared in the moving water

彼自身が流れる水の中に現れた
he was also being tied with the bondage of yearning to his distant son
彼はまた、遠く離れた息子への憧れの束縛に縛られていた。
his son appeared, lonely as well
彼の息子も孤独に現れた
the boy, greedily rushing along the burning course of his young wishes
少年は、若い願いの燃えるような道を貪欲に突き進む
each one was heading for his goal
それぞれが自分の目標に向かっていた
each one was obsessed by the goal
それぞれが目標に執着していた
each one was suffering from the pursuit
それぞれが追跡に苦しんでいた
The river sang with a voice of suffering
川は苦しみの声で歌った
longingly it sang and flowed towards its goal
切望しながら歌い、目的地に向かって流れていった
"Do you hear?" Vasudeva asked with a mute gaze
「聞こえますか？」ヴァスデーヴァは無言の視線で尋ねた
Siddhartha nodded in reply
シッダールタはうなずいて答えた。
"Listen better!" Vasudeva whispered
「よく聞きなさい！」ヴァスデーヴァはささやいた
Siddhartha made an effort to listen better
シッダールタはもっとよく聞こうと努力した
The image of his father appeared
父親の姿が浮かび上がった
his own image merged with his father's
彼自身のイメージは父親のイメージと融合した
the image of his son merged with his image
息子のイメージが彼自身のイメージと融合した

Kamala's image also appeared and was dispersed
カマラの像も現れて散布された
and the image of Govinda, and other images
ゴヴィンダの像やその他の像
and all the imaged merged with each other
そして、すべてのイメージが互いに融合した
all the imaged turned into the river
イメージしたものはすべて川に変わった
being the river, they all headed for the goal
川なので、彼らは全員ゴールに向かった
longing, desiring, suffering flowed together
憧れ、願望、苦しみが混ざり合った
and the river's voice sounded full of yearning
川の声は憧れに満ちていた
the river's voice was full of burning woe
川の声は燃えるような悲しみに満ちていた
the river's voice was full of unsatisfiable desire
川の声は満たされない欲望に満ちていた
For the goal, the river was heading
ゴールに向けて川は
Siddhartha saw the river hurrying towards its goal
シッダールタは川が目的地に向かって急いでいるのを見た
the river of him and his loved ones and of all people he had ever seen
彼と彼の愛する人たち、そして彼が今までに見たすべての人々の川
all of these waves and waters were hurrying
これらすべての波と水は急いでいた
they were all suffering towards many goals
彼らは皆、多くの目標に向かって苦しんでいた
the waterfall, the lake, the rapids, the sea
滝、湖、急流、海
and all goals were reached
そして全ての目標は達成されました

and every goal was followed by a new one
そして、それぞれの目標の後に新たな目標が続いた
and the water turned into vapour and rose to the sky
そして水は蒸気となって空に昇っていった
the water turned into rain and poured down from the sky
水は雨となって空から降り注いだ
the water turned into a source
水は水源に変わった
then the source turned into a stream
そして源は小川に変わった
the stream turned into a river
小川は川に変わった
and the river headed forwards again
そして川は再び前進した
But the longing voice had changed
しかし、切望する声は変わった
It still resounded, full of suffering, searching
それはまだ響き渡っていた、苦しみと探求に満ちた
but other voices joined the river
しかし他の声も川に加わった
there were voices of joy and of suffering
喜びの声と苦しみの声があった
good and bad voices, laughing and sad ones
良い声も悪い声も、笑っている声も悲しい声も
a hundred voices, a thousand voices
百の声、千の声
Siddhartha listened to all these voices
シッダールタはこれらすべての声に耳を傾けた
He was now nothing but a listener
彼は今やただの聞き手だった
he was completely concentrated on listening
彼は聞くことに完全に集中していた
he was completely empty now
彼は完全に空っぽになった
he felt that he had now finished learning to listen

彼は聞くことの学習は終わったと感じた
Often before, he had heard all this
彼はこれまで何度もこのことを聞いていた
he had heard these many voices in the river
彼は川でたくさんの声を聞いた
today the voices in the river sounded new
今日、川の声が新しく聞こえた
Already, he could no longer tell the many voices apart
すでに彼は多くの声を区別することができなくなっていた
there was no difference between the happy voices and the weeping ones
幸せな声と泣いている声に違いはなかった
the voices of children and the voices of men were one
子どもたちの声と男たちの声は一つになった
all these voices belonged together
これらすべての声は一つにまとまっていた
the lamentation of yearning and the laughter of the knowledgeable one
憧れの嘆きと知識人の笑い
the scream of rage and the moaning of the dying ones
怒りの叫びと死にゆく者たちのうめき声
everything was one and everything was intertwined
全ては一つであり、全ては絡み合っていた
everything was connected and entangled a thousand times
すべてが千回もつながり絡み合っていた
everything together, all voices, all goals
全てを合わせて、全ての声、全ての目標
all yearning, all suffering, all pleasure
すべての憧れ、すべての苦しみ、すべての喜び
all that was good and evil
善と悪のすべて
all of this together was the world
これらすべてが世界だった
All of it together was the flow of events

これらすべてが一連の出来事の流れだった
all of it was the music of life
すべては人生の音楽だった
when Siddhartha was listening attentively to this river
シッダールタがこの川の音に注意深く耳を傾けていたとき
the song of a thousand voices
千の声の歌
when he neither listened to the suffering nor the laughter
苦しみにも笑いにも耳を傾けなかったとき
when he did not tie his soul to any particular voice
彼が自分の魂を特定の声に縛り付けていなかったとき
when he submerged his self into the river
彼が川に身を沈めたとき
but when he heard them all he perceived the whole, the oneness
しかし、彼はそれをすべて聞いたとき、全体性、一体性を認識した。
then the great song of the thousand voices consisted of a single word
千の声による偉大な歌は、一つの言葉から成っていた
this word was Om; the perfection
この言葉はオーム、つまり完璧さである

"Do you hear" Vasudeva's gaze asked again
「聞こえますか」ヴァスデーヴァの視線が再び尋ねた
Brightly, Vasudeva's smile was shining
ヴァスデーヴァの笑顔は明るく輝いていた
it was floating radiantly over all the wrinkles of his old face
それは彼の老いた顔のしわの上に輝いて浮かんでいた
the same way the Om was floating in the air over all the voices of the river
オームが川のあらゆる声の上に空中に浮かんでいたのと同じように
Brightly his smile was shining, when he looked at his friend

友人を見ると、彼の笑顔は明るく輝いていた
and brightly the same smile was now starting to shine on Siddhartha's face
そして今、シッダールタの顔には同じ笑顔が輝き始めていた。
His wound had blossomed and his suffering was shining
彼の傷は花開き、彼の苦しみは輝いていた
his self had flown into the oneness
彼の自己は一体感の中に飛び込んでいった
In this hour, Siddhartha stopped fighting his fate
この瞬間、シッダールタは運命と戦うことをやめた
at the same time he stopped suffering
同時に彼は苦しみを止めた
On his face flourished the cheerfulness of a knowledge
彼の顔には知識の明るさがあふれていた
a knowledge which was no longer opposed by any will
もはやいかなる意志にも反対されない知識
a knowledge which knows perfection
完璧を知る知識
a knowledge which is in agreement with the flow of events
出来事の流れに一致する知識
a knowledge which is with the current of life
人生の流れに沿った知識
full of sympathy for the pain of others
他人の痛みに対する同情心に満ちている
full of sympathy for the pleasure of others
他人の喜びに対する共感に満ちている
devoted to the flow, belonging to the oneness
流れに身を捧げ、一体性に属する
Vasudeva rose from the seat by the bank
ヴァスデーヴァは岸辺の椅子から立ち上がった
he looked into Siddhartha's eyes
彼はシッダールタの目を見つめた
and he saw the cheerfulness of the knowledge shining in his eyes

そして彼は知識の明るさが彼の目に輝いているのを見た
he softly touched his shoulder with his hand
彼はそっと手で肩に触れた
"I've been waiting for this hour, my dear"
「この時を待っていたんだよ、愛しい人よ」
"Now that it has come, let me leave"
「もう来たから、行かせて」
"For a long time, I've been waiting for this hour"
「長い間、この時を待っていた」
"for a long time, I've been Vasudeva the ferryman"
「私は長い間、渡し守のヴァスデーヴァでした」
"Now it's enough. Farewell"
「もう十分だ。さようなら」
"farewell river, farewell Siddhartha!"
「さようなら川、さようならシッダールタ!」
Siddhartha made a deep bow before him who bid his farewell
シッダールタは別れを告げる彼の前で深く頭を下げた
"I've known it," he said quietly
「それはわかっていた」と彼は静かに言った
"You'll go into the forests?"
「森に行くんですか?」
"I'm going into the forests"
「森へ行きます」
"I'm going into the oneness" spoke Vasudeva with a bright smile
「私は一体感の中に入っていきます」とヴァスデーヴァは明るい笑顔で語った。
With a bright smile, he left
彼は明るい笑顔で去っていった
Siddhartha watched him leaving
シッダールタは彼が去っていくのを見守った
With deep joy, with deep solemnity he watched him leave
彼は深い喜びと深い厳粛さで彼が去っていくのを見守った

he saw his steps were full of peace
彼は自分の歩みが平和に満ちていることに気づいた
he saw his head was full of lustre
彼は自分の頭が光り輝いていることに気づいた
he saw his body was full of light
彼は自分の体が光に満ちているのを見た

Govinda
ゴヴィンダ

Govinda had been with the monks for a long time
ゴヴィンダは長い間僧侶たちと一緒にいた
when not on pilgrimages, he spent his time in the pleasure-garden
巡礼に出ていないときは、彼は遊園地で時間を過ごした。
the garden which the courtesan Kamala had given the followers of Gotama
娼婦カマラがゴータマの信者に与えた庭園
he heard talk of an old ferryman, who lived a day's journey away
彼は一日の旅程の先に住む年老いた渡し守の話を聞いた
he heard many regarded him as a wise man
彼は多くの人が彼を賢者だとみなしていると聞いた
When Govinda went back, he chose the path to the ferry
ゴヴィンダが戻るとき、彼はフェリーへの道を選んだ
he was eager to see the ferryman
彼は渡し守に会いたがっていた
he had lived his entire life by the rules
彼は生涯ずっと規則に従って生きてきた
he was looked upon with veneration by the younger monks
彼は若い僧侶たちから尊敬されていた
they respected his age and modesty
彼らは彼の年齢と謙虚さを尊重した
but his restlessness had not perished from his heart
しかし彼の心の落ち着きのなさは消えていなかった
he was searching for what he had not found
彼は見つけられなかったものを探していた
He came to the river and asked the old man to ferry him over
彼は川に来て老人に渡し舟で渡ってくれるよう頼んだ
when they got off the boat on the other side, he spoke with the old man
彼らが船から反対側に降りると、彼は老人と話した

"You're very good to us monks and pilgrims"
「あなたは私たち僧侶や巡礼者にとても親切です」
"you have ferried many of us across the river"
「あなたは私たちの多くを川の向こうへ運んでくれました」
"Aren't you too, ferryman, a searcher for the right path?"
「あなたも、渡し守さん、正しい道を探し求める人ではないですか？」
smiling from his old eyes, Siddhartha spoke
シッダールタは老いた目で微笑みながら言った
"oh venerable one, do you call yourself a searcher?"
「ああ、尊敬すべき人よ、あなたは自分自身を探求者と呼ぶのですか？」
"are you still a searcher, although already well in years?"
「あなたはもうかなり年をとっていますが、まだ探求者ですか？」
"do you search while wearing the robe of Gotama's monks?"
「ゴータマの僧侶の衣を着て捜索するのですか？」
"It's true, I'm old," spoke Govinda
「本当よ、私は年寄りなの」とゴヴィンダは言った。
"but I haven't stopped searching"
「しかし私は探求をやめなかった」
"I will never stop searching"
「私は決して探求をやめない」
"this seems to be my destiny"
「これが私の運命のようだ」
"You too, so it seems to me, have been searching"
「あなたも、探していたようですね」
"Would you like to tell me something, oh honourable one?"
「名誉ある方よ、私に何かお話したいことはありますか？」
"What might I have that I could tell you, oh venerable one?"
「尊敬すべき方よ、私があなたに何をお伝えできるでしょうか？」

"Perhaps I could tell you that you're searching far too much?"
「もしかしたら、探しすぎだと言ってもいいかもしれないね?」
"Could I tell you that you don't make time for finding?"
「探す時間がないと言ってもいいですか?」
"How come?" asked Govinda
「どうして?」とゴヴィンダは尋ねた。
"When someone is searching they might only see what they search for"
「誰かが検索しているとき、検索したものだけが表示される可能性があります」
"he might not be able to let anything else enter his mind"
「彼は他のことは何も考えられないかもしれない」
"he doesn't see what he is not searching for"
「彼は探していないものは見ない」
"because he always thinks of nothing but the object of his search"
「彼は常に自分の探求の対象のことしか考えていないからだ」
"he has a goal, which he is obsessed with"
「彼には目標があり、それに夢中になっている」
"Searching means having a goal"
「探すということは目標を持つということ」
"But finding means being free, open, and having no goal"
「しかし、見つけるということは、自由で、オープンで、目標を持たないことを意味します」
"You, oh venerable one, are perhaps indeed a searcher"
「あなたは、ああ、尊敬すべき人よ、おそらく本当に探求者なのでしょう」
"because, when striving for your goal, there are many things you don't see"
「目標に向かって努力しているとき、見えなくなることがたくさんあるからです」

"you might not see things which are directly in front of your eyes"
「目の前にあるものが見えないかもしれない」
"I don't quite understand yet," said Govinda, "what do you mean by this?"
「まだよく分かりません」とゴヴィンダは言いました。「これはどういう意味ですか？」
"oh venerable one, you've been at this river before, a long time ago"
「おお、尊者よ、あなたはずっと昔にこの川に来られたことがあるのですね」
"and you have found a sleeping man by the river"
「そしてあなたは川のほとりで眠っている男を見つけた」
"you have sat down with him to guard his sleep"
「あなたは彼の眠りを守るために彼と共に座った」
"but, oh Govinda, you did not recognise the sleeping man"
「しかし、ああゴヴィンダよ、あなたは眠っている男に気づかなかった」
Govinda was astonished, as if he had been the object of a magic spell
ゴヴィンダはまるで魔法にかかったかのように驚いた。
the monk looked into the ferryman's eyes
僧侶は渡し守の目を見つめた
"Are you Siddhartha?" he asked with a timid voice
「あなたはシッダールタですか？」彼は臆病な声で尋ねた。
"I wouldn't have recognised you this time either!"
「今回も気づかなかったよ！」
"from my heart, I'm greeting you, Siddhartha"
「心から、シッダールタに挨拶します」
"from my heart, I'm happy to see you once again!"
「またお会いできて心から嬉しいです！」
"You've changed a lot, my friend"
「君は大きく変わったね、友よ」

"and you've now become a ferryman?"
「そしてあなたは今では渡し守になったのですか？」

In a friendly manner, Siddhartha laughed
シッダールタは友好的に笑った

"yes, I am a ferryman"
「はい、私は渡し守です」

"Many people, Govinda, have to change a lot"
「ゴヴィンダ、多くの人々が大きく変わらなければならない」

"they have to wear many robes"
「彼らはたくさんのローブを着なければならない」

"I am one of those who had to change a lot"
「私は大きく変わらなければならなかった人の一人です」

"Be welcome, Govinda, and spend the night in my hut"
「ゴヴィンダさん、ようこそ。私の小屋で一夜を過ごしてください」

Govinda stayed the night in the hut
ゴヴィンダは小屋で一夜を過ごした

he slept on the bed which used to be Vasudeva's bed
彼はヴァスデーヴァのベッドだったベッドで寝た

he posed many questions to the friend of his youth
彼は若い頃の友人に多くの質問を投げかけた

Siddhartha had to tell him many things from his life
シッダールタは彼の人生から多くのことを彼に伝えなければならなかった

then the next morning came
そして翌朝が来た

the time had come to start the day's journey
今日の旅を始める時間が来た

without hesitation, Govinda asked one more question
ゴヴィンダはためらうことなくもう一つの質問をした

"Before I continue on my path, Siddhartha, permit me to ask one more question"

「私が道を進む前に、シッダールタ、もう一つ質問させてください」
"Do you have a teaching that guides you?"
「あなたを導く教えはありますか？」
"Do you have a faith or a knowledge you follow"
「あなたは信仰を持っていますか、それとも従うべき知識を持っていますか」
"is there a knowledge which helps you to live and do right?"
「あなたが生き、正しいことをするのに役立つ知識はありますか？」
"You know well, my dear, I have always been distrustful of teachers"
「よくご存じのとおり、私は昔から教師を信用していませんでした」
"as a young man I already started to doubt teachers"
「私は若い頃から教師を疑い始めていました」
"when we lived with the penitents in the forest, I distrusted their teachings"
「私たちが森の中で悔悛者たちと暮らしていたとき、私は彼らの教えを信用していませんでした」
"and I turned my back to them"
「そして私は彼らに背を向けた」
"I have remained distrustful of teachers"
「私は教師に対して不信感を抱いています」
"Nevertheless, I have had many teachers since then"
「それにもかかわらず、それ以来、私は多くの先生に恵まれました」
"A beautiful courtesan has been my teacher for a long time"
「美しい遊女が長い間私の先生でした」
"a rich merchant was my teacher"
「裕福な商人が私の先生でした」
"and some gamblers with dice taught me"
「そしてサイコロを持ったギャンブラーたちが私に教えてくれた」
"Once, even a follower of Buddha has been my teacher"

「かつては仏陀の信者も私の師であった」

"he was travelling on foot, pilgering"
「彼は徒歩で巡礼をしながら旅をしていた」

"and he sat with me when I had fallen asleep in the forest"
「そして私が森の中で眠りに落ちたとき、彼は私と一緒に座っていました」

"I've also learned from him, for which I'm very grateful"
「私も彼から多くのことを学びました。とても感謝しています」

"But most of all, I have learned from this river"
「しかし何よりも、私はこの川から学んだのです」

"and I have learned most from my predecessor, the ferryman Vasudeva"
「そして私は、私の前任者である渡し守のヴァスデーヴァから多くのことを学びました」

"He was a very simple person, Vasudeva, he was no thinker"
「ヴァスデーヴァはとても単純な人でした。彼は思想家ではありませんでした。」

"but he knew what is necessary just as well as Gotama"
「しかし、彼はゴータマと同じくらい何が必要なのかを知っていた」

"he was a perfect man, a saint"
「彼は完璧な人間であり、聖人だった」

"Siddhartha still loves to mock people, it seems to me"
「シッダールタは今でも人を嘲笑するのが好きなようだ」

"I believe in you and I know that you haven't followed a teacher"
「私はあなたを信じているし、あなたが先生の教えに従っていないことも知っている」

"But haven't you found something by yourself?"
「でも、自分で何か見つけたんじゃないの?」

"though you've found no teachings, you still found certain thoughts"

「あなたは教えを見つけられなかったが、それでも特定の考えを見つけた」
"certain insights, which are your own"
「あなた自身の特定の洞察」
"insights which help you to live"
「生きるのに役立つ洞察力」
"Haven't you found something like this?"
「こんなの見つけなかったっけ？」
"If you would like to tell me, you would delight my heart"
「もし私に話したいのなら、私の心を喜ばせるでしょう」
"you are right, I have had thoughts and gained many insights"
「おっしゃる通り、私も考え、多くの洞察を得ました」
"Sometimes I have felt knowledge in me for an hour"
「時には1時間ほど知識を感じたことがある」
"at other times I have felt knowledge in me for an entire day"
「時には一日中知識を感じ続けた」
"the same knowledge one feels when one feels life in one's heart"
「心の中に生命を感じるときに感じるのと同じ知識」
"There have been many thoughts"
「いろいろな思いがありました」
"but it would be hard for me to convey these thoughts to you"
「しかし、この考えをあなたに伝えるのは難しいでしょう」
"my dear Govinda, this is one of my thoughts which I have found"
「親愛なるゴヴィンダ、これは私が見つけた考えの一つです」
"wisdom cannot be passed on"
「知恵は受け継がれない」
"Wisdom which a wise man tries to pass on always sounds like foolishness"

「賢者が伝えようとする知恵は、いつも愚かなものに聞こえる」

"Are you kidding?" asked Govinda
「冗談でしょ？」とゴヴィンダは尋ねた。

"I'm not kidding, I'm telling you what I have found"
「冗談じゃない、私が見つけたことを話しているだけ」

"Knowledge can be conveyed, but wisdom can't"
「知識は伝えられるが、知恵は伝えられない」

"wisdom can be found, it can be lived"
「知恵は見つけられ、生きることができる」

"it is possible to be carried by wisdom"
「知恵によって運ばれることは可能だ」

"miracles can be performed with wisdom"
「知恵があれば奇跡は起こせる」

"but wisdom cannot be expressed in words or taught"
「しかし知恵は言葉で表現したり教えたりすることはできない」

"This was what I sometimes suspected, even as a young man"
「若い頃でさえ、私は時々そう疑っていました」

"this is what has driven me away from the teachers"
「これが私を教師から遠ざけた原因です」

"I have found a thought which you'll regard as foolishness"
「私はあなたが愚かだと思うような考えを見つけました」

"but this thought has been my best"
「しかし、この考えは私にとって最善のものでした」

"The opposite of every truth is just as true!"
「すべての真実の反対も同様に真実である！」

"any truth can only be expressed when it is one-sided"
「いかなる真実も、一方的な場合にのみ表現できる」

"only one sided things can be put into words"
「言葉で表現できるのは一方的なことだけだ」

"Everything which can be thought is one-sided"
「考えられるものはすべて一方的である」

"it's all one-sided, so it's just one half"
「すべて一方的だから、半分だけだよ」
"it all lacks completeness, roundness, and oneness"
「すべてに完全性、円満性、一体性が欠けている」
"the exalted Gotama spoke in his teachings of the world"
「ゴータマは世界について教えを説いた」
"but he had to divide the world into Sansara and Nirvana"
「しかし彼は世界をサンサーラと涅槃に分けなければならなかった」
"he had divided the world into deception and truth"
「彼は世界を偽りと真実に分けた」
"he had divided the world into suffering and salvation"
「彼は世界を苦しみと救済に分けた」
"the world cannot be explained any other way"
「世界は他の方法では説明できない」
"there is no other way to explain it, for those who want to teach"
「教えたい人にとって、これ以外に説明する方法はありません」
"But the world itself is never one-sided"
「しかし、世界自体は決して一方的ではない」
"the world exists around us and inside of us"
「世界は私たちの周りと私たちの中に存在します」
"A person or an act is never entirely Sansara or entirely Nirvana"
「人や行為は、決して完全にサンサーラや涅槃になることはない」
"a person is never entirely holy or entirely sinful"
「人は完全に聖なることも、完全に罪深いことも決してない」
"It seems like the world can be divided into these opposites"
「世界はこれらの相反するものに分けられるようだ」
"but that's because we are subject to deception"
「しかしそれは私たちが騙されやすいからだ」
"it's as if the deception was something real"

「まるでその欺瞞が現実のものであったかのようだ」
"Time is not real, Govinda"
「時間は現実ではない、ゴヴィンダ」
"I have experienced this often and often again"
「私は何度も何度もこれを経験しました」
"when time is not real, the gap between the world and the eternity is also a deception"
「時間が現実でなければ、世界と永遠の間の隔たりもまた欺瞞である」
"the gap between suffering and blissfulness is not real"
「苦しみと至福のギャップは現実ではない」
"there is no gap between evil and good"
「善と悪の間に隔たりはない」
"all of these gaps are deceptions"
「これらのギャップはすべて欺瞞である」
"but these gaps appear to us nonetheless"
「しかし、それでもなお、こうしたギャップは私たちには見えるのです」
"How come?" asked Govinda timidly
「どうして？」ゴヴィンダは恐る恐る尋ねた。
"Listen well, my dear," answered Siddhartha
「よく聞きなさい、愛しい人よ」とシッダールタは答えた。
"The sinner, which I am and which you are, is a sinner"
「私もあなたも罪人です、罪人です」
"but in times to come the sinner will be Brahma again"
「しかし、将来、罪人は再びブラフマーとなるだろう」
"he will reach the Nirvana and be Buddha"
「彼は涅槃に達して仏陀となるだろう」
"the times to come are a deception"
「これからの時代は欺瞞である」
"the times to come are only a parable!"
「これからの時代は単なる寓話に過ぎない！」
"The sinner is not on his way to become a Buddha"
「罪人は仏陀になる道を歩んでいない」

"he is not in the process of developing"
「彼は成長過程にない」

"our capacity for thinking does not know how else to picture these things"
「私たちの思考力は、これらのことを他にどう描くべきかを知らない」

"No, within the sinner there already is the future Buddha"
「いいえ、罪人の中にすでに未来の仏陀がいます」

"his future is already all there"
「彼の将来はすでに決まっている」

"you have to worship the Buddha in the sinner"
「罪人の中にある仏を崇拝しなければならない」

"you have to worship the Buddha hidden in everyone"
「すべての人の中に隠れている仏を崇拝しなければなりません」

"the hidden Buddha which is coming into being the possible"
「可能性として現れつつある隠された仏」

"The world, my friend Govinda, is not imperfect"
「私の友人ゴヴィンダよ、世界は不完全ではない」

"the world is on no slow path towards perfection"
「世界は完璧に向かってゆっくりと進んでいない」

"no, the world is perfect in every moment"
「いいえ、世界はどの瞬間も完璧です」

"all sin already carries the divine forgiveness in itself"
「すべての罪は、すでに神の赦しを内包している」

"all small children already have the old person in themselves"
「すべての小さな子供たちはすでに自分の中に老人の姿を持っている」

"all infants already have death in them"
「すべての幼児はすでに死を宿している」

"all dying people have the eternal life"
「すべての死にゆく人々は永遠の命を持っている」

"we can't see how far another one has already progressed on his path"

「他の人がすでに自分の道をどれだけ進んでいるかは分からない」
"in the robber and dice-gambler, the Buddha is waiting"
「強盗とサイコロ賭博師の中に仏陀が待っている」
"in the Brahman, the robber is waiting"
「ブラフマンでは強盗が待ち構えている」
"in deep meditation, there is the possibility to put time out of existence"
「深い瞑想では、時間を存在から消し去る可能性がある」
"there is the possibility to see all life simultaneously"
「すべての生命を同時に見る可能性がある」
"it is possible to see all life which was, is, and will be"
「過去、現在、そして未来のあらゆる生命を見ることは可能である」
"and there everything is good, perfect, and Brahman"
「そしてそこにはすべてが善であり、完璧であり、ブラフマンである」
"Therefore, I see whatever exists as good"
「だから私は存在するものはすべて良いものだと見なす」
"death is to me like life"
「私にとって死は生と同じ」
"to me sin is like holiness"
「私にとって罪は神聖さのようなものだ」
"wisdom can be like foolishness"
「知恵は愚かさに似ている」
"everything has to be as it is"
「すべてはそのままでなければならない」
"everything only requires my consent and willingness"
「すべては私の同意と意志だけが必要です」
"all that my view requires is my loving agreement to be good for me"
「私の見解に必要なのは、私にとって良いことであるという私の愛情ある同意だけです」

"my view has to do nothing but work for my benefit"
「私の意見は私の利益のために働くだけでいい」
"and then my perception is unable to ever harm me"
「そして私の知覚は私を傷つけることはできない」
"I have experienced that I needed sin very much"
「私は罪を非常に必要としていることを経験しました」
"I have experienced this in my body and in my soul"
「私はこれを体と心で体験しました」
"I needed lust, the desire for possessions, and vanity"
「私には欲望、所有欲、虚栄心が必要だった」
"and I needed the most shameful despair"
「そして私は最も恥ずべき絶望を必要とした」
"in order to learn how to give up all resistance"
「すべての抵抗を放棄する方法を学ぶために」
"in order to learn how to love the world"
「世界を愛する方法を学ぶために」
"in order to stop comparing things to some world I wished for"
「私が望んでいた世界と物事を比較するのをやめるために」
"I imagined some kind of perfection I had made up"
「私は自分が作り上げたある種の完璧さを想像した」
"but I have learned to leave the world as it is"
「しかし私は世界をあるがままにしておくことを学んだ」
"I have learned to love the world as it is"
「私は世界をあるがままに愛することを学んだ」
"and I learned to enjoy being a part of it"
「そして私はその一部であることを楽しむことを学んだ」
"These, oh Govinda, are some of the thoughts which have come into my mind"
「ああ、ゴヴィンダよ、これらは私の心に浮かんだ考えの一部です」

Siddhartha bent down and picked up a stone from the ground
シッダールタはかがんで地面から石を拾い上げた
he weighed the stone in his hand
彼は石を手に重さを量った
"This here," he said playing with the rock, "is a stone"
「これは」と彼は石で遊びながら言った、「石だよ」
"this stone will, after a certain time, perhaps turn into soil"
「この石は、ある時間が経てば、土に変わるかもしれない」
"it will turn from soil into a plant or animal or human being"
「土から植物や動物や人間に変わる」
"In the past, I would have said this stone is just a stone"
「昔なら、この石はただの石だと言っていただろう」
"I might have said it is worthless"
「価値がないと言ったかもしれない」
"I would have told you this stone belongs to the world of the Maya"
「この石はマヤの世界のものだとあなたに伝えたかった」
"but I wouldn't have seen that it has importance"
「しかし、それが重要であるとは思わなかっただろう」
"it might be able to become a spirit in the cycle of transformations"
「変化の輪の中で精霊になれるかもしれない」
"therefore I also grant it importance"
「それゆえ、私もそれを重要視します」
"Thus, I would perhaps have thought in the past"
「だから、私はおそらく過去にそう思っていただろう」
"But today I think differently about the stone"
「しかし、今日私はその石について違った考えを持っています」
"this stone is a stone, and it is also animal, god, and Buddha"
「この石は石であり、動物であり、神であり、仏でもある」

"I do not venerate and love it because it could turn into this or that"
「私はそれがこうなるか、ああなるか分からないから崇拝したり愛したりするのではない」
"I love it because it is those things"
「それが好きだから」
"this stone is already everything"
「この石はすでにすべてだ」
"it appears to me now and today as a stone"
「それは今も今日も私には石のように見える」
"that is why I love this"
「だから私はこれが好きなんです」
"that is why I see worth and purpose in each of its veins and cavities"
「だからこそ私は、その静脈や空洞のそれぞれに価値と目的を見出しているのです」
"I see value in its yellow, gray, and hardness"
「私はその黄色、灰色、そして硬さに価値を見出しています」
"I appreciated the sound it makes when I knock at it"
「ノックしたときの音が気に入りました」
"I love the dryness or wetness of its surface"
「表面の乾燥や湿り具合が気に入っています」
"There are stones which feel like oil or soap"
「油や石鹸のような感触の石もあります」
"and other stones feel like leaves or sand"
「そして他の石は葉や砂のように感じます」
"and every stone is special and prays the Om in its own way"
「そして、すべての石は特別であり、独自の方法でオームを祈っています。」
"each stone is Brahman"
「それぞれの石はブラフマンである」
"but simultaneously, and just as much, it is a stone"
「しかし同時に、そしてそれと同じくらい、それは石なのです」

"it is a stone regardless of whether it's oily or juicy"
「油っぽくてもジューシーでも、それは石です」
"and this why I like and regard this stone"
「そしてこれが私がこの石を好み、尊重する理由です」
"it is wonderful and worthy of worship"
「それは素晴らしく、崇拝に値する」
"But let me speak no more of this"
「しかし、これ以上は話さないでおこう」
"words are not good for transmitting the secret meaning"
「言葉は秘密の意味を伝えるのに適していない」
"everything always becomes a bit different, as soon as it is put into words"
「言葉にすると、すべてはいつも少し違ってくる」
"everything gets distorted a little by words"
「言葉によってすべてが少し歪んでしまう」
"and then the explanation becomes a bit silly"
「すると説明がちょっとおかしくなる」
"yes, and this is also very good, and I like it a lot"
「はい、これもとてもいいです、とても気に入っています」
"I also very much agree with this"
「私もこれに大いに同意します」
"one man's treasure and wisdom always sounds like foolishness to another person"
「ある人の宝物や知恵は、他の人にとっては愚かなものに聞こえる」
Govinda listened silently to what Siddhartha was saying
ゴーヴィンダはシッダールタの言うことを黙って聞いていた
there was a pause and Govinda hesitantly asked a question
沈黙が続き、ゴヴィンダはためらいながら質問した。
"Why have you told me this about the stone?"
「なぜ石について私にこれを話したのですか?」
"I did it without any specific intention"
「特に意図せずにやった」

"perhaps what I meant was, that I love this stone and the river"
「おそらく私が言いたかったのは、この石と川を愛しているということだった」
"and I love all these things we are looking at"
「そして、私たちが見ているこれらすべてのものが大好きです」
"and we can learn from all these things"
「そして私たちはこれらすべてから学ぶことができます」
"I can love a stone, Govinda"
「私は石を愛することができるよ、ゴヴィンダ」
"and I can also love a tree or a piece of bark"
「そして私は木や樹皮を愛することもできる」
"These are things, and things can be loved"
「これらは物であり、物は愛することができる」
"but I cannot love words"
「でも私は言葉を愛することはできない」
"therefore, teachings are no good for me"
「だから、教えは私にとって役に立たない」
"teachings have no hardness, softness, colours, edges, smell, or taste"
「教えには硬さも柔らかさも色も角も匂いも味もない」
"teachings have nothing but words"
「教えは言葉だけである」
"perhaps it is words which keep you from finding peace"
「おそらく言葉があなたを平穏から遠ざけているのでしょう」
"because salvation and virtue are mere words"
「救いと美徳は単なる言葉に過ぎないから」
"Sansara and Nirvana are also just mere words, Govinda"
「サンサーラと涅槃もまた単なる言葉に過ぎません、ゴーヴィンダ」
"there is no thing which would be Nirvana"
「涅槃となるものは存在しない」

"therefore Nirvana is just the word"
「それゆえ涅槃とはまさにその言葉である」
Govinda objected, "Nirvana is not just a word, my friend"
ゴヴィンダは反論した。「涅槃は単なる言葉ではありません、友よ」
"Nirvana is a word, but also it is a thought"
「涅槃は言葉であるが、思考でもある」
Siddhartha continued, "it might be a thought"
シッダールタは続けた。「それは考えかもしれない」
"I must confess, I don't differentiate much between thoughts and words"
「告白しますが、私は思考と言葉をあまり区別していません」
"to be honest, I also have no high opinion of thoughts"
「正直に言うと、私も思考を高く評価していません」
"I have a better opinion of things than thoughts"
「私は物事について考えるよりも良い意見を持っています」
"Here on this ferry-boat, for instance, a man has been my predecessor"
「例えば、この渡し船では、ある男が私の前任者でした」
"he was also one of my teachers"
「彼は私の先生の一人でもありました」
"a holy man, who has for many years simply believed in the river"
「長年川の存在をただ信じてきた聖人」
"and he believed in nothing else"
「そして彼は他に何も信じなかった」
"He had noticed that the river spoke to him"
「彼は川が自分に語りかけていることに気づいた」
"he learned from the river"
「彼は川から学んだ」
"the river educated and taught him"
「川が彼を教育し、教えた」

"the river seemed to be a god to him"
「彼にとって川は神であるように思えた」
"for many years he did not know that everything was as divine as the river"
「彼は長年、すべてが川のように神聖であることを知らなかった」
"the wind, every cloud, every bird, every beetle"
「風、あらゆる雲、あらゆる鳥、あらゆる甲虫」
"they can teach just as much as the river"
「彼らは川と同じくらい多くのことを教えてくれる」
"But when this holy man went into the forests, he knew everything"
「しかし、この聖人が森に入ったとき、彼はすべてを知ったのです」
"he knew more than you and me, without teachers or books"
「彼は教師や本なしでもあなたや私よりも多くのことを知っていた」
"he knew more than us only because he had believed in the river"
「彼が私たちよりも多くのことを知っていたのは、彼が川を信じていたからに他なりません」

Govinda still had doubts and questions
ゴヴィンダはまだ疑問と質問を抱いていた
"But is that what you call things actually something real?"
「しかし、あなたが物と呼んでいるものは、実際に何か現実のものなのでしょうか？」
"do these things have existence?"
「これらのものは存在するのか？」
"Isn't it just a deception of the Maya"
「それはマヤの欺瞞ではないのか」
"aren't all these things an image and illusion?"
「これらすべてはイメージであり幻想ではないのか？」
"Your stone, your tree, your river"
「あなたの石、あなたの木、あなたの川」

"are they actually a reality?"
「それらは本当に現実なのか？」

"This too," spoke Siddhartha, "I do not care very much about"
「これも」シッダールタは言った、「私はあまり気にしていません」

"Let the things be illusions or not"
「物事が幻想であるかどうかは関係ない」

"after all, I would then also be an illusion"
「結局、私も幻想になってしまう」

"and if these things are illusions then they are like me"
「そしてもしこれらが幻想であるならば、それらは私と同じだ」

"This is what makes them so dear and worthy of veneration for me"
「これが、私にとって彼らをとても大切で、崇拝に値するものにしているのです」

"these things are like me and that is how I can love them"
「これらは私のようなものであり、だからこそ私はこれらを愛することができるのです」

"this is a teaching you will laugh about"
「これはあなたが笑ってしまう教えです」

"love, oh Govinda, seems to me to be the most important thing of all"
「ああ、ゴヴィンダよ、愛こそが私にとって何よりも大切なものなのです」

"to thoroughly understand the world may be what great thinkers do"
「世界を徹底的に理解することが偉大な思想家が行うことかもしれない」

"they explain the world and despise it"
「彼らは世界を説明して軽蔑する」

"But I'm only interested in being able to love the world"
「でも、私が興味があるのは世界を愛せるかどうかだけ」

"I am not interested in despising the world"
「私は世界を軽蔑することに興味はありません」
"I don't want to hate the world"
「世界を憎みたくない」
"and I don't want the world to hate me"
「そして私は世界に嫌われたくない」
"I want to be able to look upon the world and myself with love"
「世界と自分自身を愛の目で見ることができるようになりたい」
"I want to look upon all beings with admiration"
「私はすべての生き物を尊敬の念を持って見たい」
"I want to have a great respect for everything"
「私はすべてのものに対して大きな敬意を持ちたい」
"This I understand," spoke Govinda
「それは分かりました」とゴヴィンダは言った。
"But this very thing was discovered by the exalted one to be a deception"
「しかし、このことは高貴な者によって欺瞞であると発見された」
"He commands benevolence, clemency, sympathy, tolerance"
「彼は慈悲、寛大さ、同情、寛容さを授けます」
"but he does not command love"
「しかし彼は愛を命じない」
"he forbade us to tie our heart in love to earthly things"
「彼は、私たちが地上のものに愛の心を縛り付けることを禁じた」
"I know it, Govinda," said Siddhartha, and his smile shone golden
「わかっています、ゴーヴィンダ」シッダールタは言った。彼の笑顔は金色に輝いた。
"And behold, with this we are right in the thicket of opinions"
「そして見よ、我々はまさに意見の藪の中にいるのだ」
"now we are in the dispute about words"

「今、私たちは言葉について論争している」
"For I cannot deny, my words of love are a contradiction"
「私の愛の言葉は矛盾だと否定できない」
"they seem to be in contradiction with Gotama's words"
「それらはゴータマの言葉と矛盾しているようだ」
"For this very reason, I distrust words so much"
「だからこそ、私は言葉をとても信用しないのです」
"because I know this contradiction is a deception"
「この矛盾は欺瞞だと知っているから」
"I know that I am in agreement with Gotama"
「私はゴータマに同意していることを知っている」
"How could he not know love when he has discovered all elements of human existence"
「人間存在のあらゆる要素を発見したのに、どうして愛を知らないことができようか」
"he has discovered their transitoriness and their meaninglessness"
「彼はそれらのはかなさと無意味さを発見した」
"and yet he loved people very much"
「それでも彼は人々をとても愛していた」
"he used a long, laborious life only to help and teach them!"
「彼は長くて骨の折れる人生を、ただ彼らを助け、教えるために費やしたのです!」
"Even with your great teacher, I prefer things over the words"
「あなたの偉大な先生でさえ、私は言葉よりも物事を好みます」
"I place more importance on his acts and life than on his speeches"
「私は彼の演説よりも彼の行為と人生を重視します」
"I value the gestures of his hand more than his opinions"
「私は彼の意見よりも彼の手振りを重視する」
"for me there was nothing in his speech and thoughts"
「私にとって彼の言葉や考えには何もなかった」
"I see his greatness only in his actions and in his life"

「私は彼の偉大さを彼の行動と人生にのみ見ています」

For a long time, the two old men said nothing
長い間、二人の老人は何も言わなかった
Then Govinda spoke, while bowing for a farewell
そしてゴヴィンダは別れの挨拶をしながら話した。
"I thank you, Siddhartha, for telling me some of your thoughts"
「シッダールタ、あなたの考えを聞かせてくださってありがとうございます」
"These thoughts are partially strange to me"
「これらの考えは私にとって部分的に奇妙です」
"not all of these thoughts have been instantly understandable to me"
「これらの考えのすべてがすぐに理解できたわけではない」
"This being as it may, I thank you"
「そうは言っても、ありがとう」
"and I wish you to have calm days"
「穏やかな日々を過ごせますように」
But secretly he thought something else to himself
しかし、彼は心の中で別のことを考えていた
"This Siddhartha is a bizarre person"
「このシッダールタは奇妙な人だ」
"he expresses bizarre thoughts"
「彼は奇妙な考えを表明する」
"his teachings sound foolish"
「彼の教えは愚かに聞こえる」
"the exalted one's pure teachings sound very different"
「高貴なる者の純粋な教えは非常に異なって聞こえる」
"those teachings are clearer, purer, more comprehensible"
「それらの教えはより明確で、より純粋で、より理解しやすい」
"there is nothing strange, foolish, or silly in those teachings"

「その教えには奇妙なこと、愚かなこと、馬鹿げたことは何もない」

"But Siddhartha's hands seemed different from his thoughts"
「しかし、シッダールタの手は彼の考えとは違っていたようだ」

"his feet, his eyes, his forehead, his breath"
「彼の足、彼の目、彼の額、彼の息」

"his smile, his greeting, his walk"
「彼の笑顔、彼の挨拶、彼の歩き方」

"I haven't met another man like him since Gotama became one with the Nirvana"
「ゴータマが涅槃と一体化して以来、私は彼のような人に会ったことがない」

"since then I haven't felt the presence of a holy man"
「それ以来、私は聖人の存在を感じていない」

"I have only found Siddhartha, who is like this"
「私はこのようなシッダールタしか見つけられなかった」

"his teachings may be strange and his words may sound foolish"
「彼の教えは奇妙かもしれないし、彼の言葉は愚かに聞こえるかもしれない」

"but purity shines out of his gaze and hand"
「しかし、彼の視線と手からは純粋さが輝いている」

"his skin and his hair radiates purity"
「彼の肌と髪は純粋さを放っている」

"purity shines out of every part of him"
「彼のあらゆる部分から純粋さが輝いている」

"a calmness, cheerfulness, mildness and holiness shines from him"
「彼からは穏やかさ、明るさ、温和さ、そして神聖さが輝いている」

"something which I have seen in no other person"
「他の誰にも見たことのない何か」

"I have not seen it since the final death of our exalted teacher"
「私は、私たちの崇高な師が亡くなって以来、それを見たことはありません」
While Govinda thought like this, there was a conflict in his heart
ゴヴィンダはこのように考えていたが、心の中では葛藤があった。
he once again bowed to Siddhartha
彼は再びシッダールタに頭を下げた
he felt he was drawn forward by love
彼は愛に引き寄せられていると感じた
he bowed deeply to him who was calmly sitting
彼は静かに座っている彼に深くお辞儀をした
"Siddhartha," he spoke, "we have become old men"
「シッダールタ」と彼は言った。「我々は老人になったのだ」
"It is unlikely for one of us to see the other again in this incarnation"
「私たちのどちらかが、この生まれ変わりで再び相手に会うことはまずないでしょう」
"I see, beloved, that you have found peace"
「愛しい人よ、あなたが平和を見つけたのがわかります」
"I confess that I haven't found it"
「私は見つけられなかったと告白します」
"Tell me, oh honourable one, one more word"
「ああ、尊敬する人よ、もう一つだけ教えてください」
"give me something on my way which I can grasp"
「私が掴めるものを途中で与えてください」
"give me something which I can understand!"
「私に理解できるものをください!」
"give me something I can take with me on my path"
「私の道に持っていけるものをください」
"my path is often hard and dark, Siddhartha"

「私の道はしばしば困難で暗いのです、シッダールタ」
Siddhartha said nothing and looked at him
シッダールタは何も言わず彼を見つめた
he looked at him with his ever unchanged, quiet smile
彼はいつもと変わらない静かな笑顔で彼を見た
Govinda stared at his face with fear
ゴヴィンダは恐怖で彼の顔を見つめた
there was yearning and suffering in his eyes
彼の目には憧れと苦しみがあった
the eternal search was visible in his look
彼の表情には永遠の探求が表れていた
you could see his eternal inability to find
彼が永遠に見つけられないのがわかるだろう
Siddhartha saw it and smiled
シッダールタはそれを見て微笑んだ
"Bend down to me!" he whispered quietly in Govinda's ear
「私に屈んでください！」彼はゴヴィンダの耳元で静かに囁いた。
"Like this, and come even closer!"
「こうやって、もっと近づいて！」
"Kiss my forehead, Govinda!"
「私の額にキスして、ゴヴィンダ！」
Govinda was astonished, but drawn on by great love and expectation
ゴヴィンダは驚いたが、大きな愛と期待に引き寄せられた。
he obeyed his words and bent down closely to him
彼は彼の言葉に従い、彼に近づきました
and he touched his forehead with his lips
そして彼は唇で額に触れた
when he did this, something miraculous happened to him
彼がこれをしたとき、奇跡が起こった。
his thoughts were still dwelling on Siddhartha's wondrous words

彼の考えは依然としてシッダールタの素晴らしい言葉に留まっていた
he was still reluctantly struggling to think away time
彼はまだしぶしぶ時間を忘れようとしていた
he was still trying to imagine Nirvana and Sansara as one
彼はまだ涅槃とサンサーラを一つのものとして想像しようとしていた
there was still a certain contempt for the words of his friend
友人の言葉に対してはまだ軽蔑の念が残っていた
those words were still fighting in him
その言葉は彼の中でまだ戦っていた
those words were still fighting against an immense love and veneration
その言葉は、まだ計り知れない愛と尊敬と戦っていた
and during all these thoughts, something else happened to him
そして、こうした考えの途中で、彼に何か別のことが起こった
He no longer saw the face of his friend Siddhartha
彼はもう友人シッダールタの顔を見ることはなかった
instead of Siddhartha's face, he saw other faces
シッダールタの顔の代わりに、彼は他の顔を見た
he saw a long sequence of faces
彼は長い一連の顔を見た
he saw a flowing river of faces
彼は顔の川の流れを見た
hundreds and thousands of faces, which all came and disappeared
何百何千もの顔が現れては消えていった
and yet they all seemed to be there simultaneously
しかし、彼らは皆同時にそこにいるようだった
they constantly changed and renewed themselves
彼らは常に変化し、新しくなった
they were themselves and they were still all Siddhartha's face

彼らは彼ら自身であり、彼らはまだシッダールタの顔でした

he saw the face of a fish with an infinitely painfully opened mouth
彼は、限りなく痛々しい口を開けた魚の顔を見た。

the face of a dying fish, with fading eyes
死にゆく魚の顔、消えゆく目

he saw the face of a new-born child, red and full of wrinkles
彼は赤くしわだらけの生まれたばかりの赤ちゃんの顔を見た

it was distorted from crying
泣いて歪んでしまった

he saw the face of a murderer
彼は殺人者の顔を見た

he saw him plunging a knife into the body of another person
彼は彼が他の人の体にナイフを突き刺すのを見た

he saw, in the same moment, this criminal in bondage
彼は同じ瞬間に、この犯罪者が拘束されているのを見た

he saw him kneeling before a crowd
彼は群衆の前でひざまずいている彼を見た

and he saw his head being chopped off by the executioner
そして彼は死刑執行人によって首が切り落とされるのを見た

he saw the bodies of men and women
彼は男性と女性の死体を見た

they were naked in positions and cramps of frenzied love
彼らは熱狂的な愛の姿勢と痙攣の中で裸だった

he saw corpses stretched out, motionless, cold, void
彼は動かず、冷たく、虚ろな死体を見た

he saw the heads of animals
彼は動物の頭を見た

heads of boars, of crocodiles, and of elephants
イノシシ、ワニ、象の頭

he saw the heads of bulls and of birds

彼は雄牛と鳥の頭を見た
he saw gods; Krishna and Agni
彼は神々、クリシュナとアグニを見た
he saw all of these figures and faces in a thousand relationships with one another
彼はこれらすべての人物と顔を、互いに千の関係の中で見ていた
each figure was helping the other
それぞれの人物がお互いを助け合っていた
each figure was loving their relationship
それぞれの人物は彼らの関係を愛していた
each figure was hating their relationship, destroying it
それぞれの人物は彼らの関係を憎み、それを破壊していた
and each figure was giving re-birth to their relationship
そしてそれぞれの人物が彼らの関係に新たな生命を与えていた
each figure was a will to die
それぞれの人物は死への意志を持っていた
they were passionately painful confessions of transitoriness
それは、はかないものの情熱的で痛ましい告白だった
and yet none of them died, each one only transformed
しかし、彼らは誰も死なず、それぞれが変身しただけだった
they were always reborn and received more and more new faces
彼らは常に生まれ変わり、ますます新しい顔を獲得した
no time passed between the one face and the other
一つの顔から他の顔までの間には時間が経っていない
all of these figures and faces rested
これらの人物や顔はすべて休息していた
they flowed and generated themselves
それらは流れ、自ら生成した
they floated along and merged with each other
彼らは漂い合い、互いに融合した

and they were all constantly covered by something thin
そしてそれらはすべて常に何か薄いもので覆われていた
they had no individuality of their own
彼らには独自の個性がなかった
but yet they were existing
しかし、彼らは存在していた
they were like a thin glass or ice
薄いガラスや氷のようでした
they were like a transparent skin
透明な皮膚のようでした
they were like a shell or mould or mask of water
彼らは水の殻や型や仮面のようだった
and this mask was smiling
そしてこのマスクは笑っていた
and this mask was Siddhartha's smiling face
この仮面はシッダールタの笑顔でした
the mask which Govinda was touching with his lips
ゴヴィンダが唇で触れていた仮面
And, Govinda saw it like this
そしてゴヴィンダはこう考えました
the smile of the mask
マスクの笑顔
the smile of oneness above the flowing forms
流れる形の上にある一体感の微笑み
the smile of simultaneousness above the thousand births and deaths
千の誕生と死を超えた同時性の微笑み
the smile of Siddhartha's was precisely the same
シッダールタの笑顔はまさに同じだった
Siddhartha's smile was the same as the quiet smile of Gotama, the Buddha
シッダールタの微笑みは、ゴータマ仏陀の静かな微笑みと同じだった。
it was delicate and impenetrable smile
それは繊細で不可解な笑顔だった
perhaps it was benevolent and mocking, and wise

それは慈悲深く、嘲笑的で、賢明なものだったかもしれない

the thousand-fold smile of Gotama, the Buddha
ゴータマ仏陀の千倍の微笑み

as he had seen it himself with great respect a hundred times
彼自身がそれを何百回も尊敬の念を持って見てきたように

Like this, Govinda knew, the perfected ones are smiling
ゴヴィンダは、このように、完成された者たちは微笑んでいることを知っていた

he did not know anymore whether time existed
彼はもはや時間が存在するのかどうかわからなかった

he did not know whether the vision had lasted a second or a hundred years
彼はその幻視が一秒続いたのか百年続いたのか知らなかった

he did not know whether a Siddhartha or a Gotama existed
彼はシッダールタやゴータマが存在するかどうか知らなかった

he did not know if a me or a you existed
彼は私やあなたが存在するかどうか知らなかった

he felt in his as if he had been wounded by a divine arrow
彼はまるで神の矢に刺されたかのように感じた

the arrow pierced his innermost self
矢は彼の心の奥底を貫いた

the injury of the divine arrow tasted sweet
神の矢の傷は甘美な味だった

Govinda was enchanted and dissolved in his innermost self
ゴヴィンダは魅了され、心の奥底に溶け込んでいった

he stood still for a little while
彼はしばらくじっと立っていた

he bent over Siddhartha's quiet face, which he had just kissed
彼はシッダールタの静かな顔に顔を近づけた。彼はその顔にキスをしたばかりだった。

the face in which he had just seen the scene of all manifestations
彼が今見たすべての現象の光景の顔
the face of all transformations and all existence
すべての変化とすべての存在の顔
the face he was looking at was unchanged
彼が見ていた顔は変わっていなかった
under its surface, the depth of the thousand folds had closed up again
その表面の下では、千のひだの深さが再び閉じられていた
he smiled silently, quietly, and softly
彼は静かに、静かに、そして優しく微笑んだ
perhaps he smiled very benevolently and mockingly
おそらく彼は慈悲深く、そして嘲笑的に微笑んだのだろう
precisely this was how the exalted one smiled
まさにこの高貴な人が微笑んだのです
Deeply, Govinda bowed to Siddhartha
ゴーヴィンダはシッダールタに深く頭を下げた
tears he knew nothing of ran down his old face
何も知らなかった涙が彼の老いた顔を伝った
his tears burned like a fire of the most intimate love
彼の涙は最も深い愛の炎のように燃えた
he felt the humblest veneration in his heart
彼は心の中で謙虚な尊敬の念を感じた
Deeply, he bowed, touching the ground
彼は深くお辞儀をし、地面に触れた。
he bowed before him who was sitting motionlessly
彼は動かずに座っている彼の前で頭を下げた
his smile reminded him of everything he had ever loved in his life
彼の笑顔は彼が人生で愛したすべてのものを思い出させた。
his smile reminded him of everything in his life that he found valuable and holy

彼の笑顔は、彼が人生で価値があり神聖だと思ったすべてのことを思い出させた。

www.tranzlaty.com

www.ingramcontent.com/pod-product-compliance
Lightning Source LLC
Chambersburg PA
CBHW010019130526
44590CB00048B/3823